School Counselling in East and South-East Asia

This book explores trends in the practice of school counselling in East and Southeast Asia in response to socioeconomic changes, developments in education and schooling, the growth of technology, and the legacy of the recent COVID-19 pandemic.

The volume adopts an ecological perspective, taking into account both schools' institutional contexts and the sociocultural settings in which school counsellors work. Chapters focus on the needs, perspectives, and expectations of different stakeholders and explore the changing roles and identities of school counsellors. Contributions from Mainland China, Hong Kong SAR, Japan, Malaysia, The Philippines, Singapore, and Vietnam provide a wide-ranging account of the development of school counselling in the region and set out key themes and priorities for this fast-developing field.

Academics in the field of school counselling, practising school counsellors, academics involved in training programmes for school counsellors and students will find this an invaluable volume. More broadly, this text will be of interest to individuals involved in accrediting bodies for schools in Asia, and school leaders tasked with overseeing counselling provision and that of well-being.

Mark G. Harrison is an assistant professor at Hong Kong Shue Yan University with a research interest in school counselling in Southeast Asia. Originally from the UK, he has lived in Hong Kong for more than 20 years, where he worked in international secondary schools in various senior leadership roles before becoming an academic. He is a practising counsellor and supervisor, mainly working with parents, teens, and school counsellors.

Queenie A. Y. Lee is a lecturer of The University of Hong Kong with research interests in school counselling, school connectedness, and psychotherapy. She is a licensed schoolteacher in Hong Kong and has received training as a counselling psychologist. Her areas of expertise include school counselling, career facilitation, and somatic experiencing. She is a trainer of career facilitation and supervisor of postgraduate counselling students and in-service school counsellors.

James L. H. Yu is a clinical psychologist and associate professor (practice) at the Hang Seng University of Hong Kong. He is an editorial board member of the *Journal of Asia Pacific Counselling*. His research interests include clinical cases studies, psychodynamic therapy, evidence-based practice, and phenomenological psychology.

Routledge Series on Schools and Schooling in Asia
Series editor: Kerry J. Kennedy

Culturally Responsive Science Pedagogy in Asia
Status and Challenges for Malaysia, Indonesia and Japan
Edited by Lilia Halim, Murni Ramli and Mohd Norawi Ali

The Asia Literacy Dilemma
A Curriculum Perspective
Rebecca Cairns and Michiko Weinmann

Educating Teachers Online in Challenging Times
The Case of Hong Kong
Edited by Kevin Wai Ho Yung and Hui Xuan Xu

Cross-disciplinary STEM Learning for Asian Primary Students
Design, Practices and Outcomes
Edited by Winnie Wing Mui So, Zhi Hong Wan and Tian Luo

Teachers' Journeys into International School Teaching in China
Exploring Motivations and Mobilities
Adam Poole

Enacting Moral Education in Japan
Between State Policy and School Practice
Sam Bamkin

School Counselling in East and South-East Asia
Challenges and Opportunities
Edited by Mark G. Harrison, Queenie A. Y. Lee and James L. H. Yu

For the full list of titles in the series, please visit: www.routledge.com/Routledge-Series-on-Schools-and-Schooling-in-Asia/book-series/RSSSA

School Counselling in East and South-East Asia
Challenges and Opportunities

Edited by
Mark G. Harrison, Queenie A. Y. Lee
and James L. H. Yu

LONDON AND NEW YORK

First published 2025
by Routledge
4 Park Square, Milton Park, Abingdon, Oxon OX14 4RN

and by Routledge
605 Third Avenue, New York, NY 10158

Routledge is an imprint of the Taylor & Francis Group, an informa business

© 2025 selection and editorial matter, Mark G. Harrison, Queenie A. Y. Lee and James L. H. Yu; individual chapters, the contributors

The right of Mark G. Harrison, Queenie A. Y. Lee and James L. H. Yu to be identified as the authors of the editorial material, and of the authors for their individual chapters, has been asserted in accordance with sections 77 and 78 of the Copyright, Designs and Patents Act 1988.

All rights reserved. No part of this book may be reprinted or reproduced or utilised in any form or by any electronic, mechanical, or other means, now known or hereafter invented, including photocopying and recording, or in any information storage or retrieval system, without permission in writing from the publishers.

Trademark notice: Product or corporate names may be trademarks or registered trademarks, and are used only for identification and explanation without intent to infringe.

British Library Cataloguing-in-Publication Data
A catalogue record for this book is available from the British Library

Library of Congress Cataloging-in-Publication Data
Names: Harrison, Mark G, editor. | Lee, Queenie A. Y., editor. | Yu, James L. H., editor.
Title: School counselling in East and South-East Asia : challenges and opportunities / Edited by Mark G Harrison, Queenie A. Y. Lee and James L. H. Yu.
Description: Abingdon, Oxon ; New York, NY : Routledge, 2025. | Series: Routledge series on schools and schooling in Asia | Includes bibliographical references and index.
Identifiers: LCCN 2024015248 | ISBN 9781032403137 (hardback) | ISBN 9781032403144 (paperback) | ISBN 9781003352457 (ebook)
Subjects: LCSH: Educational counseling—Asia, East. | Educational counseling—Southeast Asia. | Education and state—Asia, East. | Education and state—Southeast Asia. | Educational change—Asia, East. | Educational change—Southeast Asia.
Classification: LCC LB1027.5 S36 2025 | DDC 371.4/220959—dc23/eng/20240429
LC record available at https://lccn.loc.gov/2024015248

ISBN: 9781032403137 (hbk)
ISBN: 9781032403144 (pbk)
ISBN: 9781003352457 (ebk)

DOI: 10.4324/9781003352457

Typeset in Galliard
by codeMantra

Contents

Editors		*vii*
Contributors		*ix*
Series Editor's Note		*xiii*
1	Introduction: School Counselling in East and Southeast Asia MARK G. HARRISON, QUEENIE LEE AND JAMES YU	1
2	Counselling in Asian Schools: A Decade Reviewed Through an Ecological Lens LOW POI KEE	16
3	Challenges of School Counselling in Malaysia: Pre and During the COVID-19 Pandemic SEW KIM LOW AND JIN KUAN KOK	32
4	Multicultural School Counselling in Singapore: Diversity, Worldviews and Meaning Making BOON-OOI LEE	51
5	School Counselling in Japan and the Impact of COVID-19 NICOLAS TAJAN, HANS RAUPACH AND TEO KNIVES	72
6	School Counselling in the Philippines: Challenges and New Directions SHEILA MARIE G. HOCSON, FRANCIS RAY D. SUBONG AND ELGIN B. CLAVECILLAS	91
7	Developments in School Counselling Practice in Vietnam MICHAEL HASS AND HOANG-MINH DANG	113

8 Professional School Counselling in Vietnam:
   A Preliminary Model   134
   ANH KIM PHAM AND HONG THUAN NGUYEN

9 Pioneering an Experiential Training Programme for
   Career Counsellors and Facilitators in Hong Kong:
   Design, Programme Development and Challenges   165
   QUEENIE LEE, JAMES YU AND MARK G. HARRISON

10 The Development of Career Education and Counselling
   in Mainland China: A Brief Overview   179
   HOUMING JIANG, QUEENIE LEE AND MANTAK YUEN

11 Conclusion: The Future of School Counselling in East
   and Southeast Asia   193
   MARK G. HARRISON, QUEENIE LEE AND JAMES YU

   Index   *205*

Editors

Mark G. Harrison
Department of Counselling and Psychology, Hong Kong Shue Yan University
Mark G. Harrison is an assistant professor at Hong Kong Shue Yan University with a research interest in school counselling in Southeast Asia. Originally from the UK, he has lived in Hong Kong for more than 20 years, where he worked in international secondary schools in various senior leadership roles before becoming an academic. He is a practising counsellor and supervisor, mainly working with parents, teens, and school counsellors.

Queenie Lee
Faculty of Education, The University of Hong Kong
Queenie Lee is a lecturer of The University of Hong Kong with research interests in school counselling, school connectedness, and psychotherapy. She is a licensed schoolteacher in Hong Kong and has received training as a counselling psychologist. Her areas of expertise include school counselling, career facilitation, and somatic experiencing. She is a trainer of career facilitation and supervisor of postgraduate counselling students and in-service school counsellors.

James Yu
School of Humanities and Social Science, The Hang Seng University of Hong Kong.
James Yu is a clinical psychologist and associate professor (practice) at the Hang Seng University of Hong Kong. He is an editorial board member of the *Journal of Asia Pacific Counselling*. His research interests include clinical cases studies, psychodynamic therapy, evidence-based practice, and phenomenological psychology.

Contributors

Elgin B. Clavecillas
Department of Guidance and Counselling, Far Eastern University
Elgin B. Clavecillas holds a master's degree and is a licensed guidance counsellor, bringing with her over a decade of expertise in counselling, case management, and career development programmes. She is currently working towards her doctorate in clinical psychology at the University of Santo Tomas while also fulfilling her role as a guidance counsellor at Far Eastern University.

Hoang-Minh Dang
Vietnam National University, University of Education, Hanoi
Hoang-Minh Dang is a clinical psychologist and an associate professor at VNU University of Education. She is also the director of Clinical Research Institute for Society, Psychology and Education (CRISP-E) at VNU University of Education. Her scholarship focuses on the development, evaluation, dissemination, and implementation of evidence-based interventions for child and adolescent mental health in low- and middle-income countries such as Vietnam.

Michael Hass
Attallah College of Educational Studies, Chapman University
Michael Hass is a professor emeritus and former coordinator of the graduate programmes in Counselling and School Psychology at Chapman University. He also holds an appointment as Visiting Professor at Vietnam National University, University of Education, Hanoi. His scholarly interests include school mental health, strength-based approaches to counselling, and resilience. Dr. Hass is the author of books on effective psychological report writing, interviewing for school counsellors, and most recently, *Student Mental Health in the Classroom: Essentials for Teachers*.

Sheila Marie G. Hocson
University Research Center, Far Eastern University & Philippine Guidance and Counseling Association

Sheila Marie G. Hocson is the past president of Philippine Guidance and Counseling Association for 2016–2018 and 2022–2023. She was also the branch leader and currently one of the mentors for the American Counseling Association. Prior to becoming a Research Fellow, she also became a Guidance Director for 14 years at Far Eastern University. She is also a graduate school professor teaching guidance & counseling and psychology courses. She is also a mental health consultant of the Office of the President, Presidential Management Staff of Malacanang, and senior technical consultant and author of the Unilab Foundation.

Houming Jiang
Keystone Academy in Beijing, China

Houming Jiang currently serves as the head of Middle School at Keystone Academy in Beijing. Before joining Keystone, he held various leadership and faculty positions in different international schools in Beijing and the Greater Bay Area. Dr. Jiang also taught in rural China on the Burmese border for two years and became an advocate for service learning. He attended Xiamen University for his bachelor's degree in accounting and completed a master's degree in private school leadership from Columbia University and a Doctor of Education from The University of Hong Kong. Dr. Jiang has his teacher licensure in China, the US and the UK and aspires to ground the best practices of international education in Chinese context.

Low Poi Kee
James Cook University, Singapore

Poi Kee is a counselling psychologist with experience and interests in psychotherapy, social care, special education, and refugee education and mental health. He is a registered psychologist, counsellor, and social service practitioner in Singapore. He is also a chartered psychologist and associate fellow with the British Psychological Society. Dr. Low is an associate professor of counselling at James Cook University Singapore. He continues to maintain a small but active private practice.

Teo Knives
Graduate School of Human and Environmental Studies, Kyoto University

Teo Knives is a clinical psychologist and a PhD candidate at Kyoto University. She holds a graduate diploma in clinical psychology and a master's degree in counselling from the Moscow Institute of Psychoanalysis, as well as a master's degree in built environment and architecture from Politecnico di Milano. Her ongoing doctoral research centres on the relationship between psychopathology and the arrangement of domestic environments.

Jin Kuan Kok
Tunku Abdul Rahman University (UTAR), Malaysia
Jin Kuan Kok retired as an associate professor from the Department of Psychology and Counselling, Faculty of Arts and Social Sciences, Universiti Tunku Abdul Rahman, Kampar, Malaysia. She is a registered counsellor and clinical supervisor from Singapore Association for Counselling.

Boon-Ooi Lee
National Institute of Education, Nanyang Technological University, Singapore
Boon-Ooi Lee, PhD, is Senior Lecturer and Programme Leader of MA in counselling and guidance at National Institute of Education, Nanyang Technological University in Singapore. He is interested in culture and mental health, in particular, Indigenous healing systems, multicultural therapy, cultural psychopathology, alteration of consciousness, health beliefs, somatisation, and the phenomenology of the body. His current research investigates the relevance of Indigenous healing practices to mental health and altered consciousness (e.g., dissociation, trance, transcendence) in mental health and psychopathology.

Sew Kim Low
Tunku Abdul Rahman University (UTAR), Malaysia
Sew Kim Low is a Malaysian registered counsellor with the Malaysian Council of Counsellors. She retired as a senior lecture from the Department of Psychology and Counselling, Faculty of Arts and Social Sciences, Universiti Tunku Abdul Rahman, Kampar, Malaysia. Her research interests include counselling, mental health, psychological wellness, and development.

Hong Thuan Nguyen
Center for Psychology and Education Research, Vietnam Institute of Educational Sciences
Nguyen Hong Thuan is a senior researcher with extensive experience in research and counselling in the field of school counselling psychology for governmental agencies and K-12 schools across Vietnam. Professor Thuan currently serves as the director of the Center for Psychology and Education Research at the Vietnam Institute of Educational Sciences.

Anh Kim Pham
Faculty of Psychology, University of Social Sciences and Humanity – HCM National University, Vietnam
Anh K. Pham is a speaker, author, senior lecturer, and educational advisor with intensive knowledge and experience in global K-12 and higher education. Dr. Anh serves as a senior lecturer teaching various subjects and maintains a wide range of research areas, including school counselling, industrial organisational psychology, leadership and entrepreneurship, and innovation.

Hans Raupach
University of Zurich

Hans Raupach is a master's student at the University of Zurich. He received his bachelor's degree in psychology from Goethe University Frankfurt. From 2022 to 2023, he studied at Osaka University. He is interested in clinical psychology and the history and practice of psychology in Japan.

Francis Ray D. Subong
Philippine Guidance and Counseling Association & Dominican International School Kaohsiung

Francis Ray D. Subong has been in the field of education for more than a decade. He is a staunch advocate of guidance and counselling in the Philippines. In 2022, he received the US State Department's Fulbright Distinguished Award for the International Teaching Programme. He is also one of the training consultants of the National Center for Mental Health's Crisis Hotline Responders.

Nicolas Tajan
Graduate School of Human and Environmental Studies, Kyoto University

Nicolas Tajan is a psychoanalyst and associate professor at Kyoto University. In 2021, Routledge JAW series published his open access book entitled *Mental Health and Social Withdrawal in Contemporary Japan: Beyond the Hikikomori Spectrum*. In 2022, he received an award from CIPPA for his work on autism.

Mantak Yuen
Faculty of Education, The University of Hong Kong.

Mantak Yuen is an associate professor and director of the Laboratory for Creativity and Talent Development, Centre for Advancement in Inclusive and Special Education, The University of Hong Kong, China. He is a registered counselling and educational psychologist, a Global Career Development Facilitator, and a certified Laughter Yoga Leader. He has developed and validated The Life Skills Development Self-Efficacy Inventories, which are the first measurement tools for assessing Asian adolescents' self-efficacy in applying life skills in the domains of academic, personal-social, and career and talent development.

Series Editor's Note

The so-called "Asian century" is providing opportunities and challenges both for the people of Asia and in the West. The success of many of Asia's young people in schooling often leads educators in the West to try and emulate Asian school practices. Yet, these practices are culturally embedded. One of the key issues to be taken on by this series, therefore, is to provide Western policy-makers and academics with insights into these culturally embedded practices in order to assist better understanding of them outside of specific cultural contexts.

There is vast diversity as well as disparities within Asia. This is a fundamental issue and for that reason it will be addressed in this series by making these diversities and disparities the subject of investigation. The "tiger" economies initially grabbed most of the media attention on Asian development and, more recently, China has become the centre of attention. Yet, there are also very poor countries in the region and their education systems seem unable to be transformed to meet new challenges. Thus, the whole of Asia will be seen as important for this series in order to address questions relevant not only to developed countries but also to developing countries. In other words, the series will take a "whole of Asia" approach.

Asia can no longer be considered in isolation. It is as subject to the forces of globalisation, migration, and transnational movements as are other regions of the world. Yet, the diversity of cultures, religions and social practices in Asia means that responses to these forces are not predictable. This series, therefore, is interested to identify the ways tradition and modernity interact to produce distinctive contexts for schools and schooling in an area of the world that impacts across the globe.

The current volume highlights issues related to school counselling across the region. It is very timely given the impact COVID has had on young people and concerns that have been raised about student wellbeing. Schools are not just about academic learning, they must be concerned with the whole student. It makes a welcome addition to the *Routledge Series on Schools and Schooling in Asia*. Its focus on student needs in an increasingly complex world will echo globally.

Kerry J. Kennedy
Series Editor
Routledge Series on Schools and Schooling in Asia

1 Introduction

School Counselling in East and Southeast Asia

Mark G. Harrison, Queenie Lee and James Yu

The Development of School Counselling in East and Southeast Asia

School counselling encompasses a wide range of activities that address the needs of young people. Over the past several decades, school counselling has evolved enormously, adapting to changing educational, social, and cultural landscapes, and responding to the unique challenges faced by students in different regions. The roots of school counselling can be traced to the early 20th century in the United States, where vocational guidance was implemented in schools to help students make informed career choices (Baker, 2018). In the mid-20th century, school counselling began to expand and shift towards a more comprehensive set of activities that focused on the holistic development of students.

The need for counselling in schools arises from an acknowledgement that students face an array of challenges that can potentially hinder their academic, social, and personal development. School counselling aims to promote the holistic well-being of students by addressing their academic, career, and psychosocial needs (American School Counselor Association [ASCA], 2019a). The roles of school counsellors have evolved from being primarily ad-hoc advisors and vocational guidance providers into advocates, collaborators, and leaders within the school community. School counsellors began to be more concerned with issues including mental health, emotional well-being, social and communication skills, and all-round personal development. School counselling no longer focuses primarily on academic and career development, but also addresses young people's socio-emotional needs, behavioural issues, and long-term goals. Counsellors work with students individually and in groups, providing counselling, conducting assessments, and implementing evidence-based and tailor-made interventions to address a wide range of issues. They also collaborate with teachers and parents to create an integrated and stable supportive network for students (Paisley & McMahon, 2001).

In East and Southeast Asia, the development of school counselling has been shaped by cultural factors, social and demographic changes, educational policies, as well as the recent impact of the COVID-19 pandemic. The changing

DOI: 10.4324/9781003352457-1

educational landscape and a recognition of the importance of holistic development have led to a shift in the roles of school counsellors. Despite shared themes and common concerns, such as a strong emphasis on academic achievement and success (Liu, 2017), there is a diversity of priorities and approaches across the region and, as elsewhere, counsellors are increasingly involved in providing personal and emotional support to students, addressing mental health issues, and promoting well-being (Liu, 2017). A major challenge faced by school counsellors is the integration of school counselling into the education system, and the recognition of its importance by different stakeholders, including teachers, parents, and school leaders.

School counselling has evolved at different pace in the West and in East and Southeast Asia. A more widespread recognition of the role of school counselling and an increasing professionalism in Western societies contrasts with the more gradual embracing of school counselling in the unique sociocultural contexts of different countries of East and Southeast Asia. As schools and society continue to evolve, school counselling must adapt to meet the diverse needs of students and promote their success and well-being in ways which are meaningful in the region's cultural contexts.

To illustrate how school counselling in the region is responding to the developing environment, we now briefly consider three areas where significant changes are taking place. First, rapid advances in technology present enormous challenges and great opportunities as technological innovation pervades and changes every aspect of young people's lives. Second, career counselling, a core part of many counsellors' roles, is evolving rapidly in response to social and demographic changes, and the disruption brought about by technological development. Third, the need for ethical practice which is fit for purpose requires school counsellors in the region to develop and implement contextual, responsive, and culturally meaningful codes of ethics.

The Challenges and Opportunities of Technology

The disruption caused by the COVID-19 pandemic had a significant impact on the well-being of students and acted as a major disrupter to society and school counselling. This disruption has created ongoing challenges and opportunities for school counsellors.

The pandemic spawned the now growing practice of tele-behavioural health and online counselling services (Bimrose, 2017; Rhodes, 2023a). With advances in electronic conferencing applications such as *Zoom* and *Microsoft Teams*, school children are able to seek psychological services virtually. The availability and accessibility of tele-behavioural health services was a vital resource to many young people during the pandemic, as the number of children and adolescents who struggled with anxiety and depression in this period soared (Rhodes, 2023b), and such services are now becoming increasingly normalised. At the same time, other children were deprived of mental health support when it was much needed, given the digital divide brought about by the wealth gaps in countries around the region. The disparity between economically better off and poorer young people was clear during the pandemic (Liu et al., 2021), and this digital divide will continue to be a challenge as the use of online counselling grows.

During the pandemic, school counsellors needed to rapidly adapt to remote counselling as they supported students through the challenges of online learning and social isolation (Karaman et al., 2021). Liu and colleagues (2021) investigated the impact of the pandemic on school counselling in several Asian countries including China, South Korea, and Japan. They found that online counselling created many challenges for school counsellors, including the pressure to quickly learn and adapt to new technologies, and the difficulties in building rapport with students through virtual platforms. Overall, the pandemic had a profound impact on school counselling in Asia, presenting enormous challenges.

Closely related to the rise of tele-behavioural health is the development of generative artificial intelligence (AI) in the realm of counselling and psychotherapy. With easy installation and payment of subscription fees, mental health consultation and advising by AI is becoming more common. While convenient, there are risks in areas such as privacy and confidentiality, and structural biases against some ethnic, national, and racial groups as a result of AI's reliance on databases and corpuses which may reflect racism in human discourse and societies (Giovannetti, 2023).

The changes to counsellors' practice brought about by rapid advances in technology, and accelerated by the pandemic, will continue to shape the future of the field. Counsellors will increasingly need to embrace new ways of operating, learn new skills, and adopt flexible attitudes towards their practice in order to serve the young people in the region most effectively.

The Development of Career Counselling

Career guidance, which is a well-developed specialty in the field of counselling, has undergone significant changes in both theory and practice in the last few decades. Schools in East and Southeast Asia tend to focus – explicitly and implicitly – on academic success and, reflecting this emphasis, school counselling has traditionally focused on academic guidance and career development, aligning with the emphasis on academic achievement (Wong & Yuen, 2019) and conforming to sociocultural ideals of success rather than addressing individual needs and values (Liu, 2017). Career education and counselling has evolved from a traditional person-environment fit paradigm in the early 20th century when Frank Parsons (1909) wrote his ground-breaking work, *Choosing a Vocation*, to current postmodern constructivist approaches which emphasise personal agency, meaning-making, and life design (Hartung & Santilli, 2017; Savickas, 2012, 2019).

Rapid advances in technology, particularly the evolution of AI, provide an urgent challenge to the way school counsellors approach career guidance and call for continuous evolution of counsellors' practices in this area. Technological development will inevitably have an increasing impact on both the needs of young people and the practices of school counsellors, as it reshapes society in pervasive and profound ways. For example, automation in many industries has changed the kinds of careers to which young people might aspire and has led to some precarity in the world of work. The pervasive presence of technology in the workplace is resulting in qualitative changes in the contractual relationships between employers and their staff and is leading to shifts in the psychology of employees related to how work brings meaning to their life. There is also an increasing expectation that work and other aspects of life should be integrated in such practices as remote working arrangements.

These profound shifts highlight the need for school counsellors to keep abreast of the latest development of assessment tools in career counselling, the necessary skills and knowledge current and future workers need to acquire, information about the labour market and the world of work on a global level, and how young people can search for and maintain jobs they enjoy doing (McMahon & Patton, 2017). For example, Lent (2018) has suggested that, in response to the rise of technology and its inevitable and profound influence on the work of the future, career counsellors need to actively participate in "dialogues to transform educational institutions" (p. 205), and extend the range of counselling interventions they provide in order to prepare young people for an unstable and unpredictable career future that may be far less stable for increasing numbers of workers.

Social and demographic changes, such as urbanisation and globalisation, have also influenced the development of career counselling in East and Southeast Asia. Rapid societal changes have resulted in the emergence of new challenges for students (Liu, 2017). School counsellors must adapt their approaches to address these complicated evolving needs. For example, in the Philippines, globalisation has shifted the economic landscape with the rise of the business process outsourcing (BPO) industry (Errighi et al., 2016). School counsellors must be up to date with their knowledge of career opportunities and desirable vocational skills to facilitate effective counselling with students. Urbanisation has resulted in increased migration of families from rural areas to crowded cities, putting the unique needs of migrant students, such as language barriers and acculturative stress, to the forefront of the school counselling process (Melgar, 2013).

School counsellors are expected to expand their repertoire such that their work is not confined to a traditional assessment of personal attributes such as personality and interests, but makes use of a wider range of methodologies and techniques such as the *Career Construction Interview* (CCI; Savickas, 2013, 2019) and other qualitative assessments whereby clients are given the time and space to explore, narrate, and construct their life design in accordance with their understanding about themselves, significant people or events that have shaped their personality and development, and demands from the global and labour markets, so as to construct a life that brings meaning and fulfilment.

The Challenge of Ethical Practice

Ethical practice is at the centre of all good counselling. In the course of their work, school counsellors grapple with many complex ethical issues that affect their professional practice. Some important ethical considerations that are particularly relevant to school counsellors include: informed consent (especially in the case of mandated counselling), confidentiality and its limits (e.g., revelation of suicidal ideation and/or attempts and self-injurious behaviours in minors), the need for multicultural awareness and practices and advocacy for social justice and the rights of marginalised groups and minorities, working within one's scope of knowledge and expertise and the need to make a referral when the welfare of the client is at stake (e.g., when working with clients engaged in behaviours that might be in conflict with a counsellor's religious background, or working with a case that requires neurobiological intervention beyond the scope and knowledge of a counsellor dealing with the case) and, importantly, managing dual roles effectively.

While many well-established codes of ethics are available which deal comprehensively with these issues (e.g., The American Counselling Association *Code of Ethics* (ACA, 2014); The British Association for Counselling and Psychotherapy *Ethical Framework for the Counselling Professions* (BACP; 2018; ASCA Ethical Standards for School Counselors (ASCA, 2014)), they may not be best suited to the cultural contexts of counsellors in the East and Southeast Asia. The ethical principles on which codes of ethics are built need to be enacted in those contexts, which might be quite different from those elsewhere. For example, promoting a young person's autonomy and encouraging self-advocacy, which might be empowering in a Western setting and seen as a school counsellors' ethical duty, might be out of place – and perhaps even harmful – in a Confucian context, where notions of self are construed more interdependently, and putting personal needs above those of the community can be considered shameful (Cross et al., 2011). It is necessary, therefore, to develop codes of ethics more suited to the cultural characteristics of the young people with whom school counsellors in the region work.

As the scope of school counsellors' work continues to increase, responsive and culturally meaningful codes of ethical practice are becoming more important. Counsellors are also increasingly called upon to be involved in safeguarding, issues related to minority or marginalised communities such as LGBTQ students, and to have a focus on issues of equity, diversity, and inclusion.

The rise of technology also brings with it ethical problems. As online counselling became commonplace during the recent COVID-19 pandemic, counsellors were faced with ethical dilemmas which emerged from this. Issues include privacy, confidentiality, and security; the need for proper training and the technical competence of counsellors; communication issues specific to the use of technological applications such as *Zoom* and *Microsoft Teams*; and emergency issues, where the counsellor's effectiveness is limited by physical distance

(Stoll et al., 2020). As online counselling becomes more normalised, a robust consideration of the ethics of online counselling needs to be undertaken.

A consideration of ethical conduct related to these areas is well developed in Western school counselling, but much less so in Asia, providing a challenge for school counsellors. Responding effectively to these issues in any school setting can be complex. In the context of schools in Asia, where counsellors have a relatively weak identity, are more likely to carry out dual roles, and less likely to receive good supervision, the challenges can be magnified.

Responding Effectively to the Changing Environment

Responding to the many issues brought about by a rapidly changing society presents a set of complex challenges, as the above sections illustrate. We suggest that the development of school counselling can best respond to these challenges when it is built on two foundational pillars: (1) an ecological perspective and (2) the indigenisation of counselling. Throughout this edited book, the authors explore these two pillars in different settings, and how they support effective responses to the myriad challenges faced by school counsellors. We now briefly outline the characteristics of each one.

An Ecological Perspective on School Counselling

Schools are made up of diverse intersecting and interacting systems and dynamic relationships between stakeholders (McMahon & Mason, 2014). These systems and relationships make up an ecosystem (Bronfenbrenner, 1979) which influences the experiences of counsellors and the young people with whom they work and shapes the nature of counselling. In almost any school, counsellors carry out a highly multifunctional role, and they tend to lean heavily on family systems approaches in their daily work (Martin, 2017).

In the United States, school counselling has moved towards a collaborative approach aiming to bring about systemic change (ASCA, 2019a), and an ecological approach to school counselling has been increasingly recognised as an effective means of doing so (McMahon & Mason, 2014). An ecological approach to school counselling acknowledges the complexity of a school and the interdependence of its systems and stakeholders, and assumes that counsellors cannot work effectively with young people without a thorough understating of, and engagement with, all the parts that constitute the ecology of the school within its wider sociocultural setting.

The extent to which counsellors are embedded in school ecosystems is an important consideration. In South and Southeast Asia, where counselling is less developed, there is much variation in how counsellors are positioned relative to the school ecosystem. They may be embedded into the school as part of its staff or located more peripherally. They may be performing roles which ASCA (2019b) describes as systemic change agents, holding positions of influence or even formal leadership, or (far more likely) they may be marginalised and treated as a supporting, auxiliary service. Schools may adopt an ownership model, where counselling is well integrated into the school's systems, or counsellors may be more independent and less well connected to the school. Some research suggests that the former is better able to support young people's needs (Spratt et al., 2006) since counsellors are better acquainted with a school's routines and culture, have better access to students, and can work more closely with teachers and parents (e.g., Knight et al., 2018). Other studies, however, have found that young people value counsellors' independence from the school, citing concerns about confidentiality and confusion about counsellors' dual roles (e.g., Griffiths, 2013: Harrison, 2020). Most studies have been carried out in Western settings, but the cultural context of East and Southeast Asia is profoundly different, and it is not obvious how the integration of counsellors into schools might influence their effectiveness.

In an ecological approach to school counselling, different groups of stakeholders, such as teachers, counsellors, social workers, etc., school be clearly distinguished from each other, and the diversity of professional roles in a school should be leveraged as a source of strength, everyone having a different and important role to play (McMahon et al., 2014; McMahon & Mason, 2019). In Asia, school counsellors often have a weak professional identity, are poorly differentiated form that other school staff such as teachers, and are often undervalued and marginalised. Counsellors have struggled to clearly articulate a professional identity, even in Western settings (Gale & Austin, 2003). School counsellors have arguably struggled more, given their ambiguous position, straddled between educator and mental health professional (DeKruyf et al., 2013). In Asia, where school counselling is in various stages of development (Harris, 2014), there is little consensus on the professional identity of school counsellors (Harrison, 2022).

Because school counsellors' professional identity is often not well differentiated from other professionals, they are frequently given roles which are not commensurate with their expertise and experience, and are therefore not utilised in the most effective ways. There is a wide variation in the roles of school counsellors across Asia (Amat et al., 2018; Harris, 2014; Kok, 2013; van Schalkwyk & Sit, 2013; Yeo & Lee, 2014; Yuen, Chan, & Lee, 2014). Counsellors work with individuals and small groups, deliver psychoeducation to large groups, work strategically with school leaders, build partnerships with teachers and parents, and work with the wider community (Harris, 2014). However, they are often assigned to administrative duties or given teaching assistant roles. Part of the problem is that counsellors are commonly managed by teachers, administrators, or social workers with little understanding of counsellors' function. In addition, it is uncommon for school counsellors to receive much professional development or appropriate supervision within their schools (Harrison, 2022).

Several components of school counsellor's identity are essential to the effective implementation of an ecological approach. The roles they carry out must be congruent with their expertise and training; they must be well differentiated from other professionals working in schools and the field of mental health; they should be recognised by school leaders as professionals with a distinct and specialised role; and they should have the ability to influence school policy and practice (Fitzgerald, 2020; Mellin et al., 2011; Woo et al., 2014). These are areas in need of much development in the region.

Another key area of an ecological approach to school counselling is collaboration between counsellors and different stakeholders, including parents, teachers, and school leaders. When embedded into the school ecosystem, counsellors can build rapport with teachers, ensure their availability and visibility, and solicit feedback from and provide consultation to teachers (Cholewa et al., 2017). Students are better supported when a whole school approach involving a clear and well communicated common vision is in place (Bryan & Henry, 2008). A principal's leadership in advocating for counselling to the school community, setting up clear role descriptions for counsellors, engaging in collaborative practices, and empowering counsellors, is vital in enabling counselling provision to be effective.

Research shows that when parents are more involved in school, children experience better well-being and academic achievement (El Nokali et al., 2010; Ma et al., 2016), and that the latter is influenced more strongly by parental involvement than by socioeconomic status, ethnicity, or parents' educational background (Amatea & West, 2007). Epstein et al. (2018) have proposed a theory of overlapping spheres of influence, where alignment in the values and philosophies of home, school, and community environments is associated with better student outcomes. It is therefore essential that strong and equal partnerships should exist between counsellors and parents. More effective partnerships with parents happen when counsellors have a clear role, and the confidence and authority to initiate partnerships (Bryan & Henry, 2008; Bryan & Holcomb-McCoy; 2007). However, while the importance of these partnerships is not in dispute, how to achieve them effectively in the cultural context of East and Southeast Asia has not been explored.

In summary, several key principles need to be borne in mind as school counsellors in Asia adopt an ecological approach (McMahon et al., 2014). Counsellors need to understand the multiple contexts within which students live and use this knowledge and understanding in their work with students. This means that counsellors need a deep understanding of the sociocultural setting and the characteristics of the school and the education system. They should also engage in leadership, advocacy, and collaboration to promote a healthy school system conducive to students' success, often requiring the skilful use of social capital and a sound ability in navigating organisational politics. The adoption of an ecological model of school counselling may be far from a reality in many of the region's schools, but a greater focus on this approach may enable counsellors to rise to many of the challenges they face.

The Indigenisation of School Counselling in East and Southeast Asia

A second pillar essential to the effective development of school counselling is the indigenisation of counselling models and practices (Leung & Chen, 2009). Most counselling practices in the East and Southeast Asian area originate from the U.S. and U.K. These practices are enacted within school counselling frameworks such as the ASCA National Model (2019a) or, in many cases, not within the context of any model at all. Some countries and regions have developed frameworks, such as the Comprehensive School Guidance Service (CSGS; Hong Kong Education Bureau, 2023) devised by Gysbers and Henderson (1997) used in Hong Kong. These frameworks are generally well thought out, with empirical evidence for their design and implementation. In many ways, however, these models fail to suit the ecologies of schools in the Asian region which are both very diverse and markedly different from countries in the West in terms of cultures and customs, value systems and beliefs, operation of the school systems, and day-to-day life (e.g., long school hours for children which leave quite little room for play and the sedentary lifestyle of many Asian people who rely on digital devices for information and entertainment that result in problems of different kinds such as internet addiction and alienation from social groups). Often, these differences have implications for the physical and mental health of children that school counsellors have to address on a personal and school system level, and school counselling frameworks are needed which are informed by culturally relevant and meaningful notions of help seeking, mental health, and wellness. Such frameworks should also take into account the characteristics of the education system and the level of maturity of school counselling as a profession, and its relation to other supportive services. The development of indigenised school counselling frameworks tailored to each country or region is important since each faces unique challenges that universal models may not adequately address (Leung & Chen, 2009).

For example, the CSGS adopted in Hong Kong (Gysbers & Henderson, 1997; Hong Kong Education Bureau, 2023) comprises four components: (1) policy and organisation; (2) supportive service; (3) personal growth education; and (4) responsive service. Although this framework has been adopted by the Education Bureau in Hong Kong for nearly three decades, elements of the programme are not actualised in practice due to constraints in resources. For example, despite the need for school guidance teachers and counsellors to provide responsive services to students in need (commonly emotional and behavioural problems and difficult family circumstances), many frontline teachers who need to provide counselling to students are without professional training. This situation is even more concerning in mainland China, where school counselling is a relatively new practice, and the existing psychological services provided by teachers and guidance personnel in many provinces can be qualitatively different from the ideologies and implementation of school counselling from the West, yet no framework exists to guide school counsellors.

Clearly, then, frameworks which consider the cultural context and the organisational features of schools in the region may be more effective. Leung and Chen (2009) have drawn attention to the need for both "indigenization from within" where "researchers develop theories, concepts, and methods internally within a culture, using indigenous information as primary sources of knowledge," and also "indigenization from without," where Western frameworks and theories of counselling are adapted to the local cultural setting (p. 951).

The aim of developing indigenous school counselling frameworks is to understand how people function in their local cultural contexts, including the beliefs, knowledge and skills people have about themselves (Ho, 1998; Kim et al., 2006; Leung & Chen, 2009), and to respond to constantly changing societal needs and emerging issues in the local context. As the scope of school counselling grows, counsellors' work, such as properly serving the diverse needs of young people, and responding effectively to unpredictable challenges and crises such as the COVID-19 pandemic, the importance of a culturally meaningful framework in which to locate counselling practice is becoming more important.

Overview of the Book

In the chapters which follow, contributors from a wide range of countries across East and Southeast Asia outline many of the challenges faced by school counsellors in the region, and discuss the opportunities presented to counsellors as we near the end of the first quarter of the 21st century. The two foundational pillars of adopting an ecological perspective and indigenising school counselling are themes which tie the chapters together.

In Chapter 2, Low Poi Kee shows how we can see key developments in school counselling in the region, including the rise of technology and social change, through an ecological lens. The chapter emphasises the importance of seeing counselling as extending beyond the counselling room and being informed by the context in which young people and counsellors live and work.

In Chapter 3, Sew Kim Low and Jin Kuan Kwok present an overview of the challenges faced by school counsellors in Malaysia as they adapted to using technology to offer effective services during the pandemic. The authors describe how the pandemic brought to light structural challenges to providing counselling, and map out a way forward.

Boon-Ooi Lee writes in Chapter 4 about the challenges and opportunities of multicultural school counselling in Singapore, where cultural diversity is a central facet of counselling practice. He explores the concept of culture and, through the presentation of case studies, shows the importance of cultural humility and epistemological flexibility in making sense of how students make sense of their life experiences, and in being able to help them most effectively.

In Chapter 5, Nichloas Tajan, Hans Raupach, and Teo Knives give an overview of the development of school counselling in Japan, highlighting the challenges faced by counsellors in their own words. The authors use interviews

Introduction: School Counselling in East and Southeast Asia 11

with practising counsellors to highlight the importance of collaboration with teachers and parents, the need for better integration of technology, and the need to address issues of workload and burnout.

The authors of Chapter 6, Sheila Marie Hocson, Frances Ray Subong, and Elgin Clavesillas, provide an overview of the history and development of school counselling in the Philippines, highlighting the need for role clarity, appropriate remuneration and career progression in counselling. The authors also highlight the importance of professional counselling organisations and the need to work effectively with government to enact policy which supports the practice of counselling in schools.

In Chapter 7, Michael Hass and Hoang-Minh Dang examine the development of school counselling in Vietnam. They give an overview of the needs of young people and the history of school counselling in the country, and highlight the need for better collaboration between practitioners, school leaders, and government in establishing counsellors' roles and scope of practice. They also highlight the need for uniform training standards for counsellors, and for more research into the effectiveness of counselling in schools.

Anh Kim Pham and Hong Thuan Nguyen present the development of a school counselling framework for Vietnam in Chapter 8. They show how the framework addresses Vietnamese school counsellors' needs, including clearer role descriptions and stronger professional identities, good quality professional development, working with other stakeholders, and assessing the effectiveness of school counselling provision.

In Chapter 9, Queenie Lee, James Yu, and Mark Harrison describe the development and implementation of a professional training programme for school counsellors in providing career guidance in Hong Kong. The programme facilitates the development of importance competencies, including familiarity with career development theories, ethical issues in career facilitation, multicultural awareness, helping skills, the use of technology, and working with the community. The authors show how this programme can address some of the challenges to career counselling in Hong Kong.

In Chapter 10, Houming Jiang, Queenie Lee, and Mantak Yuen present an overview of the development of career counselling in mainland China. Through an examination of government documents, teacher guidelines and student textbooks as used in high schools, the authors chart the development of career counselling as it has responded to the profound changes in Chinese society in the last few decades. They draw attention to the opportunities for improvement in the development of career counselling in China.

In the final chapter, the editors present an overview of the themes presented throughout the book. School counsellors need to be reflective practitioners (Savickas, 2016) who keep abreast of latest developments and trends in the field and seek supervision regularly to deliver psychological services that can enhance the well-being of young people in order to help them develop into independent, well-adjusted and well-functioning individuals who are able to find meaning as they navigate through life. Carrying out this role in the diverse and rapidly changing societies of East and Southeast Asia is no easy task, as the chapters in this edited volume convey. We believe that the authors give a good sense of the scope and speed of school counselling development across the region of East and Southeast Asia as the field responds to significant change and challenge. Above all, we hope that this volume showcases the passion and creativity of school counsellors as they rise to these challenges.

References

Amat, S. (2018). Guidance and counseling in schools. In *3rd International Conference on Current Issues in Education (ICCIE 2018), Advances in Social Science, Education and Humanities Research* (p. 326). Atlantis Press. https://doi.org/10.2991/iccie-18.2019.3

Amatea, E. S., & West, C. A. (2007). Joining the conversation about educating our poorest children: Emerging leadership roles for school counselors in high poverty schools. *Professional School Counseling, 11*(2), 81–89. https://doi.org/10.5330/PSC.n.2010-11.81

American Counseling Association. (2014). *Code of ethics.* https://www.counseling.org/knowledge-center/ethics/code-of-ethics-resources.

American School Counselor Association (2019a). *ASCA national model: A framework for school counseling programs* (4th ed.). https://schoolcounselor.org/About-School-Counseling/ASCA-National-Model-for-School-Counseling-Programs

American School Counselor Association. (2019b). The Role of the School Counselor. https://www.schoolcounselor.org/asca/

Baker, S. B. (2018). A brief history of school counseling in the United States. In S. B. Baker & W. T. Erford (Eds.), *Transforming the School Counseling Profession* (5th ed., pp. 3–20). Pearson.

Bimrose, J. (2017). Constructivism in online career counselling. In M. McMahon (eds.), *Career Counselling: Constructivist Approaches* (pp. 210–221). Routledge.

British Association for Counselling and Psychotherapy (2018, July 1). *Ethical framework for the counselling professions.* https://www.bacp.co.uk/events-and-resources/ethics-and-standards/ethical-framework-for-the-counselling-professions/

Bronfenbrenner, U. (1979). *The ecology of human development.* Harvard University Press.

Bryan, J., & Henry, L. (2008). Strengths-based partnerships: A school-family-community partnership approach to empowering students. *Professional School Counseling, 12*(2), 149–156. https://doi.org/10.1177/2156759X0801200202

Bryan, J., & Holcomb-McCoy, C. (2007). An examination of school counselor involvement in school-family-community partnerships. *Professional School Counseling, 10*(5), 441–454. https://doi.org/10.1177/2156759X0701000501

Cholewa, B., Goodman-Scott, E., Thomas, A., & Cook, J. (2017). Teachers' perceptions and experiences consulting with school counselors: A qualitative study (Featured Research). *Professional School Counseling, 20*(1), 77–88. https://doi.org/10.5330/1096-2409-20.1.77

Cross, S. E., Hardin, E. E., & Gercek-Swing, B. (2011). The what, how, why, and where of self-construal. *Personality & Social Psychology Review, 15*(2), 142–179. https://doi.org/10.1177/1088868310373752

DeKruyf, L., Auger, R. W., & Trice-Black, S. (2013). The role of school counselors in meeting students' mental health needs: Examining issues of professional identity. *Professional School Counseling, 16*(5), 271–281. https://doi.org/10.1177/2156759X0001600502

El Nokali, N. E., Bachman. H. J., & Votruba-Drzai E. (2010). Parent involvement and children's academic and social development in elementary school. *Child Development, 81*(3), 988–1005. https://doi.org/10.1111/j.1467-8624.2010.01447.x

Epstein, J. L., Sanders, M. G., Sheldon, S. B., Simon, B. S., Salinas, K. C., Jansorn, N. R., Van Voorhis, F. L., Martin, C. S., Thomas, B. G., Greenfeld, M. D., & Hutchins, D. J. (2018). *School, family, and community partnerships: Your handbook for action.* Corwin Press.

Errighi, L., Khatiwada, S., & Bodwell, C. (2016). Business process outsourcing in the Philippines: Challenges for decent work. *ILO Asia-Pacific Working Paper Series.* https://doi.org/ 10.13140/RG.2.2.13337.93287

Fitzgerald, A. (2020). Professional identity: A concept analysis. *Nursing Forum, 55*(3), 447–472. https://doi.org/10.1111/nuf.12450

Gale, A. U., & Austin, B. D. (2003). Professionalism's challenges to professional counselors' collective identity. *Journal of Counseling & Development, 81*(1), 3–10. https://doi.org/10.1002/j.1556-6678.2003.tb00219.x

Giovannetti, M. (2023, April). Artificial intelligence and mental health. *Counseling Today, 65*(10), 21–22.

Griffiths, G. (2013). *Scoping report for MindEd: Helpful and unhelpful factors in school-based counselling: clients' perspectives.* BACP.

Gysbers, N. C., & Henderson, P. (1997). *Comprehensive guidance programs that work II.* ERIC/CASS Publications.

Harris, B. (2014). Locating school counseling in the Asian-Pacific region in a global context. Brief reflections on a scoping review of school counseling internationally. *Journal of Asia Pacific Counseling, 4*(2), 1–26. https://doi.org/10.18401/2014.4.2.11

Harrison, M. G. (2020). Relationship in context: Processes in school-based counselling in Hong Kong. *Counselling and Psychotherapy Research 19*(4), 474–483. https://doi.org/10.1002/capr.12234

Harrison, M. G. (2022). The professional identity of school counsellors in East and Southeast Asia. *Counselling and Psychotherapy Research, 22*(3), 543–547. https://doi.org/10.1002/capr.12546

Hartung, P. J., & Santilli, S. (2017). The theory and practice of career construction. In M. McMahon (Eds.), *Career Counselling: Constructivist Approaches* (pp. 174–184). Routledge.

Ho, D. Y. F. (1998). Indigenous psychologies: Asian perspectives. *Journal of Cross-Cultural Psychology, 29*, 88–103. https://doi.org/10.1177/0022022198291005

Hong Kong Education Bureau (2023). *Guide on comprehensive student guidance service.* https://www.edb.gov.hk/attachment/tc/teacher/student-guidance-discipline-services/projects-services/sgs/comprehensive-student-guidance/CSGS_Guide_en.pdf

Karaman, M. A., Eşici, H., Tomar, İ. H., & Aliyev, R. (2021). COVID-19: Are school counseling services ready? Students' psychological symptoms, school counselors' views, and solutions. *Frontiers in Psychology, 12*, 1–14. https://doi.org/10.3389/fpsyg.2021.647740

Knight, K., Gibson, K., & Cartwright, C. (2018). "It's like a refuge": Young people's relationships with school counsellors. *Counselling and Psychotherapy Research, 18*(4), 377–386. https://doi.org/10.1002/capr.12186

Kok, J. K. (2013). The role of the school counsellor in the Singapore secondary school system. *British Journal of Guidance & Counselling, 41*(5), 530–543. https://doi.org/10.1080/03069885.2013.773286

Lent, R. W. (2018). Future of work in the digital world: Preparing for instability and opportunity. *The Career Development Quarterly*, 66(3), 205–219. https://doi.org/10.1002/cdq.12143

Leung, S. A., & Chen, P. H. (2009). Counseling psychology in Chinese communities in Asia: Indigenous, multicultural, and cross-cultural considerations. *The Counseling Psychologist*, 37(7), 944–966. https://doi.org/10.1177/0011000009339973

Liu, X., Zhang, Y., & Li, Z. (2021). The impact of COVID-19 on school counseling in Asia: A comparative study. *Journal of School Counseling*, 19(4), 1–19.

Liu, Y. (2017). School counseling in Asia: Development, current status, and future challenges. In S. B. Baker & A. T. Dahir (Eds.), *Comprehensive School Counseling Programs: K-12 Delivery Systems in Action* (3rd ed., pp. 289–307). Pearson.

Ma, X., Shen, J., Krenn, H. Y., Hu, S., & Yuan, J. (2016). A meta-analysis of the relationship between learning outcomes and parental involvement during early childhood education and early elementary education. *Educational Psychology Review*, 28, 771–801. https://doi.org/10.1007/s10648-015-9351-1

Martin, D. M. (2017). School counselors' perceptions of family systems perspectives. *The Family Journal*, 25(3), 271–277. https://doi.org/10.1177/1066480717711109

McMahon, H. G., & Mason, E. C. M. (2019). Ecological school counseling. In C. T. Dollarhide & M. E. Lemberger-Truelove (Eds.), *Theories of School Counseling for the 21st Century* (pp. 241–265). Oxford University Press. https://psycnet.apa.org/record/2019-31289-011

McMahon, H. G., Mason, E. C., Daluga-Guenther, N., & Ruiz, A. (2014). An ecological model of professional school counseling. *Journal of Counseling & Development*, 92(4), 459–471. https://doi.org/10.1002/j.1556-6676.2014.00172.x

McMahon, M., & Patton, W. (2017). Qualitative career assessment. In M. McMahon (Ed.), *Career Counselling: Constructivist Approaches* (pp. 235–249). Routledge.

Melgar, M. I. E. (2013). Counseling and psychotherapy in the Philippines: A discipline in transition. In R. Moodley, U. P. Gielen, & R. Wu (Eds.), *Handbook of Counseling and Psychotherapy in an International Context* (pp. 237–246). Routledge.

Mellin, E. A., Hunt, B., & Nichols, L. M. (2011). Counselor professional identity: Findings and implications for counseling and interprofessional collaboration. *Journal of Counseling & Development*, 89(2), 140–147. https://doi.org/10.1002/j.1556-6678.2011.tb00071.x

Paisley, P. O., & McMahon, G. (2001). School counseling for the 21st century: Challenges and opportunities. *Professional School Counseling*, 5(2), 106.

Parsons, Frank. (1909). *Choosing a vocation*. Houghton Mifflin Company.

Rhodes, L. R. (2023a, April). The impact of telebehavioral health on clinical practice. *Counseling Today*, 65(10), 23–30.

Rhodes, L. R. (2023b, August). Treating anxiety in children. *Counseling Today*, 66(2), 24–29.

Savickas, M. L. (2012). Life design: A paradigm for career intervention in the 21st century. *Journal of Counseling and Development*, 90(1), 13–19. https://doi.org/10.1111/j.1556-6676.2012.00002.x

Savickas, M. L. (2013). The theory and practice of career construction. In S. Brown & R. Lent (Eds), *Career Development and Counseling: Putting Theory and Research to Work* (2nd ed., pp. 147–183). John Wiley.

Savickas, M. L. (2016). Reflection and reflexivity during life-design interventions: Comments on career construction counseling. *Journal of Vocational Behavior*, 97, 84–89. https://doi.org/10.1016/j.jvb.2016.09.001

Savickas, M. L. (2019). *Career counseling* (2nd ed.). American Psychological Association.

Spratt, J., Shucksmith, J., Philip, K., & Watson, C. (2006). 'Part of who we are as a school should include responsibility for well-being': Links between the school environment, mental health and behaviour. *Pastoral Care in Education, 24*(3), 14–21. https://doi.org/10.1111/j.1468-0122.2006.00374.x

Stoll, J., Müller, J. A., & Trachsel, M. (2020). Ethical issues in online psychotherapy: A narrative review. *Frontiers in Psychiatry, 10*, 498439. https://doi.org/10.3389/fpsyt.2019.00993

van Schalkwyk, G. J., & Sit, H. H. Y. (2013). Evaluating school-based psychological and counselling services in Macao using a qualitative approach. *School Psychology International, 34*, 154. https://doi.org/10.1177/0143034312453395

Wong, L. P., & Yuen, M. (2019). Career guidance and counseling in secondary schools in Hong Kong: A historical overview. *Journal of Asia Pacific Counseling, 9*(1), 1–19. https://doi.org/10.18401/2019.9.1.1

Woo, H., Henfield, M. S., & Choi, N. (2014). Developing a unified professional identity in counseling: A review of the literature. *Journal of Counselor Leadership and Advocacy, 1*(1), 1–15. https://doi.org/10.1080/2326716X.2014.895452

Yeo, L. S., & Lee, B. O. (2014). School-based counseling in Singapore. *Journal of Asia Pacific Counseling, 4*(2), 159–167. https://doi.org/10.18401/2014.4.2.7

Yuen, M. T., Chan, R. T. H., & Lee, B. S. F. (2014). Guidance and counseling in Hong Kong secondary schools. *Journal of Asia Pacific Counseling, 4*(2), 103–112. https://doi.org/10.18401/2014.4.2.3

2 Counselling in Asian Schools
A Decade Reviewed Through an Ecological Lens

Low Poi Kee

Acknowledgement. The author would like to express his sincerest gratitude for the time and effort Mr Tan Chun Kiat has put into reviewing multiple drafts of this chapter.

Introduction

School counselling has grown very rapidly in the last decade in Asia (Harrison, 2021). In this chapter, I seek to discuss some of these changes observed by clinicians, academicians, and other stakeholders through a set of ecological lenses. While some similarities seem to exist between the situations in Asia and those found elsewhere around the world, it is interesting to note some particularities in Asian cultures and how societies play a part in shaping school counselling.

This chapter uses a dual-dimension structure, much like a coat hanger, to hold the discussions together for easy consumption. I will discuss the developments and changes that have, arguably, most impacted the practice of counselling in schools in the region. An ecological framework is applied to extend and deepen the discussions within each segment. Developments surrounding the growth of counselling in Asian schools are aplenty. For ease of discussion, they are put into three baskets, namely developments in Information Technology, Clinical Progress & Focus, and Demographic & Social changes. The impact of changes in these areas and responses from counselling researchers and educators, practitioners, and policymakers will be discussed in greater detail in the section dedicated to them.

In 2009, I offered the triangle of interaction for practitioners, school leaders, and other stakeholders such as policy makers as a way of organising the challenges to and resources available for the delivery of school counselling services (Figure 2.1; Low, 2009). I noted four domains, namely Internal, External, Systems, and Personal in the framework. I suggested that one can map and analyse the origin(s) of challenges and potential solutions in school counselling using the framework as a model. The ecological underpinning of the model is useful for the discussion of the observations made in this chapter about trends in counselling. Using this model, I will present and make

DOI: 10.4324/9781003352457-2

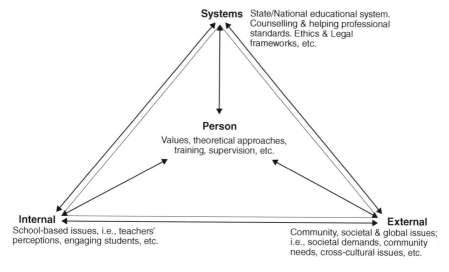

Figure 2.1 Triangle of interaction for practitioners, school leaders, and other stakeholders

sense of the happenings in the three identified areas of development with a spotlight on key research in East, South and Southeast Asian regions where appropriate. This framework has been considered by others when they examined school counselling in mainland China (Leuwerke & Shi, 2010), Nigeria (Anagbogu et al., 2013), Australia (Mah, 2015), Kenya (Boitt, 2016), and Ethiopia (Arfasa & Weldmeskel, 2020). It was also used as the underlying model to examine school counselling and school counsellors in Macau (van Schalkwyk, 2013) and in the Philippines (Bustos, 2016).

Before we proceed further, it will be essential to understand this model/ framework and how it is applied. The framework comprises four domains. Three of them, Internal, External, and Systems, are each an apex of the triangular model, while the last domain, Personal, referring to the counselling practitioner, is centred in the middle of the triangle. The Internal and External domains refer to the space within and outside the school, while the Systems domain refers to other social-political structures such as educational, social care and the justice systems, amongst others. I had suggested locating challenges, their origins and contributing factors in these domains to provide clarity and insights which would be useful to generate and design corresponding solutions and measures (Low, 2009).

Further, the importance of examining the interactions or dynamics between domains with regard to how challenges originated and/or are sustained was emphasised. I also suggested that resources and solutions may reside in these interactions in which resolutions and/or resources to resolve challenges may be found (Low, 2009). One example is how community vendors or service providers (External domain) may be able to lend support when an emergency occurs in the school that requires reinforcement for counsellors operating in the Internal domain. This illustrates the need for greater internal-external collaborations among stakeholders so they can better respond in times of crisis. By extension, should the Systems domain be considered, such practices can be institutionalised (as we have seen in some places) between the schools and communities to realise seamless service delivery for children and families. Using the terminologies and mechanics of this model, I will discuss how developments in Information Technology, Clinical Progress & Focus, and finally Demographic & Social changes have shaped and are shaping school counselling landscapes in Asia.

Developments in Information Technology & Counselling

School counselling in Asia, as in other parts of the world, has had to quickly adapt to changes in the information, communication, and technology arena in the past decade. We have seen the encroachment of technology in schools and further into the counselling environment in many Asian countries. The speed, impact, and response, however, vary from country to country and city to city. A Malaysian study of university students suggested that online counselling was becoming an effective adjunct to face-to-face counselling and was helpful in widening access to counselling services for young people (Wong et al., 2018). On the other hand, concerns arose quite expectedly about the use of online or virtual psychological services as technology advanced. A study based in Australia suggested that these concerns were valid and deserved greater attention (Furlonger & Budisa, 2016). It is particularly important to note that the widening access to mental health services did not equate to service credibility and quality.

A global event that must be mentioned here is the role of the COVID-19 pandemic on the spread, adoption, and adaptation of technology in schools and, in-turn, in counselling practices and processes. Many studies have reported the usefulness and needfulness as well as documented the pace of this adaptation of technology by school counsellors prior and during this period (e.g., Beidoğlu et al., 2015; Puhy et al., 2021) including several in Asia (e.g., Lin et al., 2021; Putri et al., 2022; Supriyanto, et al., 2020).

A study in Indonesia investigated how school counsellors used YouTube and WhatsApp to engage and support students during the pandemic (Putri et al., 2022). Another study from this country covered a broader set of information and communication technologies. They were grouped into asynchronous media (WhatsApp, Facebook, Instagram or social media) and synchronous media (Zoom, Webex, Google Meet or Hangouts). The study found that WhatsApp and YouTube were the mediums of choice as students had greater access to these platforms. Consequently, the authors called for greater use of these technologies in the arena of school counselling (Supriyanto et al., 2020). The effects of the pandemic and the associated restrictions imposed by governments have directly impacted the Internal domain of school counselling and more importantly influenced directly and indirectly the Personal domain in how a school counsellor would engage his/her practice and service delivery. The latter study further advised the government, through education policies, to provide internet access and the development of literacy skills for students and teachers to enable greater access to services. This offers us an illustration of the interactions between the domains of Internal, External, and Systems in this area.

On the not-so-distant horizon, approaching quickly are other technological advances and the associated attempts to apply them in providing mental health services or to enhance the current access to these services. For example, a chatbot was deployed in Taiwan to specifically address academic stress among college students (Lin et al., 2021). This and other attempts, well-meaning as they are, must be evaluated through practice over time to ensure school counsellors harness the effectiveness of these technologies, reduce any unwanted effects, and remain focused on the well-being of individuals in care. An ecological review of these aspects of technology assisted school counselling should be regularly conducted as we roll out more in the years to come.

Growing Clinical Knowledge

As a thriving care profession, new research and discoveries and, by extension, new treatment approaches have rapidly emerged from all corners of the world over the years, a little too rapidly some may suggest (Martin, 2020). This is while school counselling is becoming more commonly available globally, including in many parts of Asia (Harris, 2013). The following paragraphs offer brief discussions on four areas of clinical development that have influenced and shaped counselling in schools in recent years. These include Trauma-informed care, Bullying and Violence, Child and Adolescent Mental Health, and the trend of School-based Family Counselling in Asia.

Trauma-informed practices have over the past decade populated across counselling sub-sectors including school counselling (Rawson, 2021; Rumsey & Milsom, 2018; Wells, 2022). Increasingly, it is recognised that individuals affected by past trauma are present in all population groups, hence counsellors ought to adopt trauma-informed practice regardless of their setting (Koch et al., 2020). This includes school counsellors. While practising different modalities or approaches, counsellors would benefit from using a trauma-informed lens as they work in many settings, including schools (Rawson, 2021; Wells, 2022).

The adoption of trauma-informed care was observed to be more comprehensive in certain parts in the region. For example, it seems to permeate the Internal, External, and Systems domains of the school counselling ecology in the case of Singapore. Family Service Centres as well as Out-of-Home care services have been familiarising themselves with trauma-informed care over the past decade (Ng-Tay et al., 2019; Peh et al., 2022). Collaboration between community-based and school counsellors are considered important, even essential (Low, 2014, 2015; Low & van der Laan, 2023). Naturally, this development is expected to facilitate greater personal and professional development in this aspect among counselling practitioners in schools. Thus, we could say that trauma-informed care is effecting a wholesome and ecological change to the school counselling landscape in Singapore and perhaps in other Asian cities.

Mental health concerns among children and young people are on the rise in parts of Asia. School counselling is part of a wider response to mental health support for young people. A rising concern in youth mental health in Singapore (Ang, 2022) led to efforts to respond within the Internal and Systems domains of the school counselling ecosystem in recent years (Lee, 2021; Neo et al., 2022). Nearby Malaysia reported that the most common mental health problem affecting adolescents is anxiety, followed by depression and stress (Fadzilah et al., 2022). It appears that anxiety has overtaken depression, which was noted to be a growing concern among adolescents in earlier studies (Teoh, 2010; Kaur, et al., 2014). In Vietnam, stress among high school students was found to correlate with their demand for counselling in schools (Van et al., 2019). A further investigation into the provision of career guidance and counselling also found that school counselling in Vietnam required urgent and large-scale enhancement. It called policymakers' attention to the need for wider availability and accessibility to counselling services in schools to support students' psychological and emotional needs as well as career guidance (Tran et al., 2020).

In Japan, Tajan (2015) noted the crucial role of school counselling in junior high schools in the prevention of school dropouts and suggested strengthening school counselling services in practical ways, such as ensuring continuity in employment contracts and standardising certifications for practitioners in schools. These measures, targeted at the Systems domain, are likely to impact service delivery in the Internal domain as well as counsellors themselves in the Personal domain. However, the growth of school counselling was reported to be hindered by the general public's lack of appreciation of the service. A study revealed that the public accorded a relatively low monetary value to school counselling services (Sueki, 2016). Interestingly, over in South Asia, Jayawardena and Gamage (2022) also reported the state's reluctance in investing in mental health and counselling services in Sri Lankan schools. They also suggested cultural implications such as a low focus on personal well-being and a high emphasis on one's social image, amongst other issues that reside in the External as well as Systems domains, inevitably influencing help-seeking behaviours as well as help in the provision of counselling.

A study comparing Southeast Asian nations to Japan suggested that different countries organise their support system according to available resources and the level of awareness of mental health concerns among the student population. Most of these centred on the deployment and training of professionals such as guidance counsellors, school psychologists, and teachers who took up the responsibility of delivering mental health education and/or interventions (Nishio et al., 2020).

As discussed above, the mental health of young people in schools is receiving greater attention within the Internal, Personal, and arguably the Systems domains in Asia. However, as seen in the experience of several Asian countries, school counselling requires support from actors in the External domains, such as other community services, parents, and even taxpayers for it to be effective in prevention and intervention work relating to improving child and youth mental well-being.

Similarly, bullying continues to grow as a concern in schools globally. The situation in Asia is similar to that in the Americas, Australia, and Europe. In Korea, while school bullying has seen a marked reduction from 2011 to 2017, a trend of bullying occurring earlier in schooling lives has been reported. An increase in cyber bullying was noted while a decrease in physical bullying was recorded in the same study by Lee and Trevisan (2019). In another Korean study from a slightly different period (2013–2017), sexual bullying was noted to be increasing rapidly and both physical and cyber bullying were growing concerns (Kim et al., 2019). Similarly, online bullying in India has been on the rise, but more is becoming known in terms of the association between the roles of the initial bully, secondary bully, and the victim, as well as bystanders. Bhat and colleagues (2017) found that when someone engaged in one of the roles, the likelihood of their engaging in another role increased as well.

For South Asia, a large study conducted in Bangladesh and Nepal found that school bullying was relatively common, and the impact of these victimisation experiences on negative health outcomes such as physical violence, tobacco use, alcohol use, drug use, suicidal ideation, loneliness, and sleeping difficulty, were identified (Rahman et al., 2020). A similar study conducted in three other South Asian countries, namely Myanmar, Pakistan, and Sri Lanka, reported that adolescents who were bullied were more likely to report symptoms of depression (Murshid, 2017).

The situation reported in Southeast Asia seems to reflect a similar trajectory. A study covering Indonesia, Laos, Philippines, Thailand, and Timor-Leste reported that bullying victimisation was associated with tobacco, alcohol and drug use, violence, truancy, anxiety, loneliness, suicidal ideation, sedentary behaviour, and weight issues (Pengpid & Peltzer, 2019). School bullying victimisation experience has also been found to be associated with truancy among Timor-Leste school-going adolescents (Owusu et al., 2022).

Recent studies highlighted the role that culture and tradition may have on the occurrence of school bullying or the prevention of bullying. Some literature suggested that East Asian education, tradition, or culture may be a factor in school bullying. For example, Sokantat and colleagues (2021) in Thailand suggested that some aspects of the Thai culture may be linked to bullying in Thai schools. In particular, the normalisation of some bullying behaviours as a form of joke or fun and the generally high-power distances in society were highlighted as potential contributing factors. On the other hand, Noboru and colleagues (2021) found that based on the Global School-based Health Survey, Indonesia reported a lower proportion of adolescents (aged

13–17 years old) bullied as compared to other Southeast Asian countries. They further suggested that moral education and cultural activities were useful avenues for the prevention of school bullying in Indonesia. Another interesting study by Rappleye and Komatsu (2020) reported that rates of bullying and suicide in East Asian societies such as Japan, Korea, and Taiwan were no higher than societies in the West such as Australia, England, New Zealand, Canada, Finland, Estonia, and the United States. The debate remains open as Asian societies are different in many ways from one another. Research in the External and Systems domains, particularly in how elements in those domains influenced bullying occurring in the Internal domains of the school would add clarity to this discourse.

Nevertheless, the problem and impact of bullying remain a current and growing concern for school counsellors in Asia. The preceding paragraphs summarised how school bullying experiences are negatively affecting the health of adolescents and young adults in many parts of Asia. Bullying can be seen largely as occurring inside schools (Internal domain) and is closely associated with the competency and readiness of counsellors (Personal domain).

Sokantat and colleagues (2021) suggested that culture (External domain) inevitably shapes the growing phenomenon of bullying, as is the case in Thailand, and thus solutions or interventions should be designed accordingly. Noboru and colleagues (2021) also illustrated the value of examining the local culture when trying to understand school bullying in Indonesia.

This global and persistent phenomenon requires a stronger ecological or multi-disciplinary response, coordinated among stakeholders in the Internal, External, and Systems domains. Within school counselling practitioners' Personal domain, the need to build skills such as mediation, restorative practice, trauma-informed care, and school-based family counselling may become more apparent in the next decade.

The trend of school-based family counselling is growing in some parts of Asia. In Singapore and Korea, while some counsellors have started to adopt a more adaptive response to meet the needs of families, there appears to be room for growth within the Systems domain (Chong et al., 2013; Lee, et al., 2013; Low, 2015). With the maturing of counselling in schools across many urban centres like Singapore and Hong Kong in Asia (Harrison, 2021), it may be a worthwhile area of study to explore ways to build ecosystems that facilitate better school-community collaboration and create more seamless delivery of services for children and their families.

To that end, the relatively well-known issue of role clarity in school counselling deserves a mention before the end of this section. As the practice of implementing counselling in schools grows in many countries and territories (Harris, 2013), there is more interest in how this problem affects each country or territory (Chaudhary & Chadha, 2014) in the Internal, Personal, and Systems domains. Hsi and Boman (2023), in their study of counsellors in tertiary institutions in Singapore, suggested that the development of professional identity is an ecological process in which the counsellors' sense of self in the

Personal domain interacted with job demands, expectations, and resources in the other domains. Harrison (2022) also recently drew attention to a lack of role clarity across East and Southeast Asia. We can only look forward to more local studies to inform practitioners, policymakers, and counsellor-educators, on ways to improve counselling provision with efforts applied to all domains in the ecosystem, contextualised to each location.

Social and Demographic Changes

Much has happened in the past decade in this area. Yeung and colleagues (2018) offered us a good overview of these developments in the region in their recent report. Baby-boomers are moving into late adulthood, adding the pressure of an ageing society in many advanced economies in Asia. Along with this development, there is a trend towards smaller nuclear families in some cities, while people have moved from rural to urban centres for work and to pursue education.

Regional and international students' movement has ensured that some local schools are less local than before, and international schools have mushroomed in many Asian cities in the past decade (The New Local, 2014). So-called third culture kids (TCK) have received much interest in research. Tan and colleagues (2021) conducted a review of related studies between 2000 and 2018 in which they noted a general increase in research conducted over the years in this area. Publications on TCK related to school counselling offer further direction in future research (Miller et al., 2020) or guidance for practice (Limberg & Lambie, 2011). In Asia, a study conducted in Singapore and Shanghai noted that international school staff may lack training in skills and knowledge pertaining to TCK (McNulty & Carter, 2018).

In Macau, school counsellors and psychologists may be helpful in supporting TCK with potential relationship difficulties and their families (Lijadi & Schalkwyk, 2014). In another study, Lijadi and Schalkwyk (2018) suggested that international schools in some parts of Asia were becoming less international as more local students began attending these schools. This fluidity, clearly originating from the External domain of the school counselling environment, has greatly impacted the way school counselling is being resourced and practised within the Internal as well as Personal domains. Whether globally or in Asia, the call for better and more specific support for TCK seems to be growing stronger, a call to which both international and local school counsellors and school leaders alike will have to respond effectively in the coming years.

Another development is a gradual increase in acceptance of the LGBTQ population, often accompanied by greater advocacy from both the supporting and the opposing sides. This is influential in the External domain and is potentially impacting education and counselling practices in schools. While more is needed, some timely Asian research has been informing school counselling practices in this area in recent years.

The work of Kwok and collaborators (2012) offered valuable insights into feelings among LGBQ students in Hong Kong which were helpful in enhancing training, practice, and ethics for school counselling. A larger and more recent study in China called for changes at policy level to offer training and enhance practices in education and counselling to better help LGBTQ youth in Chinese schools (Wei & Liu, 2019). A phenomenological study of sexual minority students in colleges in Korea also made a similar call for counsellors to be more skilled and sensitive to individual differences in the delivery of counselling services in schools and colleges (Choi & Oh, 2021). As school counselling is often seen as a personal encounter between a young person and an adult and could potentially be educational (or influential) in nature, cultural, and societal norms and expectations rest strongly with the counsellor. Additional training for counsellors might be especially important in countries with a dominant religion that might view LGBTQ as an unnatural phenomenon such as Indonesia (Ardi et al., 2018).

The dynamics between the External and Systems domains acting on Internal and Personal domains in the school counselling ecosystem cannot be underestimated. Societal values are often held tightly by parents who are key stakeholders. National religion in some cases is influential to all aspects of children's lives, including education and counselling. Hence, the management of the moral conflicts within the Personal domain is a key competence of a counsellor working with young persons in schools with LGBTQ or sexual identity concerns. More local research is needed to guide practitioners and would also add to a more robust global discourse on this subject.

Social inequality has also been flagged more prominently in several parts of Asia in the last few years. Determining how inequalities are impacting children's development, growth, and education deserves greater attention. While these issues are observed outside school walls (External domain), the impact and effects felt within schools' Internal domain are well reported. One of the ways socioeconomic status can affect the processes and outcomes of education – highly relevant to school counselling – is that of parental involvement in children's schooling (Goldstone et al., 2023). This was observed in China in a recent study on parental involvement on social networking sites in relation to their children's lives in schools (Huang & Lin, 2019). In Hong Kong, parental involvement was found to be partially aligned to socioeconomic status, but it was reported that parental involvement across all groups seem to be more strategic in nature, specifically focusing on helping their children do better academically (Kwan & Wong, 2016).

The roles in the Systems domain have also been spotlighted in some places such as Singapore. Teo (2018) shared her findings that a student's lived experience of poverty and inequality in schools should be better understood and harnessed by those seeking to offer help on the ground as well as those involved in policy making. In China, an interesting study conducted by Loyalka and colleagues (2013) found that counselling was linked to an increase in dropouts and lower academic achievements in some rural schools. The counselling experience appeared to have made students less optimistic about the cost-benefits of having a formal educational qualification, considering the growing wages among unskilled labour in the economy. The reason why students may have chosen work over further studies could be attributed to the career information and statistics provided to the students during the counselling process. This observation further demonstrates the social ecological impact events in the External as well as Systems domains have in the microspace of counselling in schools. Therefore, school counsellors' awareness, knowledge, and information (Personal domain) of developments in the External and Systems domains are equally important to their growth in clinical know-how and skills.

The notion that school counselling and guidance has a role in reducing social inequalities, if not at least limiting related impacts, has been discussed in the counselling literature (Fitzgibbon & Winter, 2023; Restori et al., 2008). Hence, it is possible to see that the school counsellor as part of the system, operating in the internal school setting and subject to wider external environmental changes, would be involved in one way or another in influencing social (in)equalities as they present themselves in counselling sessions, group programmes, and other professional or educational contexts.

Awareness of the interactions between the ecological domains in relation to demographic changes in our societies is essential in ensuring school counselling practices and services remain relevant and responsive. The ability to analyse, appreciate, and put in action necessary steps, such as timely training to further cultural sensitivity, and recognition of the specific needs of vulnerable groups, would gradually become a marker of an expert practitioner in the realm of school counselling in Asia.

Beyond the School Counselling Room

We live in a dynamic and ever-changing world. Adopting an ecological mindset and using a suitable framework can allow us to capture the moving parts and their interaction with each other as we function as clinicians in listening, attending, and helping young people. To intervene meaningfully in a young person's and his/her family's relational and emotional space requires consideration beyond the presenting issues which the young person brings to counselling sessions.

The discussions in this chapter strive to illustrate the potential of understanding the interaction between domains while crafting purposeful interventions in school counselling. This appreciation of the dynamics between domains requires a careful examination and interpretation of the school ecology so that meaningful insights can inform counselling practice, policy changes, and service development in schools.

The COVID-19 pandemic can be cited as a good example of how the different ecological domains interact. With the pandemic originating in the External domain, schools had to adapt to measures imposed by the Systems domain into the Internal domain of the school environment. As observed in

Asia, this interaction culminated in the growth of school counsellors' capabilities, from picking up skills to operate in the virtual environment or online platforms, to new clinical skills in providing therapy remotely and becoming more sensitive to emotional cues, considering that much of the faces of both counsellors and clients were covered during that period.

School counselling is more than just a conversation between a safe and trusted adult and a young person in a small quiet room in the school. One must embrace the ecological influences surrounding each of these unique conversations and how they shape the young person's dynamic and fast-changing External domain. This is particularly important to school counselling in Asia, which is seeing rapid growth today, and will change at a quicker pace in the coming years.

References

Anagbogu, Nwokolo, Anyamene, Anyachebelu, & Umezulike, R. Q. (2013). Professional challenges to counselling practice in primary schools in Anambra State, Nigeria: The way forward. *International Journal of Psychology and Behavioral Sciences*, 5, 89–96. https://doi.org/10.5897/IJPC13.001

Ang, Q. (2022, May 20). About 1 in 3 young people in Singapore has mental health symptoms: Study. *The Straits Times.* https://www.straitstimes.com/singapore/about-1-in-3-youths-in-singapore-has-mental-health-symptoms-study

Ardi, Z., Yendi, F., & Febriani, R. (2018). Fenomena LGBTQ dalam perspektif konseling dan psikoterapi: realitas dan tantangan konselor. *Jurnal Pendidikan Indonesia*, 4(2), 77–82. https://doi.org/10.29210/120182260

Arfasa, A. J., & Weldmeskel, F. M. (2020). Practices and challenges of guidance and counselling services in secondary schools. *Emerging Science Journal*, 4(3), 183–191. https://doi.org/10.28991/esj-2020-01222

Beidoğlu, M., Dinçyürek, S., & Akıntuğ, Y. (2015). The opinions of school counselling on the use of information and communication technologies in school counselling practices: North Cyprus Schools. *Computers in Human Behavior*, 52, 466–471. https://doi.org/10.1016/j.chb.2015.06.022

Bhat, C. S., Ragan, M. A., Selvaraj, P. R., & Shultz, B. J. (2017). Online bullying among high-school students in India. *International Journal for the Advancement of Counselling*, 39, 112–124. https://doi.org/10.1007/s10447-017-9286-y

Boitt, M. L. (2016). Evaluation of the challenges in the implementation of the guidance and counselling programme in Baringo county secondary schools, Kenya. *Journal of Education and Practice*. 7(30), 27–34. https://eric.ed.gov/?id=EJ1118929

Bronfenbrenner, U. (1981). *The ecology of human development*. Harvard University Press.

Bustos, I. G. (2016). Development of the guidance counsellors' occupational and life satisfaction scale. *Journal of Universality of Global Education Issues*, 3(1), 1–30. https://ugei-ojs-shsu.tdl.org/ugei/article/view/6

Chaudhary, N., & Chadha, N. K. (2014). Conflicting role of counselors: Scenario of Indian schools. *International Journal of Education and Management Studies*, 4(2), 98–102.

Choi, K., & Oh, I. (2021). A phenomenological approach to understanding sexual minority college students in South Korea. *Journal of Multicultural Counselling & Development*. 49(4), 225–238. https://doi.org/10.1002/jmcd.12227

Chong, W., Lee, B., Tan, S., Wong, S., & Yeo, L. (2013). School psychology and school-based child and family interventions in Singapore. *School Psychology International*, *34*(2), 177–189. https://doi.org/10.1177/014303431245339

Fadzilah, M., Syifa, M. A., Rahima, D., Zarina, I. I., Hayati, K. S., Nainey, K. K., Amirah, S. N., Najwa, S. M. S., Hana, S. N., & Muhammad, A. (2022). Mental health status among Malaysia youth – A nationwide cross-sectional study. *Malaysian Family Physician*, *17*, 15–16.

Fitzgibbon, A., & Winter, L. A. (2023). Practical applications of a social justice agenda in counselling and psychotherapy: The relational equality in education framework (REEF). *British Journal of Guidance & Counselling*, *51*(5), 665–674. https://doi.org/10.1080/03069885.2021.1981230

Furlonger, B., & Budisa, S. (2016). Internet sites and apps available to students seeking counselling, and what school counsellors should know about them. *Journal of Psychologists and Counsellors in Schools*, *26*(1), 68–83. https://doi.org/10.1017/jgc.2015.22

Goldstone, R., Baker, W., & Barg, K. (2023). A comparative perspective on social class inequalities in parental involvement in education: Structural dynamics, institutional design, and cultural factors. *Educational Review*, *75*(5), 976–992. https://doi.org/10.1080/00131911.2021.1974347

Harris, B. (2013). *International school-based counselling*. British Association for Counselling & Psychotherapy. https://www.academia.edu/48547005/School_based_counselling_internationally_a_scoping_review

Harrison, M. G. (2021). *School counselling in an Asian cultural context: Insights from Hong Kong and Asia-Pacific Region*. Routledge.

Harrison, M. G. (2022). The professional identity of school counsellors in East and Southeast Asia. *Counselling & Psychotherapy Research*, *22*(3), 543–547. https://doi.org/10.1002/capr.12546

Hsi, T., & Boman, P. (2023). The development of professional identity among counsellors in tertiary educational institutions in Singapore. *Counselling & Psychotherapy Review Singapore*, *1*(1), 19–27. https://doi.org/10.1142/S2810968623500031

Huang, H., & Lin, X. (2019). Chinese parental involvement and class-based inequality in education: The role of social networking sites. *Learning, Media and Technology*, *44*(4), 489–501. https://doi.org/10.1080/17439884.2019.1620767

Jayawardena, H. K., & Gamage, G. P. (2022). Exploring challenges in mental health service provisions for school-going adolescents in Sri Lanka. *School Psychology International*, *43*(1), 18–37. https://doi.org/10.1177/0143034321104306

Kaur, J., Cheong, S. M., Mahadir Naidu, B., Kaur, G., Manickam, M. A., Mat Noor, M., Ali, O. (2014). Prevalence and correlates of depression among adolescents in Malaysia. *Asia-Pacific Journal of Public Health*, *26*(5_Suppl.), 53S–62S. https://doi.org/10.1177/1010539514544356

Kim, H., Han, Y., Song, J., & Song, T. M. (2019). Application of social big data to identify trends of school bullying forms in South Korea. *International Journal of Environmental Research and Public Health*, *16*(14), 2596. https://doi.org/10.3390/ijerph16142596

Koch, M. C., Vajda, A. J., & Koch, L. C. (2020). Trauma-informed rehabilitation counselling. *Journal of Applied Rehabilitation Counselling*, *51*(3), 192–207. https://doi.org/10.1891/JARC-D-19-00025

Kwan, P., & Wong, Y.-L. (2016). Parental involvement in schools and class inequality in education: Some recent findings from Hong Kong. *International Journal of Pedagogies and Learning*, *11*(2), 91–102. https://doi.org/10.1080/22040552.2016.1227250

Kwok, D. K., Winter, S., & Yuen, M. (2012). Heterosexism in school: The counselling experience of Chinese tongzhi students in Hong Kong. *British Journal of Guidance & Counselling, 40*(5), 561–575. https://doi.org/10.1080/03069885.2012.718735

Lee, S. M., & Trevisan, M. (2019). Evaluation in support of school counselling in Korea: A proposal. *KEDI Journal of Educational Policy, 16*(1), 63–80. https://doi.org/10.22804/kjep.2019.16.1.004

Lee, S., Chun, Y., Chung, H., Shin, S., Lee, I., Lee, D., & Choi, Y. (2013). The profession of family therapy in South Korea: Current status and future directions. *Contemporary Family Therapy, 35*, 388–399. https://doi.org/10.1007/s10591-013-9270-6

Lee, V. (2021, August 9). More than counselling: How schools help students with mental health woes. *The Straits Times.* https://www.straitstimes.com/singapore/parenting-education/more-than-counselling-how-schools-help-students-with-mental-health

Leuwerke, W., & Shi, Q. (2010). The practice and perceptions of school counsellors: A view from urban China. *International Journal for the Advancement of Counselling, 32*, 75–89. https://doi.org/10.1007/s10447-009-9091-3

Lijadi, A. A., & Schalkwyk, G. J. (2014). Narratives of third culture kids: Commitment and reticence in social relationships. *The Qualitative Report, 19*(25), 1–18. https://doi.org/10.46743/2160-3715/2014.1213

Lijadi, A. A., & Schalkwyk, G. J. (2018). "The international schools are not so international after all": The educational experiences of third culture kids. *International Journal of School & Educational Psychology, 6*(1), 50–61. https://doi.org/10.1080/21683603.2016.1261056

Limberg, D., & Lambie, G. W. (2011). Third culture kids: Implications for professional school counselling. *Professional School Counselling, 15*(1), 45–54. https://doi.org/10.1177/2156759X1101500102

Lin, A. P., Trappey, C. V., Luan, C.-C., Trappey, A. J., & Tu, K. L. (2021). A test platform for managing school stress using a virtual reality group chatbot counselling system. *Applied Sciences, 11*(19), 9071. https://doi.org/10.3390/app11199071

Low, P. K. (2009). Considering the challenges of counselling practice. *International Journal for the Advancement of Counselling, 31*, 71–79. https://doi.org/10.1007/s10447-009-9069-1

Low, P. K. (2014). Looking in from the outside: Community counsellors' opinions and attitudes to school counselling in Singapore. *Pastoral Care in Education, 32*(4), 295–305. https://doi.org/10.1080/02643944.2014.974663

Low, P. K. (2015). Stakeholders' perceptions of school counselling in Singapore. *Journal of Psychologists and Counsellors in Schools, 25*(2), 200–216. https://doi.org/10.1017/jgc.2014.21

Low, P. K., & van der Laan, L. (2023). Community-school collaborations: Community counsellors' perceptions of school counselling in Singapore. *Asia Pacific Journal of Counselling and Psychotherapy, 14*(1), 70–78. https://doi.org/10.1080/21507686.2023.2193755

Loyalka, P., Liu, C., Song, Y., Yi, H., Huang, X., Wei, J., & Rozelle, S. (2013). Can information and counselling help students from poor rural areas go to high school? Evidence from China. *Journal of Comparative Economics, 41*(4), 1012–1025. https://doi.org/10.1016/j.jce.2013.06.004

Mah, A. (2015). *Counselling and well-being support services in Australian Muslim schools.* University of Western Australia.

Martin, F. A. (2020). *Therapy thieves.* Oxford University Press.

McNulty, Y., & Carter, M. A. (2018). Do international school staff receive professional development training about third culture kids (TCKs)? Perspectives from faculty and parents. In K. J. Kennedy, & J. Lee (Eds.), *The Routledge Handbook on Schools and Schooling in Asia* (pp. 280–292). Routledge.

Miller, S. T., Wiggins, G. M., & Feather, K. A. (2020). Growing up globally: Third culture kids' experience with transition, identity, and well-being. *International Journal for the Advancement of Counselling, 42*, 414–423. https://doi.org/10.1007/s10447-020-09412-y

Murshid, N. S. (2017). Bullying victimization and mental health outcomes of adolescents in Myanmar, Pakistan, and Sri Lanka. *Children and Youth Services Review, 76*, 163–169. https://doi.org/10.1016/j.childyouth.2017.03.003

Neo, C. C., Yip, C., & Goh, C. T. (2022, May 3). 'It's Really About Normalising Mental Health': What schools are doing so students seek help. *Channel News Asia.* https://www.channelnewsasia.com/can-insider/mental-health-what-schools-doing-help-students-2655911

Ng-Tay, C., Teo, J., & Ng, Y. (2019). Trauma-informed child welfare practice model in Methodist Welfare Services Covenant Family Service Centre (Singapore). *Children Australia, 44*(2), 81–83. https://doi.org/0.1017/cha.2019.10

Nishio, A., Kakimoto, M., Bermardo, T. M. S. and Kobayashi, J. (2020), Current situation and comparison of school mental health in ASEAN countries. *Pediatrics International, 62*, 438–443. https://doi.org/10.1111/ped.14137

Noboru, T., Amalia, E., Hernandez, P. M., Nurbaiti, L., Affarah, W. S., Nonaka, D., Kobayashi, J. (2021). School-based education to prevent bullying in high schools in Indonesia. *Pediatrics International, 63*(4), 459–468 https://doi.org/10.1111/ped.14475

Owusu, D. N., Owusu Ansah, K., Dey, N. E., Duah, H. O., & Agbadi, P. (2022). Bullying and truancy amongst school-going adolescents in Timor-Leste: Results from the 2015 global school-based health survey. *Heliyon 8*(1), e08797 https://doi.org/10.1016/j.heliyon.2022.e08797

Peh, C. X., Tan, J., Lei, T., Wong, E., & Henn-Haase, C. M. (2022). Evaluating the use of trauma-informed mental health assessment measures in care planning for children and adolescents in out-of-home residential care in Singapore. *Child Abuse Review, 31*, 150–168. https://doi.org/10.1002/car.2732

Pengpid, S., & Peltzer, K. (2019). Bullying victimization and externalizing and internalizing symptoms among in-school adolescents from five ASEAN countries. *Children and Youth Services Review, 106*, 104473. https://doi.org/10.1016/j.childyouth.2019.104473

Puhy, C. E., Litke, S. G., Silverstein, M. J., Kiely, J. R., Pardes, A., McGeoch, E., & Daly, B. P. (2021). Counsellor and student perceptions of an eHealth technology platform used in a school counselling setting. *Psychology in the Schools, 58*(7), 1284–1298. https://doi.org/10.1002/pits.22541

Putri, T. R., Supriyanto, A., Martaningsih, S. T., & Rosada, U. D. (2022). School counsellor professional competence (PC-SC): Social media utilization in guidance and counselling services (GC-S). *Counsellia: Jurnal Bimbingan dan Konseling, 12*(1), 36–47. https://doi.org/10.25273/counsellia.v12i110846

Rahman, M. M., Rahman, M. M., Khan, M. M., Hasan, M., & Choudhury, K. N. (2020). Bullying victimization and adverse health behaviors among school-going adolescents in South Asia: Findings from the global school-based student health survey. *Depression and Anxiety, 37*(10), 995–1006. https://doi.org/10.1002/da.23033

Rappleye, J., & Komatsu, H. (2020). Is bullying and suicide a problem for East Asia's schools? Evidence from TIMSS and PISA. *Discourse, 41*(2), 310–331. https://doi.org/10.1080/01596306.2020.1711515

Rawson, S. (2021). *Applying trauma-sensitive practices in school counselling: Interventions for achieving change.* Routledge.

Restori, A., Gresham, F., & Cook, C. (2008). "Old habits die hard:" Past and current issues pertaining to response-to-intervention. *The California School Psychologist, 13*, 67–78. https://doi.org/10.1007/BF03340943

Rumsey, A. D., & Milsom, A. (2018). Supporting school engagement and high school completion through trauma-informed school counselling. *Professional School Counselling, 22*(1), 1–10. https://doi.org/10.1177/2156759x19867254

Sokantat, N., Kanyajit, S., Poonyarith, S., Thanyasiri, P., & Unmarerng, N. (2021). Thai culture: The foundation of school bullying. *International Journal of Criminal Justice Science, 16*(2), 369–384. https://doi.org/10.5281/zenodo.4756082/IJCJS

Sueki, H. (2016). Willingness to pay for school counselling services in Japan: A contingent valuation study. *Asia Pacific Journal of counselling and psychotherapy, 7*(1), 15–25. https://doi.org/10.1080/21507686.2016.1199438

Supriyanto, A., Hartini, S., Irdasari, W. N., Miftahul, A., Oktapiana, S., & Mumpuni, S. D. (2020). Teacher professional quality: Counselling services with technology in Pandemic COVID-19. *Counsellia: Jurnal Bimbingan dan Konseling (Online), 10*(2), 176–189.

Tajan, N. (2015). Adolescents' school non-attendance and the spread of psychological counselling in Japan. *Asia Pacific Journal of Counselling and Psychotherapy, 6*(1), 58–69. https://doi.org/10.1080/21507686.2015.1029502

Tan, E. C., Wang, K. T., & Cottrell, A. B. (2021). A systematic review of third culture kids empirical research. *International Journal of Intercultural Relations, 82*, 81–98. https://doi.org/10.1016/j.ijintrel.2021.03.002

Teo, Y. (2018). *This is what inequality looks like.* Ethos Books.

Teoh, H. (2010). A survey of urban child and adolescent mental health problems in an urban Malaysian population. *Malaysian Journal of Psychiatry. 19*(1), 1–13.

The New Local; International Schools. (2014, December 20). *The Economist*, 413(8918), 88(US). https://link.gale.com/apps/doc/A393916198/AONE?u=james_cook&sid=bookmark-AONE&xid=ff142388

Tran, L., Huynh, V.-S., Giang, T.-V., Nguyen-Thi, M.-L., & Nguyen-Thi, D.-M. (2020). Vocational orientation and the need for establishing career counselling office in Vietnamese schools. *Journal of Technical Education and Training, 12*(2), 46–54.

Van, S., Thien, V., Tat, T., Tran, L., & Duc, H. (2019). The stress problems and the needs for stress counselling of high school students in Vietnam. *European Journal of Educational Research, 8*(4), 1053–1061. https://doi.org/10.12973/eu-jer.8.4.1053

Van Schalkwyk, G. J. (2013). School-based counselling and psychological services in Macao. *International Journal of School & Educational Psychology, 1*(3), 207–216. https://doi.org/10.1080/21683603.2013.822840

Wei, C., & Liu, W. (2019). Coming out in mainland China: A national survey of LGBTQ students. *Journal of LGBT Youth, 16*(2), 192–219. https://doi.org/10.1080/19361653.2019.1565795

Wells, T. (2022). School counsellor perceptions and knowledge of trauma-informed practices. *Professional School Counselling. 26*(1), https://doi.org/10.1177/2156759X221096352

Wong, K. P., Bonn, G., Tam, C. L., & Wong, C. P. (2018). Preferences for online and/or face-to-face counselling among university students in Malaysia. *Frontiers in Psychology. 9*, 64. https://doi.org/10.3389/fpsyg.2018.00064

Yeung, W.-J. J., Desai, S., & Jones, G. W. (2018). Families in Southeast and South Asia. *Annual Review of Sociology, 44,* 469–495. https://doi.org/10.1146/annurev-soc-073117-041124

3 Challenges of School Counselling in Malaysia
Pre and During the COVID-19 Pandemic

Sew Kim Low and Jin Kuan Kok

Introduction

Counselling services, being part of the mental health profession, are vital for the development of personal mental health wellness. The cultivation of mental well-being begins from a young age and its growth is influenced by the home and school environments in which a child is fully immersed. In Malaysia, formal public-school education is compulsory for children from the age of seven years, beginning with Year 1. Primary education is from Year 1 to Year 6 where the focus of education is academic. Upon completion of Year 6, students move to secondary education where counselling and guidance services start being introduced as studies have shown a bidirectional relationship between academic and mental health functioning (Stiles & Gudino, 2018). Poor mental health can affect academic achievement, and vice versa.

In the multicultural context of Malaysia, challenges and barriers are particularly imbedded. Online counselling in the secondary school setting, though relatively new, has the potential to develop. Currently, online counselling services are available in many universities (Kok, 2016); however, its development among secondary schools has yet to catch up. In a survey of 409 Malaysian university students, 35% of participants preferred to receive mental health counselling online (Wong et al., 2018). Research findings have shown that help-seeking behaviours have changed as many young people use digital devices such as computers and smart phones to connect with others and disclose their psychological distress. During the COVID-19 pandemic, a survey of 467 students reported the need for a counselling blog for them to access information and seek for early help (Nurul Fitriah et al., 2022). Online counselling has a disinhibition effect, creating a comfortable space which attracted school children to chat and disclose their mental health challenges. Therefore, when a Movement Control Order (MCO) was implemented during the COVID-19 period, many secondary school counsellors used online platforms to reach out and provide support for these children. This new technology advancement had many advantages and was widely used. It seemed to be effective in reaching out to the wider student population who had been isolated, with movement limited to the home. Clearly, the prospects for online

DOI: 10.4324/9781003352457-3

counselling are good. Notwithstanding this, there are legal and other related constraints that must be dealt with.

This chapter comprises three sections. The first presents an overview of the development of counselling and guidance services in Malaysia as well as challenges and barriers prior to the COVID-19 pandemic. The second section focuses on the impact of the pandemic where social and physical restrictions put in place by the government prohibited face-to-face counselling in schools. School counselling and guidance services had to depend on online platforms which came with their own challenges and implications. The last section discusses the strengths and shortcomings of Malaysian school counselling services, including suggestions on how to improve these services in the light of what has been learned throughout the pandemic.

Overview of the Development of Counselling and Guidance Service in Malaysia

In Malaysia, secondary school guidance and counselling services are based on the Missouri Comprehensive Guidance Program (Missouri Model) of the United States (Abdul Malik et al., 2013). This programme spread to Malaysia in the 1960s, with a model emphasising students' academic, career, and personal-social development. During the period of British colonial rule, guidance and counselling in Malaysian schools were handled by classroom teachers and hostel masters (Othman & Bakar, 1993). In 1963, a structured guidance service was introduced into schools with the establishment of a Guidance Unit in the Ministry of Education (Ministry of Education Report, Malaysia, 1970). With the establishment of this unit in the Educational Planning and Research Division, the Education Ministry ruled that each school should have a guidance teacher with approximately 16 hours of academic work per week and who is exempted from other activities (KP5209/35 (4), 1964). Thus, guidance services were mainly handled by classroom teachers appointed by school principals. These guidance teachers played the dual role of classroom teacher and counsellor, handling the social, emotional, and disciplinary problems of students. Guidance and counselling services later gained greater importance and became an integral part of the education system (Low et al., 2013). In 1966, a full-time school counsellor position was established whereby the counsellor was given exemption from any academic responsibility. Guidance and counselling services were predominantly school-based, with the school counsellor's roles and functions focused on three main areas: (i) academic-related issues, (ii) career guidance and developmental issues, and (iii) psychosocial issues.

In 1983, there was an emerging drug abuse scenario and increasing criminal activities among adolescents. Guidance and counselling teachers became further burdened with the responsibility of combating drugs in school. Besides performing regular counselling services, school counsellors were expected to play a vital role in the prevention, enrichment, and remediation of substance usage among students. Counsellors were to plan, perform, and manage educational programmes to prevent drug, alcohol, and cigarette abuse.

In 1993, the school counselling and guidance service was reviewed, with the main objective of providing growth and enrichment services, preventive education, orientation programmes, and crisis counselling. At present, besides the provision of the above services, greater emphasis is put on academic services such as planning performance and management of study skills, preventive programmes related to substance abuse, and involvement in school planning (See, 2004). In 2000, it was made compulsory for every public secondary school to have a full-time counsellor (See & Ng, 2010), although this policy did not extend to private and independent schools.

Studies have indicated that current school guidance and counselling services focus mainly on coordination and management, consulting, and development, with less emphasis given to assessment, appraisal, services for students with special needs and those gifted and talented, crisis intervention, and multicultural counselling competencies (Amat, 2018). A recent study of 159 Malaysian counsellors reported that counsellors have a moderate level of counselling self-efficacy pertaining to basic counselling skills (Alia Sarah Asri, 2022). Suhaila et al. (2022) proposed that the elements of self-compassion, counselling self-efficacy, emotion, and spiritual intelligence should be included in the counsellor training curriculum. The future of school counselling in Malaysia requires growth in new theoretical orientations based on local contexts, multicultural, spiritual and developmental approaches, testing, and assessment. There is a need for more local research and clinical discoveries through practice.

Although school counselling services in Malaysian secondary schools are well established with the provision of a full-time counsellor for every 500 students, the shortage of trained counsellors in some schools has resulted in the ineffective implementation of counselling services. Private or independent secondary schools may not follow this ratio of counsellors to number of students due to a lack of resources. This means some teachers who have gone through basic listening skills training will have to take on counselling jobs while also attending to other non-counselling related tasks.

According to the Counsellor Act of 1998, all counsellors have to register with the Malaysian Board of Counsellors and are granted a lifelong valid licence (The Commissioner of Law Revision Malaysia, 2006). Under the Act, it is compulsory for counsellors in settings such as higher education institutions and other workplaces to register with the Board of Counsellors. On the other hand, school counsellors are not required to register because their employment status is defined as *teachers* in their service scheme. This, unfortunately, affects the quality-of-service delivery in the school setting (Aga Mohd Jaladin, 2013). Although counselling services have improved over the years, school counsellors continue to encounter various challenges and obstacles.

Challenges and Barriers

Stigmatisation in Seeking Counselling Service

Traditional concepts of shame and the fear of stigmatisation are among the factors that hinder the seeking of psychological help. Reserved Asian societies with conservative social cultural values view psychological problems as something to be shared only among family members. Asian cultural values of restraining emotions, avoiding shame, and saving face may conflict with self-disclosure and emotional expressions in traditional counselling (Lindsey et al., 2020). Also, a lack of knowledge about the benefits of seeking early psychological help discourage the seeking of counselling services. An individual's decision to seek psychological help depends on having sufficient information and knowledge of a counsellor's qualifications, session time, and the duration of treatment.

Studies have found that students prefer to seek help from family members and friends for fear of being stigmatised as having psychological problems (Chai, 2000). This is further supported by research findings (Martin & Marshall, 2010) highlighting that issues of confidentiality and counsellors' helpfulness are barriers that keep students from seeking professional help. They tend to only seek guidance services for their schoolwork or career when the family fails to support them (Low et al., 2013).

In addition, Malaysian beliefs in supernatural power and retribution of past life transgressions (Khan et al., 2011) have resulted in the reluctance to seek professional counselling assistance for fear of being stigmatised. Similarly, a study of Malaysian school counselling services indicates students' misconception that visiting school counsellors implies the existence of problems with oneself (Chen & Kok, 2017). Students felt they should take responsibility for their own problems and that they should have the capability of solving them. Family pride and the fear of revealing one's vulnerability or inferiority and being stigmatised are barriers in seeking school counselling services. According to Putman (2010), counselling is a process where one confronts anxieties, fears, and knowing the truth about one's life, which requires a great deal of courage in this cultural setting.

Demand for Cultural Sensitivity

Malaysia has a diverse population, with multi-languages and multi-ethnic cultures and lifestyles. The country comprises 69% Bumiputra (Malay and indigenous groups), 23% Chinese and 7% Indian (Malaysian Department of Statistics, 2020). This means students in public secondary schools are culturally diverse, with different ethnicities, religions, languages, socio-economic statuses, and ages. Such diversity presents counsellors with complex issues (See & Ng, 2010). In Malaysia, intercultural counselling involves language, communication, cultural and power challenges. The language challenge includes communication styles, the use of language, and expression styles (Sulaiman et al., 2022). Counsellors are required to be multiculturally competent and confident in dealing with these issues (Chai, 2000). Low et al. (2011) indicate that gender and language are barriers often encountered by school counsellors. Female students are afraid to share their emotional and personal problems with male counsellors, thus the preference for client and counsellor to be of the same gender.

Language is another sensitive issue for effective counselling in Malaysia. According to Holmes (2001), language is an intricate part of culture. Counsellors in most public secondary schools encounter language barriers in providing effective counselling services, especially for students who are not proficient in the national language (Low et al., 2011). These students come from the vernacular primary schools where the medium of instruction is Mandarin and Tamil. In secondary schools, Bahasa Malaysia is the main language. This language barrier hinders students seeking help from counsellors as they are not sufficiently fluent to express themselves freely to be understood by the counsellor.

Besides language and gender, cultural differences are hurdles to seeking help. Among the Chinese, the preference on self-reliance, seeking help from alternative sources, low perceived need towards help-seeking, poor experiences with help-seeking, and negative attitudes towards help-seeking prevent them from engaging with counsellors (Teo et al., 2020). It was also reported that the cultural barriers to professional help-seeking included negative attitudes, poor knowledge of mental health, social and self-imposed stigma, confidentiality, misconceptions, perceived ineffectiveness of services, and apprehension of unwanted intervention (Sanghvi & Mehrotra, 2020).

Lack of Multicultural Competence

Research has demonstrated the need for counsellors to be culturally competent in specific multicultural contexts (Whaley & Davis, 2007). Multicultural competencies are imperative as they enable counsellors to evaluate the client's present issues and challenges and deliver appropriate services (Gonzalez-Prendes et al., 2011; Hwang, 2009). Knowing how culture and belief systems affect a student's daily life and interactions with school and community, a counsellor can appreciate the underlying forces that shape the academic and social development of the student (Jones & Lee, 2021). According to Sue and colleagues (2022), multicultural competencies comprise: (i) being aware of the counsellor's assumptions, values, and biases, (ii) understanding the worldview of culturally diverse clients, and (iii) developing appropriate interventions and techniques.

In Malaysia, most school counsellors are generally aware of the existence of cultural differences in society but are unable to effectively distinguish and deal with these differences. Counsellors prefer the convenient practice of cultural-match counselling (Aga Mohd Jaladin, 2013). Most Indian and Chinese school counsellors can speak well in their mother tongue, Bahasa Malaysia and English, while Malay counsellors are mostly bilingual, speaking mainly Bahasa Malaysia and English. Thus, most Malay counsellors in public secondary schools encounter a language barrier in offering effective counselling services to the ethnic minority Chinese and Indian students. Aga Mohd Jaladin (2013), in her study, reported the need to enhance school counsellors' multicultural awareness, knowledge, and skills to ensure they are more understanding of the diverse and cultural experiences of the clients. Locally, a study found that many counsellors perceive the practice of multicultural counselling as very challenging when it involves differences in specific cultural issues and their own lack of multicultural and self-awareness (Aga Mohd Jaladin et al., 2021). Nor Mazlina Ghazali (2023) reported that Malaysian counsellors must equip themselves with knowledge and skills related to interpersonal relationships, interactions, multiculturalism, and religiosity. There is a need to infuse multicultural issues and diversity in counsellor education programmes in Malaysia.

Private secondary schools should also ensure they have a sufficient number of trained counsellors, even though they do not receive funding from the Malaysian Ministry of Education. Counsellors are also needed in the many international schools to cater to students from Korea, Thailand, Indonesia, China, and other countries, and cultural sensitivities need to be observed in these settings. If school counsellors are unable to adapt their skills and knowledge to meet the needs of the culturally diverse students in the context of their unique cultural backgrounds, schools will be less able to recommend appropriate intervention plans for students (Jones & Lee, 2021).

Lack of Service for Students with Special Education Needs

Guidance and counselling services are for every student regardless of age, religion, ability, or disability. They are designed to assist individuals to overcome the emotional, psychological, and personal-social roadblocks in their daily lives. In Malaysia, *special education* refers to education for children with learning problems or disabilities which make it harder for them to learn, compared to children of the same age. This includes children with social, behavioural, and emotional difficulties, multiple learning difficulties, communication and language problems, autism spectrum disorder, attention deficit hyperactivity disorder, physical disabilities, multiple-sensory impairment, and the gifted (Hamza Alshoura, 2021).

Counselling challenges related to this category of students concern the need for appropriate counselling strategies and interventions in resolving their complex problems. The task of counselling is to provide opportunities for the individual to define, explore, discover, and adopt ways to live a more satisfying and resourceful life within the social, educational, and vocational groups with which they identify, as well as to be able to accept themselves (Bulus, 1990). The involvement of counselling with special needs students requires new strategies to improve the challenges encountered by these children. Counselling with special activities assists these students to understand themselves, others, and the school environment, and to adjust accordingly to their abilities (Agi & Chinonye, 2022).

As guidance and counselling procedures comprise advice-giving, support in time of need, encouragement, information-giving, and test interpretation, counsellors may sometimes find it difficult to handle students with special needs. Students with learning difficulties may face multi-faceted problems in academic, personal, social, financial, sexual, family, and emotional areas. Secondary school counsellors who are not professionally trained will lack the knowledge and skills to assist these special needs students. The current Malaysian school counselling services are based on the one-size-fits-all philosophy, thus ignoring children with special needs (Abu Yazid et al., 2019). Counselling services are unable to meet these students' needs. They may prefer to seek help from their parents or friends. The fact that many Malaysian school counsellors are not trained to cater to special needs students means counselling services for this group may not be well received.

Individuals with unique mental abilities or social and emotional characteristics have psychological needs that might be different from those of their peers. They need appropriate support and guidance to optimise their full potential (Abu Yazid, 2016). Although guidance and counselling services in the Malaysian secondary school system are well established, the local education system has not targeted the specific needs of this population. Despite the setting up of inclusive and remedial education in some primary schools, counsellors are not trained to cater to the special needs of these students. At present, studies on guidance and counselling for special populations are rare. Abu Yazid (2016), in his study, reported that Malaysian gifted students need an effective guidance and counselling service to support them in their academic and psychological development.

Lack of Parent, School, and Community Collaborations

Collaboration with stakeholders involved in the growth and psychological development of school children is essential to ensure the implementation of effective counselling programmes. The lack of cooperation between schoolteachers, administrators, and parents and poor response from students are constraints which hinder counsellors' implementation of effective counselling programmes at the school level. A study by Low et al. (2013) indicated parents' refusal to cooperate with school counsellors because they viewed counselling services as something which is only for problem students. A study of the role of family life on juvenile delinquency in Malaysia showed parental un-involvement, parental separation, and peer pressure were the main factors for involvement in delinquency. The findings of the study revealed the need for parental collaboration in the counselling process to help adolescents to cope with life challenges (Ezarina et al., 2022).

According to the Ministry of Education circular KP(BPSH-SPPK)201/005/02 Jld 4(5) (Kementerian Pelajaran Malaysia, 2012), 90% of a counsellor's responsibility is to provide guidance and counselling services. Counsellors need to design activities and interventions to instil moral values and good discipline (Abdul Malek et al., 2013). In addition, counsellors have to coordinate activities to promote the social, emotional, and behavioural management of students. Other activities include documentation of students' profiles, conducting preventive and remedial activities, and consultation with parents, the local community, and governmental policymakers.

Although full-time school counsellors are responsible for planning and implementing guidance and counselling services, cooperation from teachers, administrators, and students is essential to plan and promote harmony, tolerance, and understanding of differences in the school environment. School counsellor roles are shaped by the organisational ecologies of the workplace. Hence, collaborative relationships between counsellors, teachers, principals, and community enable counsellors to be more effective (Harrison, 2022). Collaboration with the resources in the community, non-governmental, and professional organisations such as libraries, local universities, faith-based organisations, and businesses help to identify specific requirements and mobilise the available resources to meet the needs of students and their families (Low & Kok, 2020). Local universities can help provide the latest career information to assist students in early preparation for their career paths while business personnel can advise students on the demands and expectations of business organisations.

The uneven distribution of school counsellors and the lack of trained counsellors have resulted in some schools not having sufficient counsellors. The Ministry of Education should set the standard for the provision of psychological services to schools according to the school psychology framework to ensure best practices and efficient services to students. In addition, the provision of counsellors should also consider the language and cultural sensitivity of the students to enable those facing language barriers to participate in counselling. Considering that many school counsellors are not trained in the assessment and early identification of children with special needs, the assistance required by this category of students remains largely unresolved. As suggested by Amat (2018), effective counselling with students with special needs requires clarification of the counsellors' feelings and attitudes, and the acquisition of relevant knowledge and skills in providing services for these children. School counsellors must consider the students' profile, presenting issues, the therapeutic environment, proposed interventions, the termination process, and follow-up. Counsellors' training programmes should therefore incorporate knowledge and skills specific to students with different types of special needs.

School Counselling Services during the COVID-19 Pandemic

The sudden advent of COVID-19 quickly escalated to a potential threat to global public health (Peng, 2020). On 28 February 2020, the World Health Organisation raised the COVID-19 risk to the highest level. As the pandemic spread, Malaysia implemented the MCO from March 2020 until August 2021. The need for social and physical distancing and lockdowns altered human social relationships. With the abandonment of physical classes, school counselling services were also interrupted. The introduction of stringent standard operating procedures (SOPs) changed the school setting, and classes were conducted virtually, partially (hybrid mode), or in a staggered return to school. In terms of counselling services, the relationship between counsellors and clients saw a change.

Due to the MCO, it was reported that the mental health of school children in Malaysia suffered (UNICEF, 2020). Among the 266 cases of suicides and deaths between March 18 and October 30 of 2020, one in four were teenagers between the ages of 15 and 18. This could be because many children were confined to their home, with no avenue or space to release stress and no interaction with friends. Needless to say, the provision of counselling during this pandemic period was crucial in meeting these children's needs.

Without a doubt, the pandemic had a serious impact on school children. The psychological, motor, and academic problems caused by the pandemic situation on children under 12 years old have been discussed in the literature (Cachon-Zagalaz et al., 2020). Online learning and limited physical connection with friends brought about feelings of isolation. Children from poor families and those living in rural areas were frustrated by limited internet resources and facilities, leaving them with a sense of helplessness. Family economic status affected learning support. A comparative study between students from mainland China and Taiwan showed that social capital and learning support are related (Xu et al, 2021). Being confined at home with family members may result in trying experiences and conflicts such as siblings fighting for private space and the usage of a computer.

With the introduction of online classes, students were required to stay at home, and counsellors had to conduct online counselling or e-counselling as an alternative. In Malaysia, an e-counselling service was established in the 1990s (Zainuddin et al., 2019). E-counselling is especially useful during movement control periods (Rahmat & Osman, 2012). This form of counselling can take the form of synchronous chat and asynchronous mail. In synchronous chat, the counsellor and client interact online at the same time (Glasheen et al., 2017), making use of social networking services and instant messaging. Synchronous chats can be delivered via video conferencing using a web camera. On the other hand, in an asynchronous mail mode of e-counselling, the counselling session is mediated through the exchange of electronic mails.

Challenges of E-Counselling

Conducting online counselling during the pandemic led to school counsellors facing different challenges. Studies have shown that counsellors experience challenges in the implementation of e-counselling. These challenges include legal considerations, a lack of accessibility, technological challenges, security issues, the absence of verbal and non-verbal behavioural cues, and the risk of misinterpretation or misunderstanding between counsellors and clients (Alia et al., 2022).

Legal and Ethical Considerations

According to the Malaysian Board of Counsellors guidelines, a student needs to complete a declaration form before seeking assistance from a counsellor. As with face-to-face counselling, the counsellor also needs to obtain the client's informed consent which includes communicating the risks and benefits of participating in online counselling, such as increased misunderstanding, miscommunication, and breaches to online security (Halabuza, 2015; Reamer, 2013).

The counsellor must ensure that clients understand the risks and benefits of online counselling so that they can act with self-determination and not be coerced into seeking help (Reamer, 2013). Non-verbal behaviour is a central factor influencing the therapeutic relationship in counselling (Ramseyer, 2020). With limited verbal and non-verbal cues, the problem of assessing the client's capacity to consent will arise, especially as the counsellor and client may encounter language barriers. This could result in the client misunderstanding the concepts outlined in the consent process and declaration form. If the client does not fully comprehend this, then the consent is not an act of self-determination. With online counselling and the absence of verbal and non-verbal cues, a counsellor may have difficulty assessing the client's present concerns.

Age of consent is another challenge for the counsellor conducting online counselling. Most Malaysian secondary school students serve young people between the ages of 13 and 17, who are likely to access counselling services without parental consent. This could be problematic from a legal point of view. Furthermore, there is a possibility that clients may provide false information about gender, culture, and religious affiliation. With false information counsellors face ethical dilemmas regarding the counselling process. This is especially true if such misinformation impairs the counselling progress and leads to safety concerns for the clients and the school community (Conlin & Bones, 2020)

Technological Barriers and Inaccessibility

With online counselling services, counsellor and client are not constrained by geography and physical mobility, but for schools in remote places, the availability of internet services and technology devices can be limited. Counsellors encounter accessibility challenges as they have to compete with classroom teachers for the usage of internet services. Furthermore, research suggests that limited technological literacy of both the counsellor and client may put pressure on the counselling process (Elleven & Allen, 2004). Challenges such as internet connection issues or computer problems are inevitable

(Riemer-Reiss, 2000). Studies have shown that technology is an immediate barrier to establishing rapport online (Haberstroh et al., 2007), especially when client concerns require immediate attention. Richello and his associates (2021) in their study on the barriers and enablers to the delivery of webchat counselling for young people concluded that participants lamented the lack of prompt support in dealing with risks and technical issues that negatively impacted the quality of the counselling services.

In the beginning stages of the pandemic, counsellors were plunged into the deep end, having to conduct online counselling without prior training and skills. Many counsellors were unable to troubleshoot when encountering computer problems and internet service failure, resulting in psychological distress.

Asynchronous Communication

Online counselling services that are asynchronous, where the counselling session is conducted through the exchange of electronic mails, can lead to potential anxiety for both the counsellor and the client (Richards & Vigano, 2013). Although asynchronous communication allows clients to process the implications of their thoughts, thus creating more self-awareness, the delayed response may cause concern for the counsellors' abilities to engage in the intervention effectively. In synchronous online communication, the effect of time lag can also create a hindrance in providing effective intervention (Bambling et al., 2008). Studies have indicated that with online counselling, school counsellors were worried about the lack of time boundaries in addition to their heavy workload and the ability to manage urgent and emergency cases after working hours (Foon et al., 2020). Clients with immediate or urgent needs may not feel supported to a degree consistent with crisis situations since counsellors may not be able to respond immediately to assist them in a meaningful way (Finn & Barak, 2010).

Misunderstanding and Misinterpretation

The lack of verbal and non-verbal information in online counselling services brings added challenges to the counsellor. It may cause the counsellor and client to construct an understanding of information based on their own interpretations and assumptions (Recupero & Rainey, 2005). This miscommunication and misconception between the counsellor's intentions and client's understanding, and vice versa, may result in early termination of counselling. In other words, the counsellor might find it challenging to develop an appropriate clinical understanding of the client for fear of miscommunication due to being unfamiliar with students' online language (Foon et al., 2020). According to Wright and Griffiths (2010), counsellors can experience a lack of emotional connectedness when they do not have sufficient essential information about their clients.

Verbal and non-verbal cues are crucial in communication, especially in multilingual environments where language may pose a problem. Clients with difficulties in verbal communication can be unable to express their emotions accurately and appropriately, resulting in the counsellor's misinterpretation of the issue. Situations involving cultural issues and the lack of verbal and non-verbal cues can leave the counsellor vulnerable to cultural insensitivity and unintentional discrimination (Mishna et al., 2013). The absence of non-verbal cues in online counselling can prevent the counsellor from forming an accurate assessment. That being the case, it may not be appropriate to counsel individuals with serious mental health illnesses such as depression, anxiety disorders, and suicidal tendencies online. In a comprehensive literature review, Stoll and colleagues (2020) have drawn attention to the need for more research into and a more robust consideration of practices associated with the ethics of online counselling. They identify five specific ethical areas where online engagement is problematic: issues of privacy and security; the technical competency of counsellors and the need for special training; communication problems specific to technological applications; gaps in research; and emergency issues.

Benefits of Online Counselling

Despite the challenges faced by online counselling, we need also to view it as a novel opportunity in the provision of counselling services. Online counselling offers accessibility and anonymity. It creates a security net for students to discuss sensitive and emotional topics with a counsellor without feeling stigmatised. The anonymous environment offers an opportunity for young people to disclose sensitive issues like depression and suicide ideation (Kraus et al., 2011). Clients become more open and honest in their expressions (Richard & Vigaro, 2013) as they feel less vulnerable and embarrassed (Dowling & Rickwood, 2013).

Online counselling reduces the barriers to service utilisation, reduces stigma, and provides more flexibility and convenience in scheduling (Chang, 2005; Glasheen & Champbell, 2009). Online counselling appointment booking systems and various online tools such as Facebook Messenger, Microsoft Teams, Zoom, Google meets, etc., can be used as they are user-friendly platforms that match the trend of the internet-savvy generation. This will enhance the effectiveness of counselling provision as interventions can be provided to young people as early as possible.

Research suggests online counselling does not pose a serious threat to traditional face-to-face counselling (Murphy et al., 2009) and is effective in the prevention, assessment, and treatment of mental health issues for individuals who are socially, emotionally or physically isolated (Mallen et al., 2005). During the COVID-19 pandemic, online classes and online counselling became necessary tools for teachers and counsellors to offer their services (Stephen, 2020). Online counselling can complement face-to-face counselling as it matches the emergent IT-savvy culture. Asynchronous counselling also serves the needs of individuals with disabilities or those who reside in remote areas (Ali et al., 2005).

Research findings show that online psychoeducation information is being sought by many teenagers. Its effect is found to be equal to traditional face-to-face counselling (Glasheen, 2016). Online counselling chatlines provide students with the opportunity to read or rewrite their transcripts, thus giving them more time for reflection. The effect can be beneficial and therapeutic when the feedback given by counsellors in writing can be read repeatedly.

The Strengths and Shortcomings of Online Counselling: A Way Forward

This chapter captures the changing scenario of Malaysian school counselling services, from traditional face-to-face interactions to online services driven by the COVID-19 pandemic. With the current technology-savvy generation and the need to reach out to students in remote areas, online counselling is becoming more popular. Nevertheless, the usage of different counselling platforms comes with various challenges and hurdles. Although online counselling is beneficial to clients who have concerns about privacy, the fear of being vulnerable may inhibit students from seeking help. The counsellor's choice of counselling service models has to depend on the needs of the clients, anonymity, accessibility of technology, asynchronous communication, security, informed consent, challenges of licensure, liability, and regulation (Harris & Birnbaum, 2014).

To overcome the barriers and challenges of online counselling, these services could be used effectively in conjunction with face-to-face models. For example, the use of face-to-face assessment to ensure an accurate evaluation of clients can be followed up with ongoing flexible and accessible online counselling services. The building of therapeutic rapport through face-to-face counselling sessions and the online support can work together to serve to meet the client's needs.

More research can be carried out to identify solutions to the inherent ethical and legal issues that exist in online counselling services. More evidence on the comparative efficacy of online counselling and face-to-face counselling services such as telephone and video conferencing, the development of positive and effective therapeutic alliance, and the provision of accurate clients' assessments should be highlighted in future studies. Moreover, cross-cultural studies on the use of online counselling services across borders from intercultural perspectives can also be further researched by counsellors as cultural sensitivity is important. Culture influences all aspects of human life where people have their own world views, expectations, norms, and taboos which will affect the counselling process. Culture may influence help-seeking pathways, the process of assessment, and choices about case management. This can enhance the importance of counselling services in schools and communal mental health services where the cultural system itself may be a barrier. Examples of such can include but are not limited to, the languages spoken by different communities, or the religions held by different groups of people (Low et al., 2011).

Conclusion

Online counselling in Malaysia is still in its infancy and faces technological, legal, and ethical challenges. It served as an alternative means of service provision during the pandemic and was found to have benefitted clients despite several shortcomings. Therefore, it is recommended that online counselling services should be used in conjunction with face-to-face counselling in the school setting. With the continual advancement in technology, school counsellors need to be constantly equipped with technical knowledge and skills in establishing rapport and building relationships with clients in an online environment. Furthermore, there is a need for more innovative approaches to assist counsellors to handle the ethical tensions that exist in online counselling (Harris & Birnbaum, 2014). Counsellors need to be aware of their limits and boundaries in online counselling, including the ability to manage and control risk-related situations, enhance attending skills and reflective practices and, most importantly, to let go of the fear of online counselling. We are hopeful that guidelines will be established in the future for online counselling in Malaysia to ensure safe, effective, and ethical practice.

References

Abdul Malik, A., R., Atan, A., & Mohd Isa, N. J. (2013). A guidance and counselling model practiced within Malaysian schools. *International Journal of Education and Research*, 1(4), 1–12.

Abu Yazid, A. B. (2016). Counseling and guidance for Malaysian gifted students: A conceptual framework. *Journal for the Education of Gifted Young Scientist*, 4(1), 21–29. http://dx.doi.org/10.17478/JEGYS.2016115332

Abu Yazid, A. B., Siti Nurliyana, A., & Mohd Izwan, M. (2019). School guidance and counselling services for special education students in Malaysia: A literature review. *International Journal of Innovation, Creativity and Change*, 5(6), 421–433. https://www.ijicc.net/images/vol5iss6/5647_Bakar_2019_E_R.pdf

Aga Mohd Jaladin, R. (2013). Barriers and challenges in the practice of multicultural counselling in Malaysia: A qualitative interview study. *Counselling Psychology Quarterly*, 26, 174–189. https://doi.org/10.1080/09515070.2013.793046

Aga Mohd Jaladin, R. A., Simmonds, J. G., Greenway, P., & Barkatsas, T. (2021). Exploring counsellors' understanding and practice of multicultural counselling in Malaysia. *Journal of Nusantara Studies (JONUS)*, 6(1), 323-35. https://doi.org/10.24200/jonus.vol6iss1pp323-350

Agi, C. W., & Chinonye, F. (2022). Influence of guidance and counselling services on development of personal skills of children with special needs in Rivers State, Nigeria. *International Journal of Innovative Psychology & Social Development*, 10(3),47–53. www.seahipaj.org

Ali, N., Mustafa, M. S., & Ahmad, R. (2005). Interview approach as a case study method: A perception of guidance and counseling services among female students http://eprints.utm.my/2212/1/91.DrMuhdSharif%26Roslee.pdf

Alia Sarah, A., Zaida Nor, Z.,Wan Norhayati, W. O.,Yusni, M. Y.,Nor Azima, A., & Siti Aishah, H. (2022). A comparison of counselling self-efficacy across social factors among e-counsellors in Malaysia. *Journal of Positive Psychology,* 6(4), 3475–3489.

Amat, S. (2018). Guidance and counseling in schools. *Advances in Social Science, Education and Humanities Research,* 326, 13–18. https://doi.org/10.2991/iccie-18.2019.3

Atkinson, D. R., & Lowe, S. M. (1995). The role of ethnicity, cultural knowledge, and conventional techniques in counseling and psychotherapy. In J. G. Ponterotto, J. M. Casas, L. A. Suzuki, & C. M. Alexander (Eds.), *Handbook of Multicultural Counseling* (pp. 387–414). Sage Publications, Inc.

Bambling, M., King, R., Reid, W., & Wegner, K. (2008). Online counselling: The experience of counsellors providing synchronous single-session counselling to young people. *Counselling and Psychotherapy Research,* 8(2), 110–116. https://doi.org/10.1080/14733140802055011

Bulus, I. (1990). *Guidance Practice in School.* Ehindero Press.

Cachon-Zagalaz, J., Sanchez-Zafra, M., Sanabrias-Moreno, D., Gonzaliz-Valero, G., Lara-Sanchez, A., & Zagalaz-Sanchez, M. (2020). Syetematic review of the literature about the effects of the COVID-19 pandemic on the lives of school children. *Educational Psychology,* 11, 1–8. https://doi.org/10.3389/fpsyg.2020.569348

Chai, M. S. (2000). *Fears of psychological treatment and attitudes toward seeking professional help among students* [Unpublished master's thesis]. University Putra Malaysia.

Chang, T. (2005). Online counseling: Prioritizing psychoeducation, self-help, and mutual help for counseling, psychology research and practice. *The Counseling Psychologist,*33(6), 881–890. https://doi.org/10.1177/0011000005279962

Chen, K. S., & Kok, J. K. (2017). Barriers to seeking school counselling: Malaysian Chinese school students' perspectives. *Journal of Psychologists and Counsellors in Schools,* 27(2), 222–238. https://doi.org/10.1017/jgc.2015.21

Conlin, W. E., & Bones, C. L. (2020). Ethical considerations for addressing distorted beliefs in psychotherapy. *Psychotherapy,* 56(4), 449–458. https://doi.org/10.1037/pst0000252

Dowling, M., & Rickwood, D. (2013). Online counseling and therapy for mental health problems: A systematic review of individual synchronous interventions using chat. *Journal of Technology in Human Services,* 31(1), 1–21. https://doi.org/10.1080/15228835.2012.728508

Elleven, R., & Allen, J. (2004). Applying technology to online counselling: Suggestions for the beginning e-therapist. *Journal of Instructional Psychology,* 31(3), 223–227.

Ezarina, Z., Noor Nasihah, K., Zhooriyati Sehu, M., Masahiro, S., Balan, K., Soon Singh, B. S., Zaizul, A. R., Vikneswaran, S., Azianura Hani, S., & Mohammad Rahim, K. (2022). The role of family life and the influence of peer pressure on delinquency: Qualitative evidence from Malaysia. *International Journal of Environmental Research Public Health,* 19, 7846. https://doi.org/10.3390/ijerph19137846

Fabriz, S., Mendzheritskaya, J., Stehle, S. (2021). Impact of synchronous and asynchronous settings of online teaching and learning in higher education on students' learning experience during COVID-19. *Educational Psychology,* 12, 1–16. https://doi.org/10.3389/fpsyg.2021.733554

Finn, J., & Barak, A. (2010). A descriptive study of e-counsellor attitudes, ethics, and practice. *Counselling and Psychotherapy Research*, *10*(4), 268–277. https://doi.org/10.1080/14733140903380847

Foon, L. W., Zaida, N. Z, Yusni, M.Y, & Wan Norhayati, W. O. (2020). E-Counselling: The intention, motivation and deterrent among school counsellors. *Universal Journal of Educational Research*, *8*(3C), 44–51.

Frame, M. W. (1997). The ethics of counseling via the Internet. *The Family Journal*, *5*(4), 328–330. https://doi.org/10.1177/1066480797054009

Glasheen, K., & Champbell, M. (2009). The use of online counselling within an Australian secondary school setting: A practitioner's viewpoint. *Counseling Psychology Review*, *24*(2), 42–51.

Glasheen, K., McMahon, M., Campbell, M., Rickwood, D., & Shochet, I. (2017). Implementing online counselling in Australian secondary schools: What principals think. *International Journal for the Advancement of Counselling*, *40*, 14–25. https://doi.org/10.1007/s10447-017-9307-x

Glasheen, K., Shochet, I., & Campbell, M. (2016). Online counselling in secondary schools: Would students seek help by this medium? *British Journal of Guidance & Counselling*, *44*(1), 108–122. http://dx.doi.org/10.1080/03069885.2015.1017805

Gonzalez-Prendes, A. A., Hindo, C., & Pardo, Y. (2011). Cultural values integration in cognitive-behavioral therapy for a Latino with depression. *Clinical Case Studies*, *10*(5), 376–394. https://doi-org.eproxy.lib.hku.hk/10.1177/1534650111427075

Haberstroh, S., Duffey, T., Evan, M., Gee, R., & Trepal, H. (2007). The experience of online counseling. *Journal of Mental Health Counseling*, *29*(3), 269–282. https://doi.org/10.17744/mehc.29.3.j344651261w357v2

Halabuza, D. (2015). Guidelines for social workers' use of social networking websites. *Journal of Social Work Values and Ethics*, *11*(1), 23–32.

Hamza Alshoura, (2021). Critical review of special needs education provision in Malaysia: Discussing significant issues and challenges faced. *International Journal of Disability, Development and Education*, *70*(5), 869–884. https://doi.org/10.1080/1034912X.2021.1913718

Harris, B., & Birnbaum, R. (2014). Ethical and legal implications on the use of technology in counselling. *Clinical Social Work Journal*, *43*, 133–141. https://doi.org.//10.1007/s10615-014-0515-0

Harrison, M. G., (2022). The professional identity of school counsellors in East and Southeast Asia. *Counselling and Psychotherapy Research*, *22*(3), 543–547. https://doi.org/10.1002/capr.12546

Holmes, J. (2001). An introduction to sociolinguistics (2nd ed). Pearson Education

Hwang, K. K. (2009). The development of indigenous counseling in contemporary Confucian communities. *The Counseling Psychologist*, *37*(7), 930–943. https://doi.org./10.1177/0011000009336241

Jones, J. M., & Lee, L. H. (2021). Multicultural competency building: A multi-year study of trainee self-perceptions of cultural competence. *Contemporary School Psychology*, *25*, 288–298. https://doi.org/10.1007/s40688-020-00339-0

Khan, T., Hassali, M., Tahir, H., & Khan, A. (2011). A pilot study evaluating the stigma and public perception about the causes of depression and schizophrenia. *Iranian Journal of Public Health*, *40*, 50–56.

Kok, J. K. (2016). E-counselling modality: Following the changing learning needs of young people in higher education. In I. Amzat, & B. Yusuf (Eds.), *Fast Forwarding Higher Education Institutions for Global Challenges: Perspectives and Approaches*. Springer.

Kraus, R., Stricker, G., & Speyer, C. (2011). *Online counseling: A handbook for mental health professionals* (2nd ed.). Elsevier Academic Press.

Lindsey, S., Maeshima, B. S. & Parent, M. C. (2020). Mental health stigma and professional help-seeking behaviors among Asian American and Asian international students. *Journal of American College Health, 70*(6), 1761–1767. https://doi.org/10.1080/07448481.2020.1819820

Low, S. K., & Kok, J. K. (2020). *Parent-school-community partnerships in mental health*. Oxford Research Encyclopedia of Education. https://doi.org/10.1093/acrefore/9780190264093.013.947

Low, S. K., Kok, J. K., & Lee, M. N. (2011). *Cultural sensitivity in counselling for youth development* [Conference session]. International Conference on Youth Development 2011, Malaysia.

Low, S. K., Kok, J. K., & Lee, M. N. (2013). A holistic approach to school-based counselling and guidance services in Malaysia. *School Psychology International, 34*(2), 190–201. https://doi-org.eproxy.lib.hku.hk/10.1177/0143034312453398

Malaysian Department of Statistics. (2020), *Launching of report on the key findings population and housing census of Malaysia* 2020. https://www.dosm.gov.my/v1/index.php?r=column/cthemeByCat&cat=155&bul_id=OVByWjg5YkQ3MWFZRTN5bDJiaEVhZz09&menu_id=L0pheU43NWJwRWVSZklWdzQ4TlhUUT09

Mallen, M. J., Vogel, D. L., & Rochlen, A. B. (2005). The practical aspects of online counseling: Ethics, training, technology, and competency. *The Counseling Psychologist, 33*(6), 776–818. https://doi.org./10.1177/0011000005278625

Martin, J., & Marshall, H. (2010). Taking counselling and psychotherapy outside: Destruction of enrichment of the therapeutic frame? *European Journal of Psychotherapy and Counselling, 12*(4), 345–359. https://doi.org./10.1080/13642537.2010.530105

Ministry of Education, Malaysia. (1970). *Education in Malaysia* (Ministry of Education Report). Dewan Bahasa dan Pustaka.

Mishna, F., Tufford, L., Cook, C., & Bogo, M. (2013). Research note: A pilot cyber counseling course in a graduate social work program. *Journal of Social Work Education, 49*, 515–524. https://doi.org/10.1080/10437797.2013.796855

Murphy L. J., Parnass, P., Mitchell, D. L., Hallett, R. H., Cayley, P., & Seagram, S. (2009). Client satisfaction and outcome comparisons of online and face-to-face counselling methods. *British Journal of Guidance and Counselling, 39*(4), 627–640. https://doi.org/10.1093/bjsw/bcp041

Nor Mazlina, G., Aqilah Yusoff, Wan Marzuki W. J., Amat, S., Edris Aden & Azahrah, A. (2023). Unique components of Malaysia counsellor performance indicator: A tool to measure the performance of counsellors in Malaysia. *International Journal of Industrial Engineering & Production Research, 34*(2), 1–13.

Nurul Fitriah, A., Sharifah Muzlia, S. M., Lina Mursyidah, H. (2022). Online counselling reach out services to alleviate stress among students during online distance learning. *Asian Jourrnal of University Education, 18*(4), 954–965. https://doi.org/10.24191/ajue.v18i4.20005

Othman, A. H. & Bakar, S. B. (1993). Guidance, counselling, and counsellors education in Malaysia. In A H. Othman, & A. Awang (Eds.), *Counseling in the Asia-Pacific Region*. Greenwood Press.

Peng, M. H. (2020). Outbreak of COVID-19: An emerging global pandemic threat. *Biomedicine & Pharmacotherapy, 129,* 110499. https://doi.org/10.1016/j.biopha.2020.110499

Peterson, J. S. (2006). Addressing counseling needs of gifted students. *Professional School Counseling, 10*(1), 43–51. https://doi.org/10.1177/2156759X0601001S06

Putman, D. A. (2010). Philosophical roots of the concept of courage. In C. L. S. Pury & S. J. Lopez (Eds.), *The Psychology of Courage: Modern Research on An Ancient Virtue* (pp. 9–22). American Psychological Association. http://doi.org/10.1037/12168-001

Rahmat Reza Atiq Abdullah O. K., & Osman Kamisah. (2012). From traditional to self-regulated learners: UKM Journey toward education 3.0. *Procedia, Social and Bahavioral Sciences, 59,* 2–8.

Ramseyer, F. T. (2020). Motion energy analysis (MEA): A primer on the assessment of motion from video. *Journal of Counseling Psychology, 67*(4), 536–549. https://doi.org/10.1037/cou0000407

Reamer, F. G. (2013). Social work in a digital age: Ethical and risk management challenges. *Social Work, 58*(2), 163–172. https://doi.org/10.1093/sw/swt003

Recupero, P. R., & Rainey, S. E. (2005). Informed consent to e-therapy. *American Journal of Psychotherapy, 59*(4), 319–331. https://doi.org/10.1176/appi.psychotherapy.2005.59.4.319

Richards, D., & Vigano, N. (2013). Online counseling: A narrative and critical review of the literature. *Journal of Clinical Psychology, 69*(9), 994–1011. https://doi.org/10.1002/jclp.21974

Richello, M. G., Mawdsley, G., & Gutman, L. M. (2021). Using the behaviour change wheel to identify barriers and enablers to the delivery of webchat counselling for young people. *Counselling and Psychotherapy Research, 22*(1), 130–139. https://doi.org/10.1002/capr.12410

Riemer-Reiss, M. L. (2000). Utilising distance technology for mental health counseling. *Journal of Mental Health Counseling, 22*(3), 189–203.

Sanghvi, P. B., & Mehrotra, S. (2020). Help-seeking for mental health concerns: Review of Indian research and emergent insights. *Journal of Health Research, 36*(3), 428–441. https://doi.org/10.1108/JHR-02-2020-0040

See, C. M. (2004). School counseling in Malaysia. In *Proceedings of the Fifth International Conference on Education Research.* Seoul National University.

See, S. M., & Ng, K. M. (2010). Counseling in Malaysia: History, current status, and future trends. *Journal of Counseling & Development, 88*(1), 18–22. https://doi-org.eproxy.lib.hku.hk/10.1002/j.1556-6678.2010.tb00144.x

Stephen, O. (2020). E-counselling implementation: Consideration during the Covid-19 deepening crisis in Nigeria. *Journal of Education and Practice, 11*(17), 13–21.

Stiles, A. A., & Gudino, O. G. (2018). Examining bidirectional associations between school engagement and mental health for youth in child welfare. *School Mental Health, 10,* 372–385. https://doi.org/10.1007/s12310-018-9248-5

Stoll, J., Muller, J. A., & Trachsel, M. (2020). Ethical issues in online psychotherapy: A narrative review. *Front Psychiatry, Section Psychological Therapies, 10,* 1–16. https://doi.org/10.3389/fpsyt.2019.00993

Sue, D. W., Sue, D., Neville, H. A., & Smith, L. (2022). *Counselling the culturally diverse: Theory and practice.* (9th ed.). John Wiley & Sons Inc.

Suhaila, K., Jannah, N., Izwan, M., Amat, S., & Saadon, S. (2022). Psychological well-being of school counsellors model. *European Journal of Educational Research*, *11*(2), 621–638. https://eric.ed.gov/?id=EJ1341597

Sulaiman, S., Basu, J., Amirullah, A., & Muhammad, A. (2022). Challenges in implementing intercultural counselling in Indonesian educational contexts: University students' perceptions. *Journal of Positive Psychology*, *6*(6), 10177–10182. https://mail.journalppw.com/index.php/jpsp/article/view/9524

Teo, T., Shi, W., Huang, F., & Hoi, C. K. W. (2020). Intergenerational differences in the intention to use psychological cybercounseling: A Chinese case study. *Patient Education and Counseling*, *103*(8), 1615–1622. https://doi.org/10.1016/j.pec.2020.02.035

The Commissioner of Law Revision Malaysia. (2006). *Akta Kaunselor 1998(Akta 580) dan Peraturan-Peraturan & Counsellors Act 1998 (Act 580) and Regulations* https://www.joshualegalartgallery.com/products/counsellors-act-1998act-580-and-regulations

United Nations Children's Fund. (2020). *Mental health alert for children in Malaysia*. https://www.unicef.org/malaysia/press-releases/mental-health-alert-children-malaysia

Whaley, A. L., & Davis, K. E. (2007). Cultural competence and evidence-based practice in mental health services: A complementary perspective. *American Psychologist*, *62*, 563–574.

Wong, K. P., Bonn, G., Tam, C. L., & Wong, C. P. (2018). Preferences for online and/or face-to-face counseling among university students in Malaysia. *Frontier Psychology*, *9*, Article 64. https://doi.org/10.3389/fpsyg.2018.00064

Wright, J., & Griffiths, F. (2010). Reflective practice at a distance: Using technology in counselling supervision. *Reflective Practice*, *11*(5), 693–703. https://doi.org/10.1080/14623943.2010.516986

Xu, P., Yao, M., & Anser, M. K. (2021). Effective learning support towards sustainable student learning and well-being influenced by global pandemic of COVID-19: A comparison between mainland China and Taiwanese students. *Frontiers in Psychology*, *12*, 521689. https://doi.org/10.3389/fpsyg.2021.561289

Zainuddin, Z. N., Yusop, Y. M., Hassan, S. A., & Alias, B. S. (2019). The effectiveness of cybertherapy for the introvert and extrovert personality traits. *Malaysian Journal of Medicine and Health Sciences*, *15*(Supp 1), 105–109.

4 Multicultural School Counselling in Singapore

Diversity, Worldviews and Meaning Making

Boon-Ooi Lee

Introduction

Jia Wen, a secondary four Chinese Singaporean student, seeks help from the school counsellor for her difficulty in concentrating on study. Her academic performance has deteriorated since the term started. She has lost interest in the daily activities she used to enjoy, stopped mingling with her friends, and prefers to be by herself. When at home, her mind wanders and she has a mental fog. Recently, she has become more anxious because her GCE 'O' Level examination is around the corner.[1] She also feels stressed out when thinking about her future career. She plans to go to an art school to become an oil painting artist, but her parents want her to attend junior college and then study information technology at university. *Jia Wen* loves her parents and does not want to upset them.

Aswab, a primary three Malay Singaporean student, was referred to counselling because of poor attention in class and frequent absenteeism. He claims he has been disturbed by a child *jinni* who wants him to be her playmate.[2] She would wait for him outside the classroom and follow him home. The lonely spirit often plays with him until midnight. As a result, he is too tired to attend lessons or concentrate in class the next day. During the family session, *Aswab*'s parents reveal that his grandfather also has the special ability to see "things". Some of his teachers are skeptical about *Aswab*'s claim, thinking that he is making an excuse, or he might have some deeper emotional problems. His parents disagree with them and prefer to consult a *bomoh* to address his "spiritual issue".

Most school counsellors would perceive *Jia Wen*'s exam stress and parents' expectations as common stressors of most Singaporean students. They may diagnose her with depression and anxiety and teach her relaxation exercises to cope with exam stress. For the school counsellors, *Jia Wen*'s case is not complicated. In contrast, they may be less certain about *Aswab*'s "paranormal encounter", speculating on whether it is a symptom of some deeper problems. They may feel uncomfortable to work with *Aswab* because of their limited knowledge of Islam.

DOI: 10.4324/9781003352457-4

School counsellors may be more conscious of the cultural aspects of *Aswab*'s case because of the culturally explicit language used such as *jinni* and *bomoh*. They may not be aware that *Jia Wen*'s career dilemma reflects a conflict between her personal and the family's goals, which occurs in a collectivistic culture.[3] Their approaches to both cases are also epistemologically shaped by cultural factors. They conceptualize the students' emotional distress according to Western psychological and psychiatric paradigms (see Horwitz, 2002) and conduct counselling—a therapeutic method embedded in Euro-American worldviews, which may or may not be relevant to culturally diverse student populations (Lee, 2018; McLeod, 2019).

These two cases point to the importance of situating students' issues in the cultural context. However, what does culture mean and how should we work with it in school counselling? The problem is that culture is not a static set of beliefs and practices. Although there are cultural differences across social groups, there are also individual differences within each group, people may be exposed to more than one type of culture, and culture evolves over time. Therefore, the goal of this article is to propose that being culturally competent is more than being knowledgeable about the beliefs and practices of a social group, but it is also about developing the disposition of *cultural humility* and *epistemological flexibility* to *listen* to the ways that individuals attach *meanings* to their predicaments. Meanings are constructed by both personal and collective narratives. One way to facilitate this meaning-making process is to apply the concept of symbolic healing and explanatory models (EMs) in school counselling. Since some students and their families may draw on local idioms of distress to make sense of life issues and to seek help from traditional practices, as shown in *Aswab*'s case, this chapter will also aim to explore the relevance of indigenous healing systems to school counselling. Indigenous healing systems (e.g., traditional medicine, ritual healing) are helping beliefs and practices developed for treating the inhabitants of the given ethnocultural groups (Sue et al., 2022).[4]

This chapter is organized in the following sections. It begins with the social context of Singapore to provide background information. The second section demonstrates that culture is multidimensional and fluid. School counsellors must be careful not to overgeneralize cultural information or stereotype students in terms of fixed cultural characteristics. The third section focuses on multicultural competencies, worldviews, cultural humility and epistemological flexibility. The final section examines the relevance of the symbolic healing model, EMs and indigenous healing systems to school counselling.

Social Context of Singapore

Singapore, which is located in Southeast Asia, was a British colony from 1819 to 1963 before attaining independence in 1965. Its colonial past has influenced many aspects of the contemporary Singapore, notably its democratic parliamentary system, and the adoption of English as a main language of communication in educational and business settings. In 2020, although English was the most frequently spoken language at home among the resident population aged five and over (48.3%), many of them also spoke a mother tongue language such as Mandarin, Malay, or Tamil (Singapore Department of Statistics, 2021).

In 2020, among its total population of 5.45 million, there were 1.46 million non-residents who were mainly foreign workers and dependents of citizens, permanent residents or work pass holders. The 3.99 million residents, comprising citizens and permanent residents, were culturally diverse. Ethnic Chinese (74.3%) were the majority followed by Malays (13.5%) and Indians (9.0%).

In terms of religious affiliation, Singapore residents (aged 15–19 years) identified themselves as Buddhists (24.1%), Muslims (21.3%), Christians (19.0%), Hindus (6.3%), or Taoists (4.9%). A sizeable proportion of them (23.8%) perceived themselves as non-religious.[5] The religious composition of the Malays (aged 15 years and over) was homogenous with 98.8% of them being Muslims. By comparison, the religious compositions of the Chinese and Indians were relatively more heterogenous. Most Chinese regarded themselves as Buddhists (40.4%), Christians (21.6%), or Taoists (11.6%). Although a large proportion of Chinese considered themselves non-religious (25.7%), only a few Indians perceived themselves as non-religious (2.2%). Among the Indians, Hinduism (57.3%) was the most common religion followed by Islam (23.4%) and Christianity (12.6%).

A Singapore study found that Protestant Christians, Roman Catholics and Hindus were more likely than Buddhists and Taoists to perceive religion as an important aspect of their identities (Mathews et al., 2014). Muslims and Protestant Christians were also more likely than other religious groups to think that their faiths and religious teachers had significantly influenced their life philosophies. These findings underscore the relevance of religion and spirituality to multicultural school counselling, as shown in *Aswab*'s case.

In general, the usage of English and multi-language literacy enables intercultural communication among diverse local ethnic groups and between Singaporeans and foreigners. Singaporeans are therefore exposed to multiple cultural beliefs and practices, which shape their identities and life experiences. Since the Singapore schools are a microcosm of the multicultural society of Singapore, school counsellors must be culturally competent in meeting the needs of the culturally diverse student population.[6] Before discussing multicultural competencies in school counselling, it is necessary to understand what the term culture means.

The Meaning of Culture

Culture as a System of Shared Symbols and Meanings

There is no consensus on the definition of culture (Anderson-Levitt, 2012). For the purpose of this chapter, culture is defined as a system of *shared symbols* and *meanings* (e.g., beliefs, values, norms, linguistic and paralanguages, artefacts, practices) to enable individuals to socialize and function as a group (Keesing, 1974; Shepherd, 2014). This meaning system is not static but an adaptive process that evolves in a larger ecological context due to the changes of physical environments (e.g., urbanization, deforestation), globalization, migration and intercultural communication. As a result, culture becomes multidimensional and people are exposed to more than one type of culture, resulting in individual diversities within same social groups. Viewing those demographic categories of Singapore's population presented at the beginning of this article as static and mutually exclusive may lead to cultural stereotypes. For example, some Singaporeans have developed multiple cultural identities because of interethnic marriages (Yeoh et al., 2021), or after living abroad as so-called third culture kids (Starr et al., 2017).

The categorization of religious affiliation is problematic, as it oversimplifies people's lived religious experiences. The survey methods such as those used in the census, which only allow respondents to select one choice, may not capture the phenomenon of *multiple religious belonging* (Corcoran et al., 2021). There are people who construct their sense of religious belonging by conflating beliefs and practices from various religious traditions. For example, the artificial separation between Buddhism and Taoism in the census of the Chinese Singaporean population does not reflect the Chinese religion as an amalgam of Buddhism, Confucianism and Taoism (see Hedges, 2017), and overlooks the social functions of religion. An ordinary Chinese person worships certain deities not because they are Buddhist or Taoist gods, or participates in certain rituals not because of their Buddhist or Taoist origins, but because they offer protection and fulfil personal wishes.

Some individuals' beliefs are also incongruous with their religious doctrines. For example, one Singapore study found that only 47.5% of Buddhists and 33.0% of Hindus subscribed to the belief of reincarnation, which was supposed to be the main tenet of their religions (Mathews et al., 2014). Ironically, some Muslims (16.8%), Catholic Christians (20.1%) and Protestant Christians (6.5%) believed in reincarnation, contradicting their religious creeds.

The category of "non-religionist" is contentious. Non-religionists, who made up 20% of the Singaporean population, are indeed a heterogeneous group. They call themselves by different names: humanists, atheists, agnostics, or sceptics (Humanist Society (Singapore), n.d.). A person can be both atheist and agnostic in different ways, for example, as an "agnostic-atheist" who does not believe in god nor believe that people can ever know whether a god exists, or as a "gnostic-atheist" with a conviction that a god does not exist (Weir, 2020).

Being non-religious does not mean not believing in anything. A Singapore study indicated that 41.8% of non-religionists held onto some paranormal beliefs, for example, god, spirits, heaven, hell and reincarnation (Mathews et al., 2014). Similarly, in their transnational study in the United States, Brazil, China, Denmark, Japan and the United Kingdom, Bullivant and colleagues

(2019) found that most self-professed atheists and agnostics believed in life after death, reincarnation, astrology, or the existence of a universal life force.

These cultural diversities and paradoxes suggest the bidirectional interaction between culture and individuals' behaviours given that mind and culture are mutually constituted (see Ellis & Stam, 2015). Individuals do not passively draw on culture to create meanings in lives, but actively adapt and negotiate with their cultures to meet personal needs. When working with students in cultural context, it is essential to explore how their cultural and personal narratives collectively shape their experiences instead of taking their cultural backgrounds for granted.

This exploratory process must consider both verbal and *nonverbal* aspects of one's cultural experience. As a symbolic and meaning system, culture is not simply cognitive-discursive but is also *embodied* (Kirmayer & Ramstead, 2017).

The Embodied Culture

For example, in *Bharatanatyam*, an Indian classical dance, the cultural meaning is communicated, and the personal experience is transformed through the embodied ritual performance. David (2009) observed that

> [Participants] were surprisingly confident in performing the actions pertaining to religious rituals, but strikingly unconfident when asked to speak about their knowledge or meaning of those actions. For these devotees, their actions were their knowledge of Hinduism — the ritual practices and actions were an embodied of that knowledge and their faith.
> (223)

To work with students' cultural beliefs, school counsellors perceive culture as an embodied phenomenon that goes beyond words. Some students may be able to express their cultural values through rituals, cultural performances and traditional arts and games. In Singapore schools, co-curricular activities are a key component of holistic education. The school counsellor can creatively integrate traditional calligraphy, music and dance into Western expressive therapies (e.g., drama, art, sand and play therapies) when working with students who are more comfortable to communicate through bodily actions and sensations.

In conclusion, the notion of culture is multidimensional, equivocal and embodied. School counsellors must not perceive their students according to statistically generated demographic categories; otherwise, they may overgeneralize cultural information or stereotype students in terms of fixed cultural characteristics. Given the limitation and fluidity of demographic categories, it may be more useful and practical for school counsellors to move beyond these categories and work with the students' worldviews and personal meanings.

Multicultural Competencies and Worldviews

According to Sue and associates (2022), there are three dimensions of multicultural counselling competencies: (a) attitudes/beliefs: an understanding of one's values and assumptions about human behaviours; (b) knowledge: an understanding of the *worldviews* and cultural contexts of culturally diverse clients; and (c) skills: an ability to apply culturally appropriate intervention strategies when working with culturally diverse clients. These three dimensions have been further developed into specific multicultural competencies in the training of school counsellors, for example, racism and student resistance, racial identity development, multicultural family counselling, school-family-community partnerships, cross-cultural interpersonal interactions, social advocacy and social justice leadership (Pietrantoni, 2022; Ratts & Greenleaf, 2017).

Worldviews

The concept of *worldview* in Sue et al.'s (2022) model is particularly germane to the practice of multicultural school counselling. Worldviews refer to the way we perceive, define, make sense of and interact with our worlds (Koltko-Rivera, 2004). Worldviews comprise five dimensions: ontology, epistemology, axiology, praxeology and cosmology (Koltko-Rivera, 2004; Taves et al., 2018; Vidal, 2008) (see Table 4.1 for more details). School counsellors can guide their case conceptualizations with self-reflexive questions. For example, instead of a broad question: "what is the student's religion?" (given the problematic category of religion as mentioned earlier); a specific question will be more useful: "besides humans, who else *exists* in the student's world and what is *real* to the student?" (an ontological question); or "what is the *knowledge* that the student uses to *make sense* of the world?" (an epistemological question). Instead of assuming that a Chinese Singaporean student follows Confucian ethics, it is more useful to ask: "how does the student perceive good and bad/evil?" (an axiological question). These worldviews questions go beyond the nebulous concept of culture and consider the multiple sources of cultural influences. They also help to broaden the counsellor's theoretical models that are embedded in particular worldviews (Koltko-Rivera, 2008).

Individualism–Collectivism

Since we all live in a world populated by other experiencing beings (shared cultural ontology) (Vidal, 2008), the way we relate to groups and authorities is an essential dimension of our worldviews (Koltko-Rivera, 2004). The worldview of self-other relationship has been extensively studied under the concepts of individualism–collectivism (I-C) (Brewer & Chen, 2007; Fatehi et al., 2020) and self-construal (Cross et al., 2011; Markus & Kitayama, 1991).

I-C has been considered as a fundamental dimension of cultural variation. A cross-cultural study involving 17- to 19-year-old Singaporean and American students found that Singaporean students were more collectivistic, whereas American students were more individualistic (Soh & Leong, 2002). Although

Table 4.1 Dimensions of Worldviews

Dimension[a]	Question[a]
Ontology (The nature of being)	Who and what exists, what is real?
Epistemology (Theory of knowledge)	How do we know what is true and what is false? How do we make sense of our world? What language (e.g., daily, religious, scientific, metaphors, words, gestures) do we use to acquire knowledge and during the process of meaning making?
Axiology (Theory of values, ethics and aesthetics)	What is good and what is bad? What are our moral, ethic and aesthetic values; and how do they shape our goals and guide our actions? What are our beliefs about human nature? What is the meaning of life?
Praxeology (Theory of actions)	What actions should we take to solve practical problems according to our values?
Cosmology (Theory about origins)	Where do we come from and where do we go?

[a]Koltko-Rivera (2004), Taves et al. (2018), Vidal (2008).

these findings were consistent with the hypothesis that Westerners are more individualistic and Asians are more collectivistic, there are variations between and within ethnocultural groups, for example, some Asians were more individualistic than Westerners (Brewer & Chen, 2007; Fatehi et al., 2020).

Although it is important not to stereotype Westerners and Asians according to the I-C worldview, this concept is useful for understanding the cultural aspect of counselling. For example, school counsellors must be aware of how their I-C worldviews would influence their counselling approaches. Williams (2003) indicated that counsellors oriented towards individualistic worldviews were more likely to ascribe client issues to internal attributes than to situational and environmental factors, focus on *individuation* (i.e., to achieve a sense of personal control and autonomy) during counselling and adopt a low-context communication (i.e., open and direct communication) with clients.[7] These counsellors were also less likely to conceptualize cases from a multicultural perspective.

Despite its applicability, the I-C worldview is conceptually limited to only the self-other relationships in a *human* world. Across cultures, people's ontological worlds do not only comprise fellow humans but also divine forces, ancestral spirits, animals and nonhuman agencies (Kohn, 2013; Lee & Kirmayer, 2022), as in *Aswab*'s case. Understanding of these broader self-other relationships and their relevance to multicultural school counselling requires an approach that views the self as a cultural construction.

Cultural Construction of the Self

Markus and Kitayama's (1991) have developed the theory of interdependent and independent self-construal to understand the ways that individuals make sense of the self across cultures. Independent self-construal perceives the self as an autonomous being with a unique individual identity separated from social contexts, behaving according to relatively stable internal attributes (e.g., traits, motivation, values) and asserting one's core beliefs and needs in social relationships. In contrast, the interdependent self-construal perceives the self as an integral part of social contexts, placing group goals above personal goals and adjusting one's inner thoughts and feelings for the sake of maintaining a harmonious relationship. It is generally assumed that Westerners are more independent than Asians who are then more interdependent than Westerners. Nonetheless, due to cultural changes and methodological issues in measuring the concept of self-construal, some studies did not find Asians to be more interdependent than Westerners, or Westerners to be more independent than Asians (see review by Cross et al., 2011).

Kirmayer (2007) expanded the self-construal theory and linked it to psychotherapy and other healing practices. He maintains that every healing system is built on an implicit cultural model of self and personhood. Western psychotherapy and counselling are built on the egocentric self (conceptually similar to independent self-construal), family therapy and collective ritual healing are grounded in the sociocentric self (conceptually similar to interdependent self-construal), shamanism is embedded in the ecocentric self (connected to the land and wildlife), and divination-related practices are structured in the cosmocentric self (connected to spirits and ancestors).

Although Kirmayer (2007) has associated family therapy with the sociocentric self, this form of relational-systemic therapy, including interpersonal psychotherapy (IPT), is more likely to be embedded in the egocentric self. According to Bowen family systems therapy, well-functioning individuals hold a well-*differentiated sense of self*, recognizing the essential of interdependence with others but without conforming to others' demands, and by thinking rationally so as not to be emotionally affected by others' negative emotions (Bowen, 1976; Jankowski & Hooper, 2012). Lack of differentiation refers to "emotional overinvolvement with significant others and overidentification with one's family of origin" (Calatrava et al., 2022, p. 2) and occurs when "individual choices are set aside in the service of achieving harmony within the system" (Brown, 1999, p. 3). The notion of differentiation contradicts the Asian sociocentric self, which views

> the person not as separate from the social context but as more connected and less *differentiated* from others... Experiencing interdependence entails seeing oneself as part of an encompassing social relationship and recognizing that one's behaviour is *determined, contingent* on, and, to a large extent *organized* by what the actor perceives to be the thoughts, feelings, and actions of others in the relationship.
> (Markus & Kitayama, 1991, p. 227, emphasis added)

Apparently, the meaning of interdependence is epistemologically different between Bowen family systems therapy and the Asian self-construal. Not only is the degree of so-called over-involvement and over-identification difficult to measure, but also identification of one's family of origin is a significant aspect of Asian people's personal identity and collective memory as reflected in their practice of ancestral worship. Differentiation may be easier to achieve in families subscribing to individualistic values but not in those observing collectivistic familism and filial piety (Y. T. Lee, 2018). When working with Asian clients, the Western family system approach has to be culturally adapted by being grounded in the interdependent self-construal (Y. T. Lee, 2018). There is no empirical evidence that self-differentiation is associated with a better interpersonal relationship and well-being in Asian cultures. Most of the studies on the positive outcome of self-differentiation have been conducted in Western societies (see review by Calatrava et al., 2022).

Similarly, IPT is also embedded in the egocentric self or independent self-construal. It aims to address the "patient's ability to *assert* his or her needs and wishes in interpersonal encounters, to *validate* the patient's anger as a normal interpersonal signal and to encourage its *efficient expression*, and to encourage taking appropriate social risks" (Markowitz & Weissman, 2004, p. 137, emphasis added). However, some Asian students may prefer restraint of strong feelings to avoid damaging relational harmony, which is not congruent with the emotional expressiveness advocated in counselling (see Allan et al., 2016; Sue et al., 2022). Emotional expressiveness is an attribute of low-context communication commonly found in the individualistic culture and in counselling (Sue et al., 2022). In contrast, Asian students and families may engage in a high-context communication style characterized by indirect and implicit messages. Some students may be reluctant to openly communicate their negative feelings and thoughts to their parents, not because of lack of desire to express inner experiences but being respectful of their parents. Without understanding how self-construal influences emotional expression and motives (see Cross et al., 2011; Uchida et al., 2022), the school counsellor may see these students as lacking self-confidence, determination and assertiveness. Since the notion of the self and personhood vary cross-culturally, the goals and process of counselling must also differ (Kirmayer, 2007), which will be examined in detail in the following sections.

Cultural Humility and Epistemological Flexibility

Discussion in the preceding sections suggests that rigidly following the framework of multicultural competencies may risk stereotyping social groups. To minimize cultural generalization and stereotypes, the school counsellor is encouraged to adopt an orientation of *cultural humility*, that is, a self-reflexive *meaning-making* process. During this enquiry process, the counsellor does not know, explores what the students and their families have already known, is interested in learning from them and acknowledges them as experts in their own lifeworld (Lekas et al., 2020; Sue et al., 2022).

The notion of cultural humility is similar to the empathetic response to the client's frame of reference (Rogers, 1980), the process of bracketing in the phenomenological inquiry whereby one suspends one's preconceptions when exploring the world (Gallagher & Zahavi, 2021); the position of not-knowing (Anderson & Goolishian, 1996); and *epistemological flexibility* in which the counsellor recognizes that a counselling theory is only one of the many ways to *know* about life and is able to comfortably join the student's worldview with curiosity without experiencing any epistemological dissonance. The school counsellor can facilitate cultural humility and epistemological flexibility by applying the concept of EMs to make sense of how students make sense of their life predicaments.

Symbolic Healing and Explanatory Models

The symbolic healing model proposes that the structures of all healing systems (e.g., counselling, *bomoh*, psychiatry) across cultures share four components: a given mythic world, the sufferer-healer relationship, symbols of affliction particularized from the general myth and the manipulation of symbols of affliction by culturally recognized interventions for alleviating the suffering.

A *mythic world* is an *experiential reality* in which every healing system is constructed (Dow, 1986; Lee et al., 2010). The word "myth" implies a healing system contains a *culturally experiential truth* or rationale that provides a plausible explanation for the sufferer's distress and prescribes a ritual or procedure for addressing it (Frank & Frank, 1991). Frank and Frank originally used the word to indicate that theories of psychotherapy encompass myth and ritual in a way resembling religious or spiritual healing.

The concept of myth and other components of the symbolic healing model offer a framework to compare healing practices across cultures. For example, the structure of a mythic world takes a psychosocial form in counselling, a supernatural form in *bomoh*, or a biomedical form in psychiatry.[8] The efficacy of a healing system depends on whether the healer can establish a therapeutic relationship with the sufferer (Wampold, 2021) and evoke a culturally legitimized myth in line with the sufferer's EMs—which concern the ways in which distress is interpreted by the sufferers, healers and other people in the local social world (Dinos et al., 2017; Kleinman & Seeman, 2000). EMs, which are shaped by worldviews, are multidimensional, including label/identity, causal attribution, timeline, consequence and control (see Table 4.2 for more details).

In a *shared* mythic world, the healer (e.g., a school counsellor or a *bomoh*) attaches the sufferer's (e.g., *Aswab*'s) personal and bodily experience onto certain *symbols* of affliction (e.g., study stress or spirit disturbances) and then manipulates the symbols through culturally recognized interventions (e.g., relaxation training or spiritual cleansing) to transform the sufferer's experience (See Figure 4.1). Symbols of affliction provide *order* to the disordered situations such as emotional distress and life predicaments, or to create a coherent plot by filling ambiguous gaps in the sufferer's narrative. Accordingly, symbols of affliction transform confusion into order and culturally meaningful patterns. For example, *Aswab*'s study stress or spirit disturbances are meaningfully linked to inattentiveness.

Table 4.2 Explanatory Models in School Counselling

Dimension[a]	Exploratory Question[b]	Objective
Label/ identity	Do you have any issue? Please tell me what it is? What do you call your issue?	To find out whether the student thinks she has any issue and how she would call it. This question provides the rationale and sets the stage for counselling. Some involuntary clients may not see the need for counselling if they do not think they have any issues, or the ways they call the issues may be different from those of the referral agents (e.g., teachers).
		It is essential for the school counsellors not to impose their labels onto students; otherwise, the students would not have a sense of ownership over their issues and not be motivated to participate in counselling. Like all other EM dimensions, the label of an issue is co-constructed by the school counsellor and the student through meaning making and negotiation.
		Given the intersubjective nature of EMs and that the school counsellor may work with different stakeholders (parents, teachers, significant others), the school counsellor may ask: "Do your parents think that you have a problem; if so, what is it?"
Cause	What do you think is causing your issue? Why do you think it started when it did? Why do you think this is happening to you?	To understand how the student perceives the causes of her issue. The perceived causes may influence the perception of controllability, coping methods, timeline and severity. For example, if the student attributes her issue to an external cause such as luck or fate, she may not think she has the power to control it. Types of perceived causes may also influence preferred sources of help (Lee, 2009).
		For example, if the issue is attributed to biomedical causes, medical professionals may be the preferred sources of help. Conversely, if the issue is attributed to black magic, religious personnel may be approached. If there is more than one causal attribution, there may be multiple sources of help.
		Given the intersubjective nature of EMs and that the school counsellor may work with various stakeholders (parents, teachers, significant others), the school counsellor may ask: "What do your parents believe is happening to you?"
Timeline	Is it a short-term or a long-term issue?	To find out whether the issue is perceived as acute, temporary or chronic. This perception may shape the sense of controllability, action plan, urgency and severity.

(*Continued*)

Table 4.2 (Continued)

Dimension[a]	Exploratory Question[b]	Objective
Consequence	How serious is your issue? How has this issue affected your life?	To identify the student's concerns, and how her issue has affected her personal and social functioning.
Control	What have you done to solve this issue? Where else have you sought help? Can you manage your issue on your own? What kind of help do you think you should receive? What are the most important results you hope to receive from counselling?	To find out the student's help-seeking behaviours (the possible use of formal and informal social support networks, indigenous healing systems), coping methods and readiness for change (Lee, 2009). These questions help to understand the student's healing experience and perceived helpfulness of the supports received.

[a] Leventhal, Brissette and Leventhal (2003).
[b] Dowdy (2000), Kleinman and Seeman (2000).

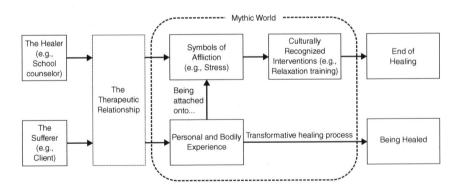

Figure 4.1 The structure and process of symbolic healing

The successful enactment of a mythic world is not about how *true* it is but whether it is socioculturally meaningful to the student and congruent with the student's EMs and depends on a strong therapeutic relationship. The connection between positive counselling relationship and outcome is well established

(Zilcha-Mano, 2017). However, similar to any forms of human relationship, the counselling relationship is culturally defined. Some Asian clients may be more comfortable with counsellors playing the role of an expert and a problem solver in a hierarchical relationship (Sue et al., 2022). They may become bemused and uncomfortable in an egalitarian and non-directive counselling relationship (Li & Kim, 2004). The perceived hierarchical relationship may be more common in Asian school counselling where students see the school counsellors as a teacher or an authoritative figure.

Shared mythic worlds and EMs help to generate shared counselling goals and tasks, which in turn facilitate positive counselling processes and outcomes (Duncan & Miller, 2000). The following section revisits the two cases introduced at the beginning of the chapter from the perspectives of worldviews, self-construal and EMs.

Case Studies

Jia Wen

Since EMs are shaped by worldviews, the counsellor explores *Jia Wen*'s worldviews and self-construal before evoking a culturally legitimized myth (i.e., a counselling theory) consistent with her EMs.

Jia Wen's self-construal is interdependent, shaped by the Confucian family-oriented value (the worldview of axiology). This collectivistic worldview may explain her inner conflict between her personal goal and parents' goal. School counsellors who are not aware of her collectivistic worldview may adopt an individualistic counselling approach by encouraging her to openly express her needs to her parents, which may make her even more anxious. In contrast, a family system theory is a more culturally responsive approach, which focuses on how individual distress is related to social relationships. However, the family system approach must be aligned with *Jia Wen*'s worldview by being grounded in an interdependent self-construal. With this adaptation, the counsellor is able to evoke a myth consistent with *Jia Wen*'s EMs (see Table 4.3).

With shared EMs, the school counsellor supports *Jia Wen* in the following ways. First, guiding her to understand how her dilemma and distress is related to her collectivistic worldview. Second, helping her to explore her parents' rationale for wanting her to study information technology. Third, encouraging her to negotiate with them to achieve a *group* goal. "Independent and interdependent individuals both experience a sense of being active agents in pursuit of their goals, but these specific goals differ depending on one's self-construal" (Cross et al., 2011, p. 145). As compared with independent people, interdependent people are more motivated by socially oriented goals.

The last two steps are conducted in a family session involving *Jia Wen* and her parents. The goal of the family session is not to ask *Jia Wen* to express and validate her personal needs to withstand family pressure, or to challenge her

64 Boon-Ooi Lee

Table 4.3 Explanatory Models of *Jia Wen* and the School Counsellor

EM Dimension	Jia Wen's EM	Counsellor's EM
Label/identity	Feeling stressed out when thinking about her future career.	Exam stress, depressive feelings.
Cause	Inner conflict between her personal goal (becoming an oil painting artist) and parents' goal (expecting her to become a data analyst).	Inner conflict between her personal goal (becoming an oil painting artist) and parents' goal (expecting her to become a data analyst). Being unsure whether to go to an art school or a junior college after her GCE 'O' Level exam.
Timeline	She will be stressed forever when she is thinking about her career choice.	The stress has a short course as the inner conflict is manageable.
Consequence	Her inner conflict has caused her study stress, which in turn has aggravated her inner conflict.	Her inner conflict has caused her study stress, which in turn has aggravated her inner conflict.
Control	Beyond her control as she does not think her parents will endorse a career in art.	She is able to manage her inner conflict by arriving a common goal with her parents via a family session.

parents' expectations, but to negotiate a group goal that both parties are comfortable with. The family session also offers *Jia Wen* an opportunity to listen to her parents. They prefer her to study information technology so that she will land a good job to support the family in the future.

Since interdependent people are more likely than independent people to develop elaborate cognitive representations of other people (Markus & Kitayama, 1991), a family session will help *Jia Wen* and her parents to develop group cognition and socially oriented goal. During this process, *Jia Wen* is unlikely to experience *dissonance-related distress* given that her wish is to maintain a harmonious relationship. Dissonance-related distress usually occurs in independent people who prefer to assert personal needs and goals against the collective norms (Cross et al., 2011).

Jia Wen and her parents finally come up with a group goal where she will attend junior college and then major in information technology with a minor in fine art at university. In the future, when working as a data analyst, she will engage in oil painting on a part-time basis.

Aswab

The worldviews of *Aswab* and his family are characterized by the cultural ontology of nonhuman beings (i.e., *jinn*); a cosmological belief in *Allah*,

Table 4.4 Explanatory Models of *Aswab*, His Parents and the School Counsellor

EM Dimension	Aswab's EM	Parents' EM	Counsellor's EM
Label/identity	Poor attention in class and frequent absenteeism.	Poor attention in class and frequent absenteeism.	Poor attention in class and frequent absenteeism.
Cause	He has been disturbed by a child *jinni* who wants him to be her playmate.	He has been disturbed by a child *jinni* who wants him to be her playmate.	He has been disturbed by a child *jinni* who wants him to be her playmate.
Timeline	Short term.	Short term.	Not sure.
Consequence	Poor attention in class and frequent absenteeism have affected his academic performance.	Poor attention in class and frequent absenteeism have affected his academic performance.	Poor attention in class and frequent absenteeism have affected his study and academic performance.
Control	Can be solved by a *bomoh*.	Can be solved by a *bomoh*.	Not sure. The counsellor will closely monitor *Aswab*'s responses to the *bomoh*'s treatments.

creation and after life; and the sacred knowledge, values and practices embedded in *Qur'an* (the worldviews of epistemology, axiology, praxeology). Their cosmocentric self is not congruous with most of the counselling theories that are structured in the egocentric self. Instead of conceptualizing *Aswab*'s paranormal encounter as hallucination or a symptom of underlying problems from a Western psychological epistemology, the school counsellor adopts the orientation of cultural humility and epistemological flexibility to learn the worldviews of *Aswab* and his parents. However, they are unable to clearly "educate" the counsellor on the phenomenon of *jinn*. It is not because they lack the knowledge, but rather, their knowledge about *jinn* has been transmitted *non-verbally* across generations. As mentioned before, since culture is both cognitive-discursive and embodied, *Aswab*'s cultural belief might have been inscribed onto his body such that he *sees* and *interacts* with a spirit. His apparition and encounter might have already reflected the Islamic belief and implied their completeness without the necessity for further explanation. Table 4.4 presents the EMs of *Aswab*, his parents and the school counsellor.

Since the school counsellor's knowledge in Islam is limited, and the family is more receptive to consult a *bomoh*, the counsellor does not object to their plan in recognition that many Singaporeans draw on local idioms of distress to make sense of their life issues and to seek help from indigenous healing systems (Picco et al., 2016).

According to his parents, the *bomoh* has managed to negotiate with the *jinni* to stop disturbing *Aswab*. Interestingly, his inattentiveness and absenteeism are solved after the healing sessions.

School counsellors can work with indigenous healing systems in two ways (Lee, 2018). First, incorporating indigenous worldviews and EMs into counselling. This integration process is challenging because of the conflicting mythic worlds between traditional practices and counselling. Nonetheless, there have been systematic attempts in integrating religious worldviews (e.g., Christianity, Islam) into psychodynamic, cognitive-behavioural and humanistic/existential therapies (Othman, 2019; Sperry & Shafranske, 2005). Counsellors may apply these spiritually oriented therapies where appropriate.

Second, school counsellors can collaborate with indigenous healers through referral, or support the student to utilize indigenous healing services. This approach is similar to networking with other professionals (e.g., psychiatrists). However, school counsellors must ensure that the indigenous therapies sought are credible, safe and ethical as these practices, except Traditional Chinese Medicine, are generally not regulated in Singapore (see Singapore Ministry of Health, 2022). When a healing method is not regulated, the risk of its misuse is high. There have been reports on bogus faith practitioners abusing and swindling consumers in Singapore (Lim, 2022; Shaffiq Alkhatib, 2020).

Conclusion

Although culture shapes the meaning, experience, expression and coping of distress, school counsellors must be aware of the dynamic nature of culture to avoid cultural generalization and stereotypes. Thus, being culturally competent is more than being knowledgeable about the beliefs and practices of a social group. The school counsellor is encouraged to adopt the dispositions of cultural humility and epistemological flexibility to learn from the student and actively make sense of how the student makes sense of their predicaments by bracketing preconception. During this learning process, the student's worldviews and EMs would naturally unfold or can be elicited with specific questions. The counsellor would then be able to evoke a mythic world consistent with the student's EMs. The shared mythic world and EMs help to generate shared counselling goals and tasks, which in turn facilitate positive counselling process and outcome.

Notes

1 GCE 'O' Level examination, or the Singapore-Cambridge General Certificate of Education Ordinary Level examination, is an annual national examination taken by secondary school students at the end of their fourth or fifth year of study (Singapore Examinations and Assessment Board, 2022).
2 In the ontological world of Islam, *jinn* (the plural of *jnni*) are a type of being created by *Allah* (Boddy, 1988). Like humans, they are born and will die; but unlike humans, they are invisible, formless and not confined by physical barriers. They can possess

and inflict sickness on humans. *Bomoh*, a shaman, is usually called on to deal with the *jinn* possession (Solehah Ishak & Muhammad Ghouse Nassuruddin, 2014).
3 I will discuss the implication of individualism-collectivism for school counselling later.
4 Although counselling can be perceived as a form of indigenous healing system originated in Euro-American cultures (Lee, 2002), the term indigenous healing systems is referred to non-Western healing practices in this article.
5 There was no information about the religious affiliations among school students aged 7 (primary one) to aged 14 years (secondary two). Since the family is students' most important agent of socialization, they may follow their parents' religious beliefs and practices. The total resident population (aged 15 years and over) comprised Buddhists (31.1%), non-religionists (20.0%), Christians (18.9%), Muslims (15.6%), Taoists (8.8%), and Hindus (5.0%).
6 For the background and development of school counselling in Singapore, refer to Kok (2013), and Yeo and Lee (2014).
7 Individuation and low-context communication may be incompatible with Asian collectivistic worldviews, which I will elaborate later.
8 Biomedicine (including psychiatry) can be perceived as a symbolic and meaning system anchored in particular ways that sickness is conceptualized and treated, patient and doctor interact, training is conducted, and practices are sanctioned (Burri & Dumit, 2007).

References

Allan, B. A., Campos, I. D., & Wimberley, T. E. (2016). Interpersonal psychotherapy: A review and multicultural critique. *Counselling Psychology Quarterly, 29*(3), 253–273. https://doi.org/10.1080/09515070.2015.1028896

Anderson, H., & Goolishian, H. (1996). The client is the expert: A not-knowing approach to therapy. In S. McNamee & K. J. Gergen (Eds.), *Therapy as Social Construction* (pp. 25–39). Sage Publications, Inc. https://psycnet.apa.org/record/1992-98567-000

Anderson-Levitt, K. M. (2012). Complicating the concept of culture. *Comparative Education, 48*(4), 441–454. https://doi.org/10.1080/03050068.2011.634285

Boddy, J. (1988). Spirits and selves in Northern Sudan: The cultural therapeutics of possession and trance. *American Ethnologist, 15*(1), 4–27. https://doi.org/10.1525/ae.1988.15.1.02a00020

Bowen, M. (1976). Theory in the practice of psychotherapy. In P. J. Guerin (Ed.) *Family Therapy: Theory and Practice* (pp. 42–90). Gardner Press.

Brewer, M. B., & Ya-Ru, Chen. (2007). Where (who) are collectives in collectivism? Toward conceptual clarification of individualism and collectivism. *Psychological Review, 114*(1), 133–151. https://doi.org/10.1037/0033-295x.114.1.133

Brown, J. (1999). *Bowen family systems theory and practice: Illustration and critique.* https://www.thefsi.com.au/wp-content/uploads/2014/01/Bowen-Family-Systems-Theory-and-Practice_Illustration-and-Critique.pdf

Bullivant, S., Farias, M., Lanman, J., & Lee, L. (2019). Understanding unbelief atheists and agnostics around the world: Interim findings from 2019 research in Brazil, China, Denmark, Japan, the United Kingdom, and the United States. https://research.kent.ac.uk/understandingunbelief/wp-content/uploads/sites/1816/2019/05/UUReportRome.pdf

Burri, R. V., & Dumit, J. (2007). *Biomedicine as culture: Instrumental practices, technoscientific knowledge, and new modes of life.* Routledge. https://www.routledge.

com/Biomedicine-as-Culture-Instrumental-Practices-Technoscientific-Knowledge/Burri-Dumit/p/book/9780415883177

Calatrava, M., Martins, M. V., Schweer-Collins, M., Duch-Ceballos, C., & Rodríguez-González, M. (2022). Differentiation of self: A scoping review of Bowen Family Systems Theory's core construct, *Clinical Psychology Review, 91*, 102101, ISSN 0272-7358, https://doi.org/10.1016/j.cpr.2021.102101.

Chong, W. H., & Lee, B. O. (2015). Social-emotional learning: Promotion of youth wellbeing in Singapore schools. In K. Wright & J. McLeod (Eds.), *Rethinking Youth Wellbeing: Critical Perspectives* (pp. 161–177). Springer. https://link.springer.com/book/10.1007/978-981-287-188-6

Corcoran, K. E., Scheitle, C. P., & Dabbs, E. (2021). Multiple (non)religious identities lead to undercounting religious nones and Asian religious identities. *Journal for the Scientific Study of Religion, 60*(2), 424–441. https://doi.org/10.1111/jssr.12719

Cross, S. E., Hardin, E. E., & Gercek-Swing, B. (2011). The what, how, why, and where of self-construal. *Personality & Social Psychology Review, 15*(2), 142–179. https://doi.org/10.1177/1088868310373752

David, A. R. (2009). Performing for the gods? Dance and embodied ritual in British Hindu Temples. *South Asian Popular Culture, 7*(3), 217–231. https://doi.org/10.1080/14746680903125580

Dinos, S., Ascoli, M., Owiti, J. A., & Bhui, K. (2017). Assessing explanatory models and health beliefs: An essential but overlooked competency for clinicians. *BJPsych Advances, 23*, 106–114. https://doi.org/10.1192/apt.bp.114.013680

Dow, J. (1986). Universal aspects of symbolic healing: A theoretical synthesis. *American Anthropologist, 88*(1), 56–69. https://doi.org/10.1525/aa.1986.88.1.02a00040

Dowdy, K. G. (2000). The culturally sensitive medical interview. *Journal of the American Academy of Physicians Assistants, 13*(6), 91–104. PMID: 11503247

Duncan, B. L., & Miller, S. D. (2000). The client's theory of change: Consulting the client in the integrative process. *Journal of Psychotherapy Integration, 10*(2), 169–187. https://doi.org/10.1023/a:1009448200244

Ellis, B. D., & Stam, H. J. (2015). Crisis? What crisis? Cross-cultural psychology's appropriation of cultural psychology. *Culture and Psychology, 21*(3), 293–317. https://doi.org/10.1177/1354067x15601198

Fatehi, K., Priestley, J. L., & Taasoobshirazi, G. (2020). The expanded view of individualism and collectivism: One, two, or four dimensions? *International Journal of Cross-Cultural Management, 20*(1), 7–24. https://doi.org/10.1177/1470595820913077

Frank, J. D., & Frank, J. B. (1991). *Persuasion and healing: A comparative study of psychotherapy* (3rd ed.). John Hopkins University.

Gallagher, S., & Zahavi, D. (2021). *The phenomenological mind* (3rd ed.). Routledge. https://www.routledge.com/The-Phenomenological-Mind/Gallagher-Zahavi/p/book/9780367334246

Hedges, P. (2017). Multiple religious belonging after religion: Theorizing strategic religious participation in a shared religious landscape as a Chinese model. *Open Theology, 3*(1), 48–72. https://doi.org/10.1515/opth-2017-0005

Horwitz, A. V. (2002). *Creating mental illness*. The University of Chicago Press. https://press.uchicago.edu/ucp/books/book/chicago/C/bo3635568.html

Jankowski, P. J., & Hooper, L. M. (2012). Differentiation of self: A validation study of the Bowen theory construct. *Couple and Family Psychology: Research and Practice, 1*(3), 226. https://doi.org/10.1037/a0027469

Keesing, R. M. (1974). Theories of culture. *Annual Review of Anthropology, 3*(1), 73–97. https://doi.org/10.1146/annurev.an.03.100174.000445

Kirmayer, L. J. (2007). Psychotherapy and the cultural concept of the person. *Transcultural Psychiatry, 44*(2), 232–257. https://doi.org/10.1177/1363461506070794

Kirmayer, L. J., & Ramstead, M. J. D. (2017). Embodiment and enactment in cultural psychiatry. In C. Durt, T. Fuchs & C. Tewes (Eds.), *Embodiment, Enaction, and Culture: Investigating the Constitution of the Shared World* (pp. 397–422). MIT Press. https://mitpress.mit.edu/9780262035552/embodiment-enaction-and-culture/

Kleinman, A., & Seeman, D. (2000). Personal experience of illness. In G. L. Albrecht, R. Fitzpatrick, & S. C. Scrimshaw (Eds.), *Handbook of Social Studies in Health and Medicine* (pp. 230–242). Sage Publications. https://dx.doi.org/10.4135/9781848608412

Kohn, E. (2013). *How forests think: Toward an anthropology beyond the human*. University of California Press. https://www.ucpress.edu/book/9780520276116/how-forests-think

Kok, J. K. (2013). The role of the school counsellor in the Singapore secondary school system. *British Journal of Guidance & Counselling, 41*(5), 530–543. https://doi.org/10.1080/03069885.2013.773286

Koltko-Rivera, M. E. (2004). The psychology of worldviews. *Reviews of General Psychology, 8*(1), 3–58. https://doi.org/10.1037/1089-2680.8.1.3

Koltko-Rivera, M. E. (2008, August 14–17). *Analysis of worldviews underlying different approaches to counselling and psychotherapy* [Poster presentation]. The 116th Annual Convention of the American Psychological Association, Boston, MA. https://www.apa.org/news/press/releases/2008/05/convention

Lee, B. O. (2002). Chinese indigenous psychotherapies in Singapore. *Counselling and Psychotherapy Research, 2*(1), 2–10. https://doi.org/10.1080/14733140212331384938

Lee, B. O. (2009). Relationships between adolescents' preferred sources of help and emotional distress, ambivalence over emotional expression, and causal attribution of symptoms: A Singapore study. *British Journal of Guidance and Counselling, 37*(4), 433–457. https://doi.org/10.1080/03069880903161393

Lee, B. O. (2018). Integrating Asian healing traditions into psychotherapy. In R. Moodley, T. Lo & N. Zhu (Eds.), *Asian Healing Traditions in Counselling and Psychotherapy* (pp. 83–95). Sage. https://dx.doi.org/10.4135/9781071800768

Lee, B. O., & Kirmayer, L. J. (2023). Spirit mediumship and mental health: Therapeutic self-transformation among *dang-ki*s in Singapore. *Culture, Medicine and Psychiatry, 47*(2), 271–300. https://doi.org/10.1007/s11013-021-09765-y

Lee, B. O., Kirmayer, L. J., & Groleau, D. (2010). Therapeutic processes and perceived helpfulness of *dang-ki* (Chinese shamanism) from the symbolic healing perspective. *Culture, Medicine and Psychiatry, 34*(1), 56–105. https://doi.org/10.1007/s11013-009-9161-3

Lee, Y.-T. (李岳庭). (2018). 反思含攝文化下的 Bowen 理論及其運用在華人文化中. *Chinese Journal of Guidance & Counselling, 53*, 23–44. https://doi.org/10.3966/172851862018100053002

Lekas, H. M., Pahl, K., & Fuller Lewis, C. (2020). Rethinking cultural competence: Shifting to cultural humility. Health services insights, 13, 1-4. https://doi.org/10.1177/1178632920970580

Leventhal, H., Brissette, I., & Leventhal, E. A. (2003). The common-sense model of self-regulation of health and illness. In L. D. Cameron & H. Leventhal (Eds.), *The Self-Regulation of Health and Illness Behavior* (pp. 42–65). Routledge. https://

www.routledge.com/The-Self-Regulation-of-Health-and-Illness-Behaviour/Cameron-Leventhal/p/book/9780415297011

Li, L. C., & Kim, B. S. K. (2004). Effects of counselling style and client adherence to Asian cultural values on counselling process with Asian American college students. *Journal of Counselling Psychology*, *51*(2), 158–167. https://doi.org/10.1037/0022-0167.51.2.158

Lim, J. (2022, October 11). Woman convinced followers she was deity and got them to give her millions, eat faeces. *The Straits Times*. https://www.straitstimes.com/singapore/courts-crime/woman-convinced-followers-she-was-deity-they-gave-her-millions-hurt-each-other-and-ate-human-faeces

Markowitz, J. C., & Weissman, M. M. (2004). Interpersonal psychotherapy: Principles and applications. *World Psychiatry*, *3*(3), 136–139. PMID: 16633477; PMCID: PMC1414693.

Markus, H. R., & Kitayama, S. (1991). Culture and the self: Implications for cognition, emotion, and motivation. *Psychological Review*, *98*(2), 224–253. https://doi.org/10.1037/0033-295x.98.2.224

Mathews, M., Khidzer, M., & Teo, K. K. (2014). *Religiosity and the management of religious harmony: Responses from the IPS survey on race, religion and language*. IPS Working Papers, No. 21. Institute of Policy Studies. https://doi.org/10.25818/qf6q-42dv

McLeod, J. (2019). *An introduction to counselling and psychotherapy: Theory, research and practice* (6th ed.). Open University Press.

Othman, N. (2019). Islamic counselling: An integrated approach in promoting psychological well-being. *International Journal of Academic Research in Business and Social Sciences*, *9*(3), 578–588. https://doi.org/10.6007/ijarbss/v9-i3/5727

Picco, L., Abdin, E., Chong, S. A., Pang, S., Vaingankar, J. A., Sagayadevan, V., Kwok, K. W., & Subramaniam, M. (2016). Beliefs about help seeking for mental disorders: Findings from a mental health literacy study in Singapore. *Psychiatric Services*, *67*(11), 1246–1253. https://doi.org/10.1176/appi.ps.201500442

Pietrantoni, A. (2022). School counsellor multicultural self-efficacy: Educational and training practices. *VISTA Online, American Counselling Association*. https://www.counselling.org/docs/default-source/vistas/school-counsellor-multicultural-self-efficacy.pdf?sfvrsn=9e9f4a2c_4

Ratts, M. J., & Greenleaf, A. T. (2017). Multicultural and social justice counselling competencies: A leadership framework for professional school counsellors. *Professional School Counselling*, *21*(1b), 1–9. https://doi.org/10.1177/2156759x18773582

Rogers, C. R. (1980). *A way of being*. Houghton Mifflin.

Shaffiq Alkhatib (2020, March 13). 'Spiritual healer' molested at least 4 women during massages, exorcism rituals. *The Straits Times*. https://www.straitstimes.com/singapore/courts-crime/spiritual-healer-molested-at-least-4-women-during-massages-exorcism-rituals

Shepherd, H. (2014). Culture and cognition: A process account of culture. *Sociological Forum*, *29*(4), 1007–1011. https://doi.org/10.1111/socf.12134

Singapore Department of Statistics (2021). *Census of population 2020: Demographic characteristics, education, language, and religion*. Singapore Department of Statistics. https://www.singstat.gov.sg/publications/reference/cop2020/cop2020-sr1/census20_stat_release1

Singapore Examinations and Assessment Board (2022, April 14). https://www.seab.gov.sg

Singapore Ministry of Health (2022, August 19). *Registration of TCM practitioners.* https://www.healthprofessionals.gov.sg/tcmpb/en/registration-of-tcm-practitioners

Soh, S., & Leong, F. T. L. (2002). Validity of vertical and horizontal individualism and collectivism in Singapore: Relationship with values and interests. *Journal of Cross-Cultural Psychology, 33*(1), 3–15. https://doi.org/10.1177/0022022102033001001

Solehah Ishak, & Muhammad Ghouse Nassuruddin (2014). Traditional Malay healing practices: Expressions of cultural and local knowledge. *Procedia: Social and Behavioral Sciences, 140*, 291–294. https://doi.org/10.1016/j.sbspro.2014.04.422

Sperry, L., & Shafranske, E. P. (2005). *Spiritually oriented psychotherapy.* American Psychological Association. https://psycnet.apa.org/doi/10.1037/10886-000

Starr, R. L., Theng, A. J., Wong, K. M., Tong, N. J. Y., Ibrahim, N. A. B., Chua, A. M. Y., Yong, C. H. M., Loke, F. W., Dominic, H., Fernandez, K. J., & Peh, M. T. J. (2017). Third culture kids in the outer circle: The development of sociolinguistic knowledge among local and expatriate children in Singapore. *Language in Society, 46*(4), 507–546. https://doi.org/10.1017/s0047404517000380

Sue, D. W., Sue, D., Neville, H. A., & Smith, L. (2022). *Counselling the culturally diverse: Theory and practice* (9th ed.). John Wiley & Sons. https://www.wiley.com/en-us/Counselling+the+Culturally+Diverse%3A+Theory+and+Practice%2C+9th+Edition-p-9781119861904

Taves, A., Asprem, E., & Ihm, E. (2018). Psychology, meaning making, and the study of worldviews: Beyond religion and non-religion. *Psychology of Religion and Spirituality, 10*(3), 207–217. https://doi.org/10.1037/rel0000201

The Humanist Society (Singapore) (n. d.). https://humanist.org.sg/about/the-society/

Uchida, Y., Nakayama, M., & Bowen, K. S. (2022). Interdependence of emotion: Conceptualization, evidence, and social implications from cultural psychology. *Current Directions in Psychological Science, 31*(5), 1–20. https://doi-org.libproxy.nie.edu.sg/10.1177/09637214221109584

Vidal, C. (2008). Wat is een wereldbeeld? [What is a worldview?]. In H. Van Belle & J. Van der Veken (Eds.), *Nieuwheid denken* (pp. 71–86). (Nieuwheid denken. De wetenschappen en het creatieve aspect van de werkelijkheid). Acco. https://researchportal.vub.be/en/publications/what-is-a-worldview

Wampold, B. E. (2021). Healing in a social context: The importance of clinician and patient relationship. *Frontiers in Pain Research, 2*, 1–10. https://doi.org/10.3389/fpain.2021.684768

Weir, K. (2020). What do you believe? *Monitor on Psychology, 51*(5), 52–57. https://doi.org/10.1201/9780203498385-6

Williams, B. (2003). The worldview dimensions of individualism and collectivism: Implications for counselling. *Journal of Counselling & Development, 81*(3), 370. https://doi-org.libproxy.nie.edu.sg/10.1002/j.1556-6678.2003.tb00263.x

Yeo, L. S., & Lee, B. O. (2014). School-based counselling in Singapore. *Journal of Asian Pacific Counselling, 4*(2), 69–79. https://doi.org/10.18401/2014.4.2.7

Yeoh, B. S. A., Acedera, K. A. F., Rocha, Z. L., & Rootham, E. (2021). Family matters: Negotiating intergenerational mixed identities among Eurasian families in Singapore. *Journal of Family Issues, 42*(8), 1880–1903. https://doi.org/10.1177/0192513x20957050

Zilcha-Mano, S. (2017). Is the alliance really therapeutic? Revisiting this question in light of recent methodological advances. *American Psychologist, 72*(4), 311–325. https://doi.org/10.1037/a0040435

5 School Counselling in Japan and the Impact of COVID-19

Nicolas Tajan, Hans Raupach and Teo Knives

Introduction

In 2014, a scoping review of school-based counselling in the Asia-Pacific region revealed a vast diversity in the nature of the work, the prerequisites for practice, and the methods of organisation and delivery of school counselling services across different countries (Harris, 2014). What remained consistent throughout the region was the continuous dedication and financial support from national governments that exhibited similarly high priorities regarding the mental well-being, overall health, and vocational guidance of children and youth. At the same time, another review pointed out that, in East and Southeast Asia, many school counsellors tended to engage in diverse yet vaguely defined functions, often finding themselves in marginalised positions within educational institutions with restricted opportunities for engagement with professional communities and limited access to professional development (Harrison, 2022).

A decade later, the poorly defined professional identity of school counsellors remains a pivotal concern in Japan. Japanese academic literature on school counselling published over the past three decades shows a growing emphasis on the need to develop a more effective collaboration between school counsellors, teachers, students, their parents, and other professionals (Mimura et al., 2019). However, achieving this collaboration is often a challenging endeavour.

A recent paper (Arai, 2022) analysed the number of articles published in Japanese scientific journals about school counsellors between 1995 and 2019. The study found that despite a steady rise in the employment of school counsellors, there was no corresponding increase in academic publications on the topic after 2001. The paper also shows a noticeable shift in the concerns of Japanese school counsellors, moving from a focus on addressing the phenomenon of school non-attendance (*futōkō*) in 2001 to actively advocating for a more efficient collaboration with school teachers.

Notably, issues such as school non-attendance, harassment, and bullying have been on the rise since the 1980s, increasingly reported in industrialised countries (e.g., USA, Canada, UK, France, Japan), where they have become a major concern of educational policies. In Japan, the phenomenon of *ijime*

DOI: 10.4324/9781003352457-5

(bullying) led to the establishment of hotlines for victims, a response observed in many other countries. Yet, in Japanese public schools, it was the homeroom teachers (*tannin no sensei*), not the school counsellors, who were at the forefront of addressing these issues due to a combination of cultural and historical factors. On top of regular academic support, homeroom teachers in Japan are traditionally expected to nurture students' psychological and social growth both during and outside of school hours (Akiba et al., 2010). They invest substantial time in individual student counselling, making home visits to check up on students and their families, and actively fostering a sense of belonging within the community. Homeroom teachers may conduct up to a hundred home visits in a year, often working overtime to accommodate these visits (Tajan, 2021, pp. 33–34). Given this peculiar tendency, it is unsurprising that in instances of bullying within a classroom, parents and school administration often assign the primary responsibility for addressing and resolving the situation to the homeroom teacher.

In this regard, homeroom teachers in Japanese public schools inevitably become important colleagues for counsellors, who arrived at this pre-established teacher-centred context only after their profession was legally recognised in 1995. As a result, the activities of school counsellors in Japan are typically structured to complement rather than overlap with the responsibilities of homeroom teachers.

According to Doi (2022), the activities of school counsellors (SCs) in Japanese schools generally include five main aspects: (1) monitoring child development; (2) supporting children with developmental disorders; (3) facilitating cooperation between kindergartens, elementary schools, and junior high schools; (4) counselling students with an awareness of the homeroom teacher-lead pedagogy; and (5) supporting, consulting, and counselling parents. Doi (2022) emphasises the vital need for collaboration with homeroom teachers, particularly in times when concerns related to social and economic issues are on the rise. Similarly, Ishikawa (2020) asserts that the primary role of school counsellors in Japan is to address problematic student behaviours within the school environment, a task that necessitates a complex cooperation among experts in education, psychology, and welfare.

Alongside existing challenges in collaboration, the diverse skill sets and work experiences of SCs in Japan pose additional obstacles to the widespread implementation of counselling across schools. There is an urgent call to improve the training systems within professional organisations and universities, and to establish greater legal stability for their employment. As Ishikawa (2020) points out, "In order to fulfil an expected important role as a counsellor, it is indispensable for a counsellor to ensure the expansion of working hours and the guarantee of status as a professional occupation" (p. 93).

In addition to the above organisational issues, the onset of the COVID-19 pandemic caused Japanese school counsellors face extreme operational challenges. All schools nationwide remained completely closed for three months from March until June 2020, with counsellors losing all contact with children and parents. Notably, no efforts were made to introduce distance learning or facilitate online communication between the school and the students during this period. After the closure, many schools temporarily implemented the *Bunsan-tōkō* system, wherein half of the students attended classes in the morning, while the other half attended in the afternoon, further disrupting the normative study process for many months to come and increasing school counsellors' overall workload.

This chapter aims to explore the specific challenges faced by school counsellors in Japan, acknowledging the unique cultural and historical context in which they operate. Furthermore, serving as a follow-up to field interviews conducted with Japanese school counsellors a decade ago (Tajan, 2021, pp. 32–58), this chapter seeks to identify distinct obstacles they had to encounter within the profession due to the impact of the COVID-19 pandemic.

The Brief History of School Counselling Regulations in Japan

The profession of school counsellor (*sukūru kaunserā*) gained recognition from the Japanese Ministry of Education, Culture, Sports, Science and Technology (MEXT) with the education reform of 1995. This development was marked by the initiation of the School Counsellor Utilisation Investigation Research Project.[1] The introduction of SCs can be viewed as a government response to escalating public concern stemming from a widespread epidemic of bullying and school non-attendance. By 2001, the placement of SCs in public junior high schools nationwide was actively promoted, with legal enforcement implemented in 2004, mandating each junior high school to provide the services of a SC (Ingrams, 2005).

In July 2007, MEXT released a document titled *Enhancement of Educational counselling for Children – Creation of a Consultation System to Nurture Lively Children (Report)* (MEXT, 2007), that clarifies general guidelines and expectations for school counselling activities. SCs' main role is presented as streamlining school operations, especially when they face disruptions caused by students' psychological issues, absenteeism, and teachers taking sick leaves due to stress and other mental health concerns. SCs are tasked with addressing these issues by supporting students, teachers, and parents. A special emphasis is placed on enhancing the visibility, accessibility, and presence of the SC for both students and parents, a measure seen as instrumental in maximising their effectiveness.

However, the relationship between the SC and the school environment, including teachers, principal, and staff, can appear somewhat ambiguous. While the SC operates for a short duration and is external to the school, they also need to be an integral part of its administrative framework. In practice, achieving the delicate balance of seamlessly integrating the SC into the school environment and ensuring they have access to all pertinent information, while still maintaining their external employment status, proves to be a formidable challenge.

According to the 2007 report, SCs tended to be employed on a part-time basis, with over 80% of them holding certifications as clinical psychologists. In most schools, counselling sessions were provided once a week, averaging four to eight hours per school. A standard work schedule for a SC includes 35 weeks annually, allocating between 8 and 12 hours per week per school. This time includes counselling, behavioural analysis, report writing and other activities. In exceptional circumstances, this commitment could be extended to up to 30 hours if deemed necessary by the school principal. The primary focus of counselling sessions with students revolved around issues of school non-attendance and bullying. Additionally, topics such as friendships, parent-child relationships, learning-related challenges, developmental disorders, mental health concerns, and self-harm, including incidents of wrist cutting, were addressed. Another task of SCs was the reduction of sick leaves due to stress-induced psychological disorders among teachers and school staff which have been rising over recent years.

As of 2006, the deployment of SCs spanned a total of 9,978 schools, distributed as follows: 7,613 in junior high schools (76.3%), 1,677 in elementary schools (16.8%), and 688 in high schools (6.9%). Given that high schools in Japan fall outside the scope of compulsory education, MEXT anticipates that SCs will predominantly be stationed in junior high schools, where behavioural issues like school non-attendance and bullying are reportedly more prevalent compared to elementary schools. Hence, as per the 2007 report, the assignment of SCs to public high schools should not exceed 10% of the overall budget provided by the MEXT school counselling project. In 2007, this budget was JPY 5051 million, which also included provisions for a 24-hour hotline for consultation (MEXT, 2023).

Due to the proactive enforcement of MEXT policies, the number of employed school counsellors in Japan surged from only 154 in 1995 to 30,681 in 2021. This expansion was accompanied by a notable increase in the total budget allocation, rising from JPY 307 million in 1995 to JPY 5278 million in 2021 (MEXT, 2021).

Following this upward trend, MEXT has been regularly updating its recommendations regarding the school counselling profession. The *Implementation Guidelines for the School Counsellor Utilisation Project*, released on April 1, 2023, sheds light on various facets of the school counsellor profession in the present day. Compared to the 2007 situation, the project encompasses several new components, such as the norms for deploying SCs to educational institutions, telephone and social media services which can also be handled by non-SCs, mobilising SCs during emergency situations, and provision of professional supervision.

The 2023 document states that now SCs can be dispatched to a wider range of public educational institutions, including elementary schools, junior high schools (where their presence is mandatory), compulsory education schools, high schools, secondary education schools, special-needs schools, and educational consultation centres established by local governments for students and their parents. Moreover, SCs can be sent to all public schools (including public kindergartens) in emergency situations to provide mental health care for children affected by a disaster. In such circumstances, they are also expected to extend guidance and aid to teachers, staff, and parents, offering advice and assistance.

The assignment of SCs should contain an investigation of effectiveness conducted by each municipality – a measure that reflects a growing concern for SCs' practical efficiency. The project underlines that when employed, SCs should actively engage and attain more visibility for students to consult them. To enhance the overall impact of the school counselling project, the report encourages local initiatives to create counselling avenues beyond the school premises, such as in community centres or libraries, as well as collaborations with other public and private projects addressing issues like bullying and school non-attendance.

Given the absence of a universally recognised school counsellor certification in Japan, most SCs are appointed based on alternative established official certifications, such as certified clinical psychologist or public psychologist. Nevertheless, individuals who do not possess any of the typical certifications can also assume roles as SCs under specific conditions. They are categorised as individuals considered equivalent to SCs. However, they are mandated to demonstrate relevant work experience and receive comparatively lower compensation than certified SCs, being defined as:

> *persons who have highly specialised knowledge and experience in the clinical psychology of children and students and are or were presidents, vice presidents, professors, associate professors, or lecturers (limited to those who work full-time) of universities as stipulated in Article 1 of the School Education Law; or persons considered by the prefecture or designated city as having at least as much knowledge and experience as the persons mentioned above.*
>
> (MEXT, 2023, p. 2)

The final clause implies that, in practice, anyone can be appointed as a SC upon the preference of the prefecture or city where the school is situated, as stated in the following section:

> *Persons equivalent to school counsellors: A person who has completed a master's degree and has at least one year of experience in clinical psychology or consultation services for children; A person who has graduated from a university or a junior college and has five years or more experience in clinical psychological services or consultation services for children; A physician who has at least one year of experience in clinical psychological services or consultation services for children; Persons considered by the prefecture or designated city as having at least as much knowledge and experience as the persons mentioned above.*
>
> (MEXT, 2023, p. 2)

A similar selection mechanism in the segment concerning individuals engaged in telephone or SMS counselling looks less surprising, as many helplines globally do not necessitate responders to hold certified psychology credentials. Instead, they are expected to receive comprehensive training in telephone counselling, tailored and confined to a service that does not involve psychotherapy. This section specifies that:

> *persons with knowledge and experience regarding telephone and SNS counselling, and who understand the aim of the project will be selected by the prefecture or designated city. The service can also be entrusted to third parties. Since counselling via SNS requires different counselling methods than face to face or telephone counselling, selected persons (including persons of third parties) who do not have the adequate skills must be trained.*
> (MEXT, 2023, p. 2)

As early as 2007, the MEXT student support hotline already operated 24/7, but today, there has been a substantial increase in the project's visibility and accessibility. Every student, regardless of their school type (public, private, spanning from elementary to high school, including special-needs schools), is informed of the availability of the telephone and SMS counselling service through Education Consultation Service Referral Cards, which are regularly distributed by the schools for easy reference. Another pivotal advancement lies in the new consultation system that employs SMS messaging. It enables two-way 24/7 online counselling through text messaging, as well as a one-way reporting system via an application to address concerns such as bullying.

A noteworthy and final enhancement since 2007 is the introduction of professional supervision and oversight for the project. The emphasis on collaboration among various actors is evident, highlighted by the regular reference to liaison conferences, seminars, and training sessions geared towards enhancing service quality and ensuring the seamless operation of the project through information exchange with relevant institutions. In specific terms, supervisors are assigned to provide guidance for SCs at both schools and within Boards of Education. Furthermore, in-school seminars are arranged to elevate the counselling proficiency of teachers, and additional educational programmes are organised to mitigate students' difficulties and alleviate stress.

The Diversity of School Counsellors and their Certifications

We have already explained elsewhere (Tajan, 2021) that Japan, which appears to be culturally homogeneous (Befu, 2001), is quite diverse in terms of the landscape of counselling, psychotherapy, and psychology. In fact, there are approximately 50 independent associations issuing a variety of certifications, including an association certifying clinical psychologists (*rinshō shinri shi*). This certification was established in 1988 largely due to the endeavours of Professor

Hayao Kawai, who founded and chaired the Association of Japanese Clinical Psychology and played an important role in the creation of a nation-wide school counselling system in 1995. The title of a certified clinical psychologist held its position as the most sought-after licensing option, especially for school counsellors, for several decades up until 2018. In 2012, there were 26,329 people holding clinical psychologist certificates (Tajan, 2021, p. 6), the largest number among any other professional licensing bodies at that time in Japan.

However, in 2018, the Japanese psychologist certification landscape underwent a significant transformation with the introduction of the first national licence. The annual national exam now grants individuals the title of *certified public psychologist*, known as *kōnin shinri shi*, a national psychologist licence (*shinri shi no kokka shikaku*). The exams conducted in 2018, 2019, 2020, and 2021 culminated in the certification of 55,352 public psychologists, and as of September 2023, the total has reached an estimated 70,000.[2] These statistics hold considerable weight because we now have a rough estimate of the number of practising psychologists in Japan. Nowadays, both the longstanding private clinical psychologist licence, which is still being issued (the total has reached 40,749 in 2023[3]), and the more recent public psychologist licence can serve as two possible pathways to becoming a school counsellor.

In 2015 and 2021, Tajan discussed a debated issue: Should every school counsellor in Japan hold a certification as a clinical psychologist? Indeed, in certain prefectures, this certification gained prevalent popularity, with many public and private institutions requiring psychologists to obtain it. This was notably the case in Kyoto prefecture, where Hayao Kawai, then professor at Kyoto University, held considerable influence. One of the original aims of this certification was to guarantee that SCs had received high-quality training, and to provide clarity for the public in the absence of a government standard. However, with the emergence of certified public psychologists, the significance of clinical psychologist certification gradually decreased both nationally and internationally.

Before the public certification was introduced, aspiring school counsellors would commonly pursue certification as clinical psychologists alongside any other additional certifications of their choosing. However, the current emphasis has shifted towards getting the title of a certified public psychologist, which has now become crucial for employment in public schools. Moreover, it may be useful to get a public psychologist licence and become a member of Japan School Counseling Association (JSCA)[4] that provides access to resources and a useful professional network. JSCA was founded in 2009 from a consolidation of nine pre-existing associations, all of which granted a range of certifications for school counsellors.[5] This merger occurred because MEXT sought to streamline communication by having these organisations present their demands through a unified channel, rather than negotiating separately with nine distinct entities. Among other groups, JSCA gathers Japanese Association of Counselling Science (JACS) producing *certified counsellors* (*nintei kaunserā*) since 1986, the Japanese Society for the Study of Career Education

(JSSCE) certifying *career counsellors* (*kyaria kaunserā*) since 1992, the Japanese Association of School Counselling (JASC) certifying *school counsellors* (*gakkō kaunserā*) since 1995, the Japanese Association of School Psychology certifying *school psychologists* (*gakkō shinri shi*) since 1997, and the Association of Clinical Developmental Psychologists that started certifying *clinical developmental psychologists* since 2022 (*rinshō hattatsu shinri shi*).

The coalition aims to preserve all these diverse professional associations and to make all their certifications nationally recognised as sufficient for school counsellor job positions. In terms of its ideological focus, JSCA emphasises providing students with guidance related to their careers and how they can contribute effectively to society as its members. According to JSCA, guidance is an educational term that refers to "activities in school education aimed at helping children understand themselves and fully utilise their abilities, enabling them to become valuable members of society" (Japan School Counseling Association, n.d., para. 1).

Interestingly, the association attempted to create its own joint licensing system by introducing *guidance counsellor* certification (*gaidansu kaunserā*) valid for ten years with a possibility for extension. Guidance counsellors, as outlined by JSCA, are recognised as specialists in both psychology and education. As integral members of the school team, they are expected to lend support to children in addressing developmental challenges across four guidance domains – study, career, psychosocial dimension, and health (Japan School Counseling Association, n.d.). As of March 2018, there were only 3,500 people who obtained the guidance counsellor certification, compared to the combined number of all the other certificate holders of the various associations included in JSCA: 10,000 educational counsellors (*kyōiku kaunserā*), 4,200 school psychologists, 3,500 clinical developmental psychologists, 820 counselling psychologists (*kaunseringu shinri shi*), 770 school counsellors (*gakkō kaunserā*), and 150 career counsellors (*kyaria kaunserā*) – around 20,000 professionals in total. It seems that both the desire of Japanese school counsellors to maintain their previous diverse professional identities and the introduction of the all-encompassing public psychologist licence makes the joint JSCA certifications as attractive as any other school counselling-related licence from associations belonging to it.

School Counselling as Seen by School Counsellors Themselves

In-depth qualitative research interviews with two experienced counsellors working in Japan were conducted in September 2023. The names of the individuals interviewed, who gave authorisation to be audio-recorded, have been anonymised. In this exploratory investigation, we used an open questionnaire in which we asked SCs to describe the following: first, the period between graduation and their present work; second, a typical day before, during, and after the COVID-19 pandemic; third, the impact of the COVID-19 pandemic on the school counselling practice; fourth, the impact of the COVID-19 pandemic on the role of the counsellor in the school; and fifth, their best and worst experiences during or after the COVID-19 pandemic.

Narrative analysis was used to understand stories SCs told about their experiences in the Japanese cultural context amidst drastic social changes brought by the pandemic. We focused on themes such as counselling before and during the pandemic, the impact of COVID-19 on mental health and school counselling practice. The use of teleconsultations (Tajan et al., 2023) were examined across the study. We share extracts from these interviews below to illustrate the impact of the COVID-19 pandemic on school counselling practices, and to highlight areas where the support to students and their parents in Japan could be improved.

ES (Elementary School Counsellor)

ES is a senior female psychologist with extensive experience working in a hospital. She served as a SC for five years at an elementary school, from 2017 to 2022. She had a typical weekly schedule for a school counsellor, working only once a week for eight hours. Working hours can vary depending on the school, and ES had to be in her office (consultation room) from 10:30 a.m. to 6:30 p.m.

Counselling Before the COVID-19 Pandemic. In the context of counselling sessions held in the consultation room by ES, meetings were typically arranged with the guardians, frequently the mothers, who were often referred to her by the homeroom teacher. However, students could also come directly to the counsellor of their own accord:

> *Pupils from the upper grades of elementary school often came to counselling directly because they said they wanted to talk. I don't really do play therapy, instead, I focus mainly on talking. In the lower grades of elementary school, the mothers came together with their children; in the case of truancy sometimes the children came together with their mothers, sometimes the children alone, sometimes the mothers came alone.*

While ES conducted regular one-hour sessions with truant children, she also took the initiative to have shorter 30-minute sessions during lunch breaks, where she would eat together with children who didn't want to miss classes to see her in the office, but still wanted to talk. When it comes to talking with the mothers, ES adopted a clinical approach where she provided realistic advice, inquired about their concerns, and attentively listened to them. In such cases, conversations often lasted for one to one and a half hours until a resolution started to emerge:

> *Additionally, because they were elementary school pupils, when the mother applied for a consultation, I often chatted informally with the child beforehand to understand their personality and also asked the homeroom teacher*

about the child. By doing so, I would form an impression of the child's academic progress, social interactions with friends, and many other details. After gathering the information, I would finally meet with the mother to hear her concerns.

ES also conducted home visits on rare occasions along with the homeroom teacher. However, in instances involving truant children, she refrained from home visits, and instead, mothers of these children would visit her at the school, which aligns with findings from accounts of Japanese SCs collected a decade ago (Tajan, 2015). When ES did request a home visit for such a case, parents declined, and the school was also hesitant to grant permission. At school accessing children in need was much easier:

> …When a child doesn't want anyone to know that he is seeing the SC, we are also allowed to meet the child without the permission of the mother. It was quite rare, but there were some children who talked to me and didn't want me to tell their parents: 'Don't tell them because my mother will worry,' they said.

On top of counselling students and their guardians, ES held a daily meeting with the coordinator and school nurse who is responsible for the school infirmary, to discuss the school's weekly situation, the needs of the children, and the ongoing problems of those who frequently visited the infirmary. After school hours when all the children had left for the day, ES also conducted "discussion meetings" with the homeroom teachers regarding the students she regularly counselled. Furthermore, occasional case review meetings with the school management, which included the principal and vice-principal, were held whenever necessary.

Counselling During the COVID-19 Pandemic. In the case of ES's school, she was given permission to freely use the counselling room during the COVID-19 pandemic. This way, even though the children were not at school, she could still continue consultations with some of the students' mothers. However, when the schools reopened with *bunsan-tōkō* (literally *divided schooling*) system, ES found it impossible to conduct individual interviews with every single child from the 5th grade, which is government-set requirement for all Japanese SCs working at public elementary schools – there was not enough time to see all the children with a half-day study program in place. Another problem was that talking to the younger children while playing with them became more difficult, as all physical contact got prohibited. Similarly, eating together and talking while facing each other was not allowed anymore:

> The children used to talk more openly while eating. Collecting information about them, solving some issues while interacting with them in a relaxed way – all of that became impossible, because we had to eat silently.

As mentioned in the introduction, in the beginning of the pandemic, schools closed for about three months – the whole of March, April, and May 2020 – reopening in June of that year. This closure was met with little opposition, as both children and parents were afraid of getting infected. Since online classes were not organised, all SCs in Japan almost completely stopped working. However, when the children were allowed to return, schools aimed to maximise the use of counsellors' services due to their predetermined working hours and fixed pay.[6] Throughout the pandemic, most children came to school at least once a month, while some, particularly younger elementary school children lacking sufficient parental support, were placed under special supervision at school and asked to come more often. In such instances, if a particular child gained this attention, ES was occasionally requested to visit the school for counselling, typically about once a month. ES recalled this as an especially vulnerable period for the students:

The rhythm of many children's everyday life kind of collapsed, and there was a certain number of children who became truant in that time. When children come to school every day, the teachers can look after them, they have contact with friends so they can preserve their everyday rhythm, even when their mothers' child rearing ability is not that high. But because they were not able to come to school, their rhythms collapsed, and some of them became truant, especially in the case of the upper grades of elementary school.

The Impact of COVID-19 on Students' Mental Health. ES's observations suggest that many children who transitioned from nursery school to first-year elementary school in March 2020 and began their academic year on April 1st, 2020, faced challenges in adapting to the school environment due to the pandemic. This transition amplified what is commonly referred to in Japan as the "first-year elementary school problem."[7] ES noted a sharp decline in spoken language skills and communication abilities in social settings like the school canteen in this group of students:

There were some children who were not good at talking and a bit reserved, who ended up not talking at all because they were wearing masks, and it was considered normal for them not to talk by others. If the COVID-19 pandemic had not occurred, these children would have probably kept talking, because they would have had to use loud voice for others to hear them, talk with others while eating lunch, despite their initial shyness. But under the circumstances at that time, talking could be avoided, and there were no opportunities to practise it.

According to ES, the widespread use of masks also slowed down language acquisition for many students, making it more difficult to see mouth movements and therefore to learn to pronounce words correctly. Moreover, implementation of pandemic-related measures in Japanese schools, such as maintaining silence in the canteen and wearing masks, also became a catalyst for the emergence of anxiety disorders and eating disorders among some children:

> *A first-year elementary school girl developed an anxiety disorder, a fear of vomiting, because she saw a friend vomiting, resulting in her not being able to eat at school anymore. In the first grade of elementary school, you normally always eat together, so even if you have such an anxiety, at some point, while eating and having fun together, you become able to eat again and normalise (…) such a pattern would be quite common, but during the COVID-19 pandemic that didn't happen because we had to eat silently. We weren't allowed to face one another (…) and in the heads of these children their fear was really whirling around. So, for these children with anxiety, I asked for a special permission from the homeroom teachers and mothers, sat next to them, talked to them, and made them laugh, trying to make the lunch more relaxed, something they don't need to be nervous about. With one child I did that for 3 months until he was finally able to eat again.*

To summarise, the pandemic has challenged the role and functions of the SC, which were relatively well defined before 2020. The disruption caused by this crisis has profoundly affected the day-to-day life of schools and destroyed an established routine that was beneficial to the students' cognitive and social development. The newly implemented rule of maintaining silence in informal settings, such as the canteen, have contributed to increased shyness of some students. The impact of the COVID-19 pandemic on students' mental health and on SC's professional practice was predominantly negative. For instance, the requirement to wear masks has led to unfortunate consequences, potentially contributing to delays in verbal language acquisition and the emergence of lasting anxiety and eating disorders among students, issues that could have been less prominent under ordinary circumstances.

GC (Elementary School Counsellor)

GC, a female elementary school counsellor, became a psychologist after working for children's welfare in different settings as an NGO employee. When she got certified to become a SC, she took on three jobs to fill the week and support herself financially: counselling at public schools, in private practice, and in a government-run specially designated "guidance classroom" (*tekiō shidō kyōshitsu*) for children with learning or behavioural difficulties between 2015 and 2023.

Counselling Before the COVID-19 Pandemic. As a former NGO worker, GC is highly motivated to help children coming from disadvantaged social backgrounds. She started the interview by recounting her work experience in the guidance classroom, where she encountered children who lacked essential life experiences due to various factors such as poverty, including hidden poverty, or family dysfunction. Some children were unable to bring their own lunch to the guidance classroom due to financial struggles or lacked basic everyday knowledge:

> *I once asked a girl who was wearing the summer uniform in winter: 'Aren't you cold?' It was a wrong question because whether she is cold or not, it was the only thing she had. There is a lot of hidden poverty. Kids at the bottom of the social pyramid do not have the typical life experiences that one would expect everyone to have.*

In her role as a school counsellor at public schools, GC noted that the nature of her work depended heavily on the attitudes and approaches of both the school principal and the teachers, which aligns with the data from our previous interviews (Tajan, 2021, pp. 32–58). Some principals that Miss GC worked with asked her to prioritise interactions with parents, while others suggested she should focus solely on the students.

In her final four years of employment, she was asked to prioritise individual counselling with students. Her contractual working hours were from 8:30 a.m. to 5 p.m., but she often started earlier for morning sessions, particularly those attended by single fathers or aimed at encouraging children facing social difficulties to arrive before their peers. GC's schedule was consistently packed with sessions, each lasting 45 minutes with a five-minute break in between. Even during lunch, students would come and talk to her while she was eating. This meant conducting nine or ten sessions a day. At the end of her workday, she would write reports and then discuss them with the homeroom teachers. In contrast to ES, GC rarely had sessions involving both parents and children. Instead, GC usually followed a practice known as "parallel consultation" (Tajan, 2021), wherein she would meet with the child individually while another counsellor held a separate session with the parent.

GC provided a valuable insight into an aspect of counselling that had previously been unclear – the presence (or absence) of fathers in Japanese counselling and family therapy settings. She was surprised to encounter many single fathers seeking support. In cases where the child had two parents, it was typically the mother who attended sessions. According to GC, it is not that single fathers are more inclined to seek help, but rather *"they worry about their children growing up without a mother, and they have their own stress of raising children."*

One of the most difficult aspects of working at a public school for GC is when counselling sessions must be terminated due to either the student or counsellor leaving the school. When rapport is already established within the school framework, referrals to the own private practice can pose an ethical dilemma for the SC. Even when referrals are permitted by school regulations, many students and their families may lack the financial means to afford private counselling. GC believes that easily accessible free school counselling is a critically important service to maintain and promote, especially for financially struggling families.

GC has acknowledged significant progress in Japan, noting that every public junior high school now has a school counsellor – a concept that was simply unimaginable three decades ago. However, she feels that the status of school counsellors remains undervalued, often seen as an entry-level position that, in her view, fails to align with the actual responsibilities of the role.

Counselling During the COVID-19 Pandemic. Despite working in a different region of Japan than ES, GC reported similar challenges faced by the Japanese public school system in adapting to the onset of the COVID-19 pandemic, as measures were implemented uniformly nationwide. At the onset of COVID, the combination of not being permitted to attend school and not being allowed to call students from her private phone made it impossible for GC to follow up on the children she was regularly seeing before:

I lost all contact. If the system was a bit more flexible or quicker to adapt to the change, they could have allowed us to work from home. For some children, home is not the safest place. So, in my opinion, it was an inappropriate time to stop the counselling service. Unfortunately, no measures were implemented for us to continue doing our job. Schools closed in March. Until they reopened in the summer, we depended on the homeroom teacher who would call the students from time to time.

Interestingly, when her school reopened, GC said her work resumed back to its hectic pre-pandemic rhythm immediately, from morning to night. Just as ES reported, GC was also expected to offer a counselling experience to all Grade 5 students throughout the academic year. There was even consideration of expanding this opportunity to other grades. However, even the regular requirement was impossible to meet given the limited days that GC worked. Instead, teachers at her school conducted the initial screening of students who were anxious and concerned about COVID-19 and then referred the more serious cases to her. The counselling sessions for all Grade 5 students lasted only five to ten minutes per person because of the dimensions of the school. GC's work became drastically busier because the requirement of being aware of the impact of COVID-19 on children got accentuated by the school's administration.

Surprisingly, despite all the work-related difficulties arising from the pandemic, GC felt that there were some positive impacts of the school closure on the students, who were chronically absent from school before the pandemic:

Many kids who couldn't enter the classroom before COVID due to various issues managed to return to the classroom after COVID. I am not sure if there's a scientific narrative about it, but I guess school closure gave them a break. Nobody could go to school. They were no longer the strange minority. No one questioned them why they could not go to school or enter the classroom.

GC believed that after the school reopened, the *bunsan-tōkō* system also helped improve the well-being of many students. To enforce increased social distancing, each class was divided into two groups. The first group of students attended in the morning, and the second group replaced them in the afternoon. As a result, all students studied in the classroom for only half of the regular school day for many months:

> *Because students only stayed half the usual time at school, the speed of the class was slow, and that probably helped. Besides, everybody was restarting after a long break. (...) So many truant kids managed to go back to the classroom after COVID. But there were new ones who couldn't enter the classroom anymore after COVID. So, there was an interesting turnover.*

The Impact of COVID-19 on School Counselling Practice. Prior to the pandemic, GC held reservations about teletherapy or online counselling, but her perspective has since changed. GC lamented the absence for online counselling opportunities in Japanese schools, expressing strong regret over the missed opportunity. In Japan, due to the external nature of their job position, SCs face limitations in accessing computers within schools. In GC's case, she had to compile handwritten reports for years until she was provided with an old, unused laptop by the school. While it was a step forward, she still had difficulties with printing and securing internet connection at work.

Technical and administrative barriers also extended to phone counselling. Since school counsellors are prohibited from using their private phones to contact children and guardians, they normally are expected to use the school phone if they need to check on someone. However, GC's school did not have a dedicated telephone line for counselling during the pandemic, when all children were forced to stay home. With only two school telephone lines available, dedicating one to counselling would mean that it will become unavailable for other uses.

Overall, GC felt that she could not perform her responsibilities and assist children and parents effectively during the pandemic due to an unfortunate combination of bureaucratic factors and the insufficient speed of administrative decision-making of the school management.

Discussion

The professional experiences of these two counsellors far exceed the passive image of SCs, who merely stand by until they are needed by the students, described in the 2007 and 2023 MEXT (Ministry of Education, Culture, Sports, Science and Technology) documents. Their accounts shed light on several crucial aspects of SCs' work, including the pivotal role of the homeroom teachers and the necessity for collaboration with them; and the challenges posed by the barriers of school visits from parents and the school itself. In addition, the accounts highlight the indispensable skills of SCs in preparing for interviews by consulting with teachers, parents, and children beforehand; their adaptability, which includes having lunch breaks with certain students and adjusting session lengths based on individual needs; and their willingness to meet with parents and socially anxious students early in the morning, outside of regular working hours. If we may summarise these and our previous interviews with a dozen of SCs over a decade (Tajan, 2021), as well as relevant academic literature, we suggest that the position of SC in Japan needs a more stable employment structure beyond part-time positions and have a greater role in decision-making after several years spent at the same school.

Japan, often celebrated for its technological prowess, unexpectedly struggled to implement online counselling in the public school system during the pandemic. Regrettably, no substantial efforts have been made to prepare for such contingencies in the future. School counsellors faced challenges in providing online consultations, and there is uncertainty about whether this will be actively promoted in the coming years, although online counselling is likely to remain relevant. Moreover, our discussions with school counsellors revealed that the first year of elementary school, a sensitive period for students even under normal circumstances, became an especially vulnerable time for children during COVID-19. Additionally, there were concerns about the potential escalation of eating and learning disorders. The hygiene measures enforced in Japan during the pandemic posed difficulties for some students. Having to eat in silence and the absence of physical contact with teachers threatened the social nature of school, where children normally enjoy growing up, studying, playing, and meeting others. Parents had to find ways to care for their children during the three months when schools were completely closed and had little to no access to the school counselling system.

Both the school counsellors we interviewed decided to leave their positions a few months after the pandemic's end, despite their long professional experience. It is undeniable that factors like exhaustion, an overwhelming workload, and a lack of societal recognition[8] of the school counsellor's profession played a significant role in their decision.

Conclusion

The working conditions for SCs in Japan present several challenges. Contracts are typically part-time, often renewed yearly, with relatively low pay considering the heavy workload. This can lead SCs to feel like they are never doing enough for students, parents, and teachers. In the Japanese public school system, SCs have been deliberately positioned as external entities to the school. They operate within a different framework from teachers and other internal school staff, which makes it easier for students to confide in them and open emotionally. This externality (*gaibusei*) has long been considered important to maintain, but it can also result in job insecurity, potentially causing counsellors to leave the profession. To offer more effective support for children's well-being, significant work is still needed to improve the perception of counselling in schools as a vital and distinct professional role. This is a crucial undertaking for professional school counselling associations, one that requires continuous collaboration with governmental agencies.

Despite these challenges, Japanese school counsellors play an important role in improving the mental health and well-being of students (Chan et al., 2015; Kato et al., 2022),[9] and help resolve crisis situations involving children, parents, and teachers, even though their societal recognition remains relatively low. It is important for further research to examine the reasons for the reluctance to use distance learning and tele-counselling in schools in a country that claims to be at the cutting edge of technological progress.

Notes

1 In Japanese: スクールカウンセラー活用調査研究委託事業. For more details see Arai (2022).
2 Details can be retrieved in Japanese at https://www.jccpp.or.jp/Top.cgi
3 Details can be retrieved in Japanese at http://fjcbcp.or.jp/rinshou/about-2/
4 Details can be retrieved in Japanese at https://jsca.guide/
5 Japanese Organization of Certifying and Managing School Psychologists (学会連合資格『学校心理士』認定運営機構)
  The Japanese Association of School Psychologists (日本学校心理士会) https://www.gakkoushinrishi.jp/
  Japanese Association of School Counseling and Guidance JASCG (日本学校教育相談学会) https://jascg.info/
  The Japanese Association of Counseling Science JACS (日本カウンセリング学会) https://www.jacs1967.jp/
  The Japanese Society for the Study of Career Education JSSCE (日本キャリア教育学会) https://jssce.jp/
  Japanese Society of Educational Counseling JSEC (日本教育カウンセリング学会) http://jsec.gr.jp/index.php?FrontPage
  Japan Educational Counselor Association JECA (NPO法人日本教育カウンセラー協会) https://www.jeca.gr.jp/
  Japanese Association of Clinical Developmental Psychologists JACDP (日本臨床発達心理士会) https://jacdp.jp/
  Japanese Organization of Clinical Developmental Psychologists JOCDP (一般社団法人臨床発達心理士認定運営機構) https://www.jocdp.jp/
6 Ordinarily, the number of hours SCs have to work at one school for a year is 280 hours, determined by the budget allocated from MEXT.
7 The term "shō ichi puroburemu" refers to an inability to adapt to school life and subsequent anxiety, found in young children shortly after entering the first grade of elementary school (https://kids.athuman.com/cecoe/articles/000196/).
8 To give an idea to the reader of an article that indirectly addresses this question, a survey on 600 participants conducted by Sueki (2016) showed that willingness to pay for school counselling services was a median of JPY 1,332 (USD 13.32) per year. How can we explain the fact that the amount the Japanese public is willing to invest in a counselling service for children and families who are sometimes in extreme distress, is close to zero? Several answers are possible. For example, counselling in schools is a service that the public considers should be free of charge, and in this case, people are not prepared to pay for it, even though they may consider

it a useful service. Alternatively, counselling is a service that the population understands must be paid for, and that it can be offered outside the school, but this service is not valued for cultural reasons: poverty or limited budget of middle-class families, stigmatisation of mental health problems, lack of clarity in the offer of counselling services; fear of medicalization of transitory problems, more general difficulties in "paying to talk" (Tajan, 2022, p. 39).

9 For instance, Chan (2015) wrote that "school guidance and counselling has shifted from problem-solving remedial services to a more developmental, preventive approach. With this approach, the aim of school guidance and counselling is regarded as establishing a system that helps students develop a positive identity through successful, rewarding learning experiences in a school that provides support and care" (p. 67). Additionally, Kato Matsumoto & Hirano (2022) offer a mindfulness-based psychological education and prevention program [the Mindfulness and Awareness Program (MAP)] which reduced depression, anxiety and enhanced emotional regulation for 12–13-year-old students (with a stronger effect on female adolescents).

References

Akiba, M., Shimizu, K., & Zhuang, Y.-L. (2010). Bullies, victims, and teachers in Japanese middle schools. *Comparative Education Review, 54*(3), 369–392. https://doi.org/10.1086/653142

Arai, M. (2022). Academic activities relating to school counselling in Japan: A systematic empirical review. *The Japanese Journal of Educational Psychology, 70*(3), 313–327. https://doi.org/10.5926/jjep.70.313

Befu, H. (2001). *Hegemony of homogeneity: An anthropological analysis of nihonjinron.* Trans Pacific Press.

Chan, M. C. R., Shinji, K., Ericson, Y., & Akane, Y. (2015). Training of school guidance and counselling workers in Japan: Concerns and challenges for future development. *Journal of Learning Science*, (8), 67–79. https://doi.org/10.15027/36764

Doi, Y. (2022). Shōgakkō no sukūru kaunserā katsudō ni okeru shinri kyōiku teki shien ni kansuru kenkyū dōkō [Research trends in psycho-educational support for school counselor activities in elementary schools – issues in multidisciplinary cooperation and collaboration]. *Journal of Culture in Our Time, 144,* 107–121. https://nfu.repo.nii.ac.jp/?action=repository_uri&item_id=3627&file_id=22&file_no=1

Harris, B. (2014). Locating school counselling in the Asian-Pacific region in a global context. Brief reflections on a scoping review of school counselling internationally. *Journal of Counselling in the Asia-Pacific Region, 4*(2), 1–26. https://doi.org/10.18401/2014.4.2.11

Harrison, M. G. (2022). The professional identity of school counsellors in East and Southeast Asia. *Counselling and Psychotherapy Research, 22*(3), 543–547. https://doi.org/10.1002/capr.12546

Ishikawa, E. (2020). *The process of introducing school counsellors in Japan and subsequent challenges and prospects.* Annual Reports of Graduate School of Humanities and Sciences, Nara Women's University, 93–106. http://hdl.handle.net/10935/5453

Japan School Counseling Association (n.d.). *Gaidansu kaunserā teigi to tokuchō [Guidance counselor – definition and characteristics].* https://jsca.guide/guidance-counselor/

Kato, K., Matsumoto, Y., & Hirano, Y. (2022). Effectiveness of school-based brief cognitive behavioural therapy with mindfulness in improving the mental health of adolescents in a Japanese school setting: A preliminary study. *Frontiers in Psychology*, *13*, 895086. https://doi.org/10.3389/fpsyg.2022.895086

Mimura, N., Horikawa, Y., Yoshida, H., Kato, M., & Shimada, H. (2019). Current status and issues of collaboration between teachers, school counselors and social school workers. *Waseda Journal of Clinical Psychology*, *19*(1), 129–139.

Ministry of Education, Culture, Sports, Science and Technology Japan (MEXT). (2007). *Jidō seito no kyōiku sōdan no jūjitsu nitsuite — ikiiki to shita kodomo wo sodateru sōdan taiseizukuri (hōkoku) [Enhancement of educational counselling for children – creation of a consultation system to nurture lively children (Report)]*. https://www.mext.go.jp/b_menu/shingi/chousa/shotou/066/gaiyou/1369810.htm

Ministry of Education, Culture, Sports, Science and Technology Japan (MEXT). (2021). *Sukūru kaunserā tō katsuyō jigyō no yosangaku oyobi haichi no suii [Budget amount and allocation trends for projects utilizing school counselors]*. https://www.mext.go.jp/a_menu/shotou/seitoshidou/20220602-mxt_kouhou02-2.pdf

Ministry of Education, Culture, Sports, Science and Technology Japan (MEXT). (2023). *Sukūru kaunserātō katsuyō jigyō jisshi yōryō [Implementation guidelines for the school counselor utilization project]*. https://www.mext.go.jp/a_menu/shotou/seitoshidou/20230406-mxt_kouhou02-1.pdf

Sueki, H. (2016). Willingness to pay for school counselling services in Japan: A contingent valuation study. *Asia Pacific Journal of Counselling and Psychotherapy*, *7*(1–2), 15–25. https://doi.org/10.1080/21507686.2016.1199438

Tajan, N. (2015). Adolescents' school non-attendance and the spread of psychological counselling in Japan. *Asia Pacific Journal of Counselling and Psychotherapy*, *6*(1–2), 58–69. https://doi.org/10.1080/21507686.2015.1029502

Tajan, N. (2021). *Mental health and social withdrawal in contemporary Japan: Beyond the Hikikomori spectrum*. Routledge: Japan Anthropology Workshop Series. https://doi.org/10.4324/9781351260800

Tajan, N. (2022). Structure of the Japanese language and psychoanalysis: "It does not preclude the analysis". *Research in Psychoanalysis*, *33*(1), 27–42. https://doi.org/10.3917/rep.033.0027

Tajan, N., Devès, M., & Potier, R. (2023). Tele-psychotherapy during the COVID-19 pandemic: A mini-review. *Frontiers in Psychiatry*, *14*, 1–11. https://doi.org/10.3389/fpsyt.2023.1060961

6 School Counselling in the Philippines

Challenges and New Directions

Sheila Marie G. Hocson, Francis Ray D. Subong and Elgin B. Clavecillas

School Counselling in the Philippines

Guidance and Counselling services in the Philippines began in the early part of the 1900s. Counselling started with a focus on occupational information in 1913–1934, such as collecting information on employment opportunities in various industries, occupational and educational guidance, and reference materials on various trades and professions. From 1913–1934, guidance and counselling services were provided for public and private schools focusing on disciplinary, academic, vocational, and emotional problems. In the period 1946–1969, counsellor training emerged and gave birth to professional organizations, the Philippine Association of Guidance Counsellors in 1953, and the Philippine Guidance and Personnel Association in 1965. From 1970 to 1986, career guidance efforts and international linkages were intensifying. The 1990s saw the expansion of counselling services like personnel career counselling services, private placement, and career services centres, government-run skills training centres, and career information online, and schools continued to offer career guidance services. From the 1990s until 2004, there was advocacy for professionalization, with the Republic Act 9258 (Official Gazette, 2004) and the Guidance and Counselling Act of 2004 being enacted (Salazar-Clemeña, 2002).

The Guidance and Counselling Act seeks to promote the improvement, advancement, and protection of guidance and counselling services as a profession. It undertakes and institutes measures that result in professional, ethical, relevant, efficient, and effective guidance and counselling services. The law recognizes the important role of guidance counsellors in nation-building, and promotes the sustained development of a reservoir of guidance counsellors in the Philippines (Professional Regulation Commission, 2007).

The Guidance and Counselling Act (R.A. 9258) defines Guidance and Counselling as a profession that involves the use of an integrated approach to the development of a well-functioning individual primarily by helping them to utilize their potential to the fullest and plan their present and future, following their abilities, interests, and needs. The functions of a guidance counsellor include counselling, psychological testing (personality, career, interest, mental

DOI: 10.4324/9781003352457-6

ability, aptitude, achievement, learning, and study orientation), research, placement and group processes, and teaching guidance and counselling courses, specifically those covered in the licensure examinations, and other services related to human development. Furthermore, it provides that the word *counselling* is considered synonymous with and interchangeable with guidance and counselling (Professional Regulation Commission, 2007).

The passing of the Guidance and Counselling Act among Filipino counsellors provided many opportunities, such as putting an emphasis on the importance of advancing and protecting the guidance and counselling profession by establishing regulatory mechanisms and standards of practice. These mechanisms include licensure examinations and registration, the Professional Regulatory Board of Guidance and Counselling, ethical standards, continuing professional development, complaints and disciplinary procedures, and rehabilitative response. These mechanisms help ensure that practitioners adhere to ethical guidelines, maintain professional competence, and provide high-quality services to their clients.

To supplement the law and maintain high standards of professional practice, the Philippine Guidance and Counselling Association (PGCA), the Accredited Integrated Professional Organization of Guidance Counsellors, maintains and continuously updates its code of ethics (PGCA, 2021). The PGCA also promotes the exchange of professional experience at the local, national, and international levels. Additionally, it mobilizes all guidance counsellors to focus on enhancing their understanding of the ethics and standards that govern the field. It also promotes professional group collaboration and improves the calibre of professional knowledge and practice. Through its collaboration with the PRC and Commission of Higher Education (CHED), it also strengthens the content standards and programme requirements in terms of the curriculum that provides qualifications to become a Filipino Registered Guidance Counsellor subject to licensure examination. In addition, it advocates for the creation of guidance counsellor positions in various settings such as schools, industries, and communities in different sectors such as government, private, and non-government organizations.

From 2005 to the present, remarkable developments in Philippine counselling have strengthened the practice and provision of services. One of the more significant developments is the passing of RA 11036, the Philippine Mental Health Act, where the State affirms the basic right of all Filipinos to mental health as well as the fundamental rights of people who require mental health services. The law further commits itself to promoting the well-being of people by ensuring that mental health is valued, promoted, and protected; mental health conditions are prevented and treated timely, affordable, high-quality, and culturally appropriate, that mental health care is made available to the public; mental health services are free from coercion and accountable to service users; and persons affected by mental health conditions are able to exercise the full range of human rights and participate fully in society and at work, free from stigmatization and discrimination. It strictly complies with the State obligations under the United Nations Declaration of Human Rights, the Convention on the Rights of Persons with Disabilities, and all other relevant international and regional human rights conventions and declarations.

The law provides for Filipinos' access to mental health and well-being services and programmes and mandates evidence-based mental health programmes in schools, industry, and the community. Guidance and counselling as one of the fields in promoting mental health and well-being has been strengthened and recognized in various settings. This has solidified the standing of guidance counsellors in the delivery of school mental health services. The law also mandates that all educational institutions shall have a complement of mental health professionals, one of which is a guidance counsellor (IRR RA 11036).

In the school setting, the Department of Education (DepEd) and the CHED issued different policies and guidelines. The DepEd has created policies to prioritize mental health in the school setting, namely the Office of the Secretary Office Order No. 2021-005, Department Memorandum No. 58 series of 2020, and the National Technical Working Group for the Development of the Employee Welfare and Wellness Policy of the Department of Education. These policies are designed to promote mental well-being among learners and employees and ensure the availability of necessary support systems within the education system.

The CHED Memo Number 8, Series of 2021 focused on the implementation of flexible delivery of Student Affairs and Services (SAS) programmes during the COVID-19 pandemic in higher education institutions. It emphasizes the importance of prioritizing mental health in SAS programmes and encourages HEIs to collaborate with other institutions, organizations, or agencies to strengthen the delivery of SAS programmes. It also encourages the use of various modes and options to ensure support services are accessible and appropriate for the student's circumstances.

To further improve the competence of Filipino counsellors and other professionals in the delivery of their professional services and to make them attuned to the development and advancements in their chosen field, the Republic Act No. 10912, otherwise known as the Continuing Professional Development (CPD) Act of 2016 (Professional Regulation Commission, 2016), mandates that professionals should participate in the continuing professional development endeavours such as seminars, conferences, research, and publication, and serve as a resource person, to name a few.

Currently, in response to the upgrading and improvement of the counselling profession, the Professional Regulatory Board of Guidance and Counselling is developing guidelines on the creation of a Career Progression and Specialization Programme (CPSP) for the profession to address the pathways and equivalencies of the Philippine Qualifications Framework (Republic Act No. 10968; Official Gazette, 2018) aligning to ASEAN Qualifications Reference Framework (Secretariat ASEAN, 2020) and qualifications frameworks of other states such as New Zealand, Australia, and Canada.

However, the Guidance and Counselling Act poses a problem for non-licensed practitioners since they cannot practise without a license and must finish their master's degree in Guidance and Counselling and pass the licensure examination. Unfortunately, only a limited number of counsellors have taken the master's degree in Guidance and Counselling Programme due to a lack of career progression and low salary grades in public educational institutions as well as some private educational institutions in the country. The salaries of guidance counsellors in the Philippine public sector are determined by the Salary Standardization Law (SSL). This law sets the salary grades and corresponding salary levels for government employees, including guidance counsellors who work in the public schools. However, in most cases, guidance counsellors in the public sector can get stuck in the same entry-level salary grade for years due to limited career progression, seniority-based promotion, budget constraints, and a lack of professional development opportunities.

To address these issues, the PGCA, in collaboration with the education sector and other allied professions, has been pushing the government for a change in guidance counsellors' positions to guidance services specialists with a starting salary grade of 16 (SG-16) amounting to P39,672 ($693.32) and to improve the career progression of guidance counsellors in public elementary and secondary schools.

Counselling in Educational Institutions

School counselling is a diverse and continually evolving profession (Cinotti, 2014; Lambie & Williamson, 2004). Most of the researches into the effectiveness of school counselling has been carried out in Western settings, where studies consistently report its value in improving the mental health of children (Cooper et al., 2021; Fedewa et al., 2016; Finning et al., 2021; Manthei et al., 2020; McLaughlin et al., 2013).

Asian nations have seen a rising trend over the past 25 years towards counsellors gaining accountability, conducting research, and creating a professional identity (Suh et al., 2014). Collaboration among professionals involved in implementing guidance programmes, such as teachers, principals, social workers, and psychologists, is becoming more necessary as a result of both international and local trends (Yuen et al., 2014).

The Filipino school guidance system was first implemented in the 1930s, but is currently plagued by labour, resource, and budgetary constraints. Only since 2004 – the year the Philippine Guidance and Counselling Act (R.A. 9258) became a law – has school counselling been recognized as a legitimate profession (Tuason et al., 2012).

Counselling in schools in the Philippines is continually growing, particularly following the enactment of Republic Act 11036, the Mental Health Act, in 2018 (LawPhil Project, n.d.) (Table 6.1).

This legislation mandates comprehensive mental health programmes in various settings including schools to address the personal, social, academic, and

Table 6.1 Current Set of Guidance Positions in the Government Sector

Items	Salary Grade	Education	Experience	Training	Eligibility
Guidance counsellor I	SG-10		None required	None required	RA 1080 (Guidance Counsellor)
Guidance counsellor II	SG-11				
Guidance counsellor III	SG-12				
Guidance coordinator I	SG-13				
Guidance coordinator II	SG-14	Master's degree in guidance and counselling	One year of relevant experience	Four hours of relevant training	
Guidance coordinator III	SG-15		None Required	None Required	
Guidance services associate I	SG-12		One year of relevant experience	Four hours of relevant training	
Guidance services associate II	SG-14				
Guidance services specialist I	SG 16				
Guidance services specialist II	SG-18		Two years of relevant experience	Eight hours of relevant training	
Guidance services specialist III	SG-20				
Guidance services specialist IV	SG-22		Three years of relevant experience	16 hours of relevant training	
Guidance services specialist V	SG-24		Four years in position/s involving management and supervision	24 hours of training in management and supervision	

career needs of students using online and face-to-face platforms. Specific evidence-based approaches and initiatives distinguish the Philippines from other Asian regions, such as peer facilitation and various support programmes that are aligned with the needs of Filipinos such as counselling programmes for children of Overseas Filipino Workers (OFWs), RACE Against Suicide in Schools, *Katatagan Kontra Droga sa Komunidad* or Resilience Against Drugs in the Community (KKDK), Remote Psychosocial Support through Play for Elementary Learners, Lusog-Isip mobile application for mental health, and other well-being and psychosocial support services in collaboration with local government units, non-government organizations (NGOs), and community-based mental health initiatives through interdisciplinary, multidisciplinary, intersectoral multisectoral, and all systems-level approaches. Counselling in the Philippines is evolving and adopting innovative strategies to address the unique needs of its diverse student population. These include integrating indigenous and cultural practices, crisis intervention, and providing protocols and procedures for responding to various types of cases. These initiatives help create a safe and supportive environment for students to process their experiences and build resilience.

Licensing of Filipino Counsellors

Guidance counsellors need to meet admission standards and be licensed by the Board of Guidance and Counselling following the Guidance and Counselling Act of 2004. Anyone wanting to use the title *guidance counsellor* must successfully complete the required licensure examination. The law, in Section 3 (a), defines guidance counselling as "a profession that involves the use of an integrated approach to the development of a well-functioning individual primarily by helping him/her potentials to the fullest and plan him/her to utilize his/her potentials to the fullest and plan his/her future by his/her abilities, interests, and needs. It includes counselling subjects and other human development services, particularly those given in the licensure examinations." A master's degree in Guidance and Counselling is also required by law as a prerequisite for taking the licensing exam. It also stipulates five examination areas, namely: philosophical, psychological, and sociological foundations of guidance; counselling theories, tools, and techniques; psychological testing; organization and administration of guidance services; group process and programme development; career guidance; and organization and administration of guidance services (Philippine Guidance and Counselling Associations, 2011). After ten days of taking the board of examination for guidance and counselling, the Professional Regulatory Board of Guidance and Counselling (PRBGC) reports the ratings obtained by each candidate to the Commission.

To pass the licensure examination for guidance and counsellors, an examinee must have obtained a weighted general average of 75%, with no grade lower than 60% in any given subject. However, if an examinee obtains a weighted average of 75% or higher but obtains a rating below 60% within two years from the date of the last examination, the course or courses retaken must each have a rating of no less than 75 to qualify as having passed the examination.

All successful examinees are required to take a professional oath before any member of the Board or any officer of the commission authorized by the PRC or any officer authorized by law. A certificate of registration as a guidance counsellor is issued to any applicant who passes the examination bearing the signature of the commission chairperson and members of the board, and the official seal of the board. A professional identification card bearing the registration number, date of issuance, and expiry date duly signed by the Commission Chairperson of the PRC is issued to every registrant who has paid the prescribed fee (RA 9258; Official Gazette, 2004).

Guidance & Counselling Programme in Schools

An expanding area of the basic education system in the Philippines is the guidance and counselling programme. The Enhanced Basic Education Act of 2013 – also known as Republic Act 10533 (Official Gazette, 2013a; 2013b) – was passed by the Philippine Congress to change the basic education curriculum from 10 to 12 years. The K-12 law seeks to establish, maintain, and support a complete, adequate, and integrted education system relevant to the needs of the learners such as diverse learning styles and abilities, career readiness, addressing societal challenges, well-being, and contextualizing education to local realities which integrates local culture, history, languages, and indigenous knowledge into the curriculum to be meaningful. Additionally, it aims to equip every graduate of basic education with the capacities and motivation to learn, as well as the competence to engage in work and be productive, the capacity to coexist with local and global communities, the capacity to engage in autonomous, creative, and critical thinking, and the ability to learn. These goals are all achieved through a programme rooted in sound educational principles and geared towards excellence which includes the K-12 basic education programme, mother tongue–based multilingual education, senior high school, alternative learning system, teacher training and professional development, and improvement of educational facilities and infrastructure. With the necessary knowledge, abilities, skills, and values for lifelong education and employment, the effective K-12 upgraded basic education system will create productive and responsible citizens.

To prepare learners to be empowered individuals, the DepEd is mandated by RA 10533 with other stakeholders to pursue programmes that expose students to the world and value of work and develop the capability of career counsellors and advocates to guide the students and equip them with the necessary life skills and values.

DepEd's efforts to create resources for the senior high school career guidance programme and the evaluation of students' mental health and the implementation of homeroom guidance during the pandemic are crucial for students' holistic development, career preparedness and well-being. Students that participate in these programmes learn how to research possibilities for their careers, create career goals, and make responsible decisions. To provide an open and encouraging learning environment, DepEd places a high priority on comprehensive student development, career preparedness, student well-being, crisis response, and adherence to international standards.

The memorandum aims to conduct a programme that provides students with knowledge, skills, and values related to their academic, personal and social, and career aspects. The approach of the homeroom guidance to students is done through the use of a Structured Learning Experience (SLE) where students undergo experiential and supervised educational activities for the personal, social, academic, and career development linked to the curriculum standards of the American School Counsellor Association (ASCA) Model (ASCA, 2012). Specifically, it also helps assess students better, and makes them feel calm and comfortable, able to express themselves, relate to people, prevent stress, make the right career choices, and succeed in various areas of student life. The programme is set for one hour per week for all kindergarten to grade-12 students and is part of every school's class programme.

The homeroom guidance programme was followed by the establishment of the Guidance and Counselling Referral System through the DepEd Undersecretary for Curriculum and Instruction (DepEd OUCI) Memorandum 2021–055 titled "Guidelines on the Counselling and Referral System of Learners for School Year 2020–2021." This ensures the systematic procedure for counselling and referral of learners in public schools; guides all public schools and all governance levels in the implementation of counselling and referral of learners; and supports mechanisms that contribute to the attainment of the Department's mental health programme which is part of the proposed DepEd Comprehensive Guidance and Counselling Programme. The policy also tries to address the many challenges in school counselling, including the scarcity of qualified and licensed guidance counsellors.

Currently, most of the guidance and counselling programmes in the school year 2022–2023 are focused on addressing the psychosocial needs of students which include emotional support, social connection, identity development, coping mechanisms, self-esteem, and academic and career counselling and back to in-person transition after two years of the pandemic to prevent maladjustments.

Challenges to the Development of School Counselling in the Philippines

Scarcity of Guidance Counsellors

The scarcity of guidance counsellors is one of the challenges in the basic education system and the spectrum of student support services. Guidance counsellors are both mental health professionals and career specialists. Only 1,096 counsellors were employed by the Philippine DepEd as of May 2020, despite the country's approximately 23 million public school students (Llego, 2021). There are more than 5,398 unfilled positions in the profession, with low pay being the main factor. These data indicate that there are not many RGCs in the nation, forcing public schools to appoint teachers as guidance advocates and carry out the duties and obligations of an RGC, particularly by enabling counselling for students (Mendijar & Manamtam, 2020). Guidance advocates are vulnerable to ethical challenges when providing counselling services because of this unusual arrangement (Malate, 2017). DepEd has cooperated with various groups, such as the Philippine Guidance Counselling Association (PGCA), which is the accredited and integrated professional organization for counsellors in the country together with its local chapters, national counselling organization, and the UNILAB Foundation, to help address the mental health and well-being needs among students and other school stakeholders (Magsambol & Chi, 2020). Initiatives include the formulation of the training toolkits for guidance counsellors, teachers, and peer facilitators; RACE Against Suicide Toolkit; and contextualized universal mental health screening tool through the Children and Adolescent Risk Screener (CARS).

A lack of career development possibilities and low pay relative to that of teachers and other professionals contribute to the scarcity of counsellors (Cardinoza, 2017). Years of stagnant career growth and a low salary have left some guidance counsellors unwilling to stay in a "dead-end" profession (Magsambol & Chi, 2020). In addition, burnout, compassion fatigue, and a lack of human resources are just a few of the ongoing issues that have a negative impact on guidance counsellors' general well-being (Lawson & Myers, 2011). In extreme cases, discouragement and dissatisfaction among guidance counsellors may lead them to decide to abandon their profession (Baker, 2000).

The scarcity of mental health professionals was further emphasized by the Chairperson of the House Committee on Basic Education and Culture, Representative Roman Romulo (2022), who is supportive of mental health advocacy in the country. This was evident through House Bill 10327 (18th Congress) and House Bill 929 (19th Congress) titled "Basic Education Mental Health and Well-Being Promotion Act" to address the need for qualified full-time guidance counsellors that will provide school-based mental health programme that is responsive, accountable, developmental and evidence-based.

Role Ambiguity

In Asia, where rates of psychological distress are high, and the COVID-19 outbreak had a significant impact, school counselling can help children's wellness (de Miranda et al., 2020). However, as adequate counselling provision is related to role clarity, it is crucial that counsellors' responsibilities are well-defined and understood by all stakeholders and counsellors themselves. Role ambiguity, on the other hand, has been associated with low job satisfaction (Cervoni & DeLucia-Waack, 2011). It can be a source of incongruence for counsellors (Lambie & Williamson, 2004) and can pose negative effects to the effectiveness of counselling programmes (Camelford & Ebrahim, 2017).

Counsellors in Southeast Asia work in the broad domains of career guidance, delivering the guidance curriculum, providing psychoeducation and direct work with students, parents, and teachers. However, it is difficult to define school counsellors' roles clearly. Indeed, a lack of role clarity has been a persistent characteristic of the profession globally and constitutes a significant impediment to the development and effectiveness of school counselling (Suh et al., 2014). In Southeast Asia, role ambiguity is associated with a weak public understanding of counselling given that counselling is largely a Western import (Suh et al., 2014). Counsellors' roles are also poorly differentiated from those of other educators (DeKruyf et al., 2013; Kanellakis & D'Aubyn, 2010). This reflects the interdisciplinary nature of school counselling (Alves & Gazzola, 2011) and is particularly pronounced in the Southeast Asian region, where counselling is often seen as part of the remit of teachers (e.g., Lung, 2013) and where guidance has traditionally been associated with a disciplinary role (e.g., Guo et al., 2013; See & Ng, 2010; Hue, 2010).

In the Philippines, upon the passage of the Republic Act 9258, Guidance and Counselling Act of 2004 (Official Gazette, 2004), practitioners need to hold a license to work as guidance counsellors, highlighting their position as experts playing a unique role in student development (Tuason et al., 2012). However, as in other Asian nations, guidance counsellors frequently conduct tasks outside of advice work, notably discipline-related tasks (Suh et al., 2014; Javier, 2021). This delegation is a direct result of cultural norms and educational policies, as well as the underfunding, understaffing, and under-resourcing of public schools (Suh et al., 2014; Javier, 2021). In addition, despite the long history of counselling, counsellors' roles in schools are not well defined or understood. This, combined with the lack of resources, leads to the routine assignment of counsellors to jobs that are not directly related to school counselling, such as substitute teaching, proctoring tests, administering discipline, and clerical work.

Although organizational structures vary, Filipino guidance counsellors in basic education units work closely with their principals. However, counsellors who work in public schools must contend with a lack of administrative, instructional, and student support, higher student-to-counsellor ratios, and a lack of knowledge of advice on their part. To work more effectively, they depend on tight collaboration with teachers.

Counsellors can work better in collaboration with various stakeholders, like teachers and parents. This increases students' academic achievement and increases their access to further education (Militello et al., 2009). Since school principals typically distribute responsibilities and resources, the interaction between counsellors and principals is particularly crucial. While principals frequently lack knowledge about school counselling (Leuwerke et al., 2009), when administrators do have such knowledge, counsellors can concentrate more on their primary responsibilities of working with students and developing counselling programmes (Hilts et al., 2019). However, the development of school counselling as a profession can only occur when counsellors' duties and fundamental skills are established. The most effective roles for counsellors are those that emphasize autonomy, teamwork, and acknowledgment (Wingfield et al., 2010). Nevertheless, when school counsellors' roles are defined, improvements in the areas of accountability procedures, advocating for educational policy, and legislation supportive of counselling, in-service training, and the indigenization of school counselling can be addressed (Suh et al., 2014).

A study by Gomez (2007) noted that Filipino counsellors take on roles that are not part of the usual practice of counsellors but which they do because their pre-service training and the nature of their work call for it. Some of the tasks in the pre-service training are handling disciplinary functions such as investigating cases and settling small conflicts among students or even among teachers themselves. In some ways, this causes job dissatisfaction and discouragement on the part of the guidance counsellor (Bustos, 2016).

Based on this literature, evidence shows valuable insights into the practice of guidance and counselling in the Philippines. The Guidance and Counselling Act of 2004 prohibited the practice of the profession without a license on the part of the practitioners. In effect, the government and other sectors deem it necessary to continuously advocate for the promotion and development of the knowledge, competencies, ethics of practice, and professionalization of counsellors in the country. The rise of mental health issues among students in this age of disruption and uncertainty highlight the need for the presence of mental health professionals in schools.

To address role ambiguity, the PRC Board of Guidance and Counselling in collaboration with PGCA and other national counselling organizations are currently on the phase of the creation of guidelines regarding career progression and specialization for the guidance and counselling profession to address the pathways and equivalencies of the Philippine Qualifications Framework.

Compensation and Lack of Career Progression

For public schools that are about to employ guidance counsellors as mental health professionals, there is a need to provide an enhanced compensation package that aligns with career progression. Few guidance counsellors seek to become school counsellors because of salary-related concerns and the limited opportunities for growth and promotion (PGCA, 2020).

Despite the higher academic requirement for RGCs and a master's degree in guidance and counselling, an entry-level guidance counsellor receives a salary of only PHP 27,000 (Salary Grade 11), similar to an entry-level teacher with a bachelor's degree in education. There were two sets of guidance and counselling-related positions provided by the Department of Budget and Management (DBM) on its Index of Occupational Services, Occupational Groups,

Table 6.2 Current Set of Guidance Counsellor Positions in the DepEd

	School, college, and university teaching (SCUT)[a]		
Items	*Salary Grade*	*Philippine Peso (PHP)*[b]	*US Dollar (USD)*[c]
Guidance counsellor I	SG-11	27,000	471.86
Guidance counsellor II	SG-12	29,165	509.69
Guidance counsellor III	SG-13	31,320	547.35
Guidance coordinator I	SG-14	33,843	591.45
Guidance coordinator II	SG-15	36,619	639.96
Guidance coordinator III	SG-16	39,672	693.32

[a] Department of Budget and Management Index of Occupational Services, Occupational Groups, Classes, and Salary Grades, Calendar Year 2022 Edition

[b] Based on Republic Act 11466, otherwise known as the Salary Standardization Act of 2019, commonly called as Salary Standardization Law V or SSL V. The fourth and last tranche is implemented on January 1, 2023,

[c] Exchange rate of PhP 56.07 = 1 USD as of January 2024.

Classes, and Salary Grades, CY 2022 Edition (DBM-IOS). These items were grouped under the School, College, and University Teaching (SCUT) and Guidance Services (GS) (See Tables 6.2 and 6.4). The DepEd uses the guidance counsellor positions under the School, College, and University Teaching (SCUT) group (See Table 2). Aside from the salary issue, there simply is not enough RGCs to hire, with only 4,474 registered guidance counsellors. This may change if salaries are raised and career progression is available. Such salary increases can signal a market demand for schools and other settings.

> The differences in the entry-level salary and career progression are evident when guidance counsellors are compared to education, mental health, or equivalent professionals. Table 6.2 shows the salary differences between guidance counsellors and guidance coordinators in the Philippines, with a gradual increase in salary as counsellors move up the career ladder. Guidance counsellors are advocating for better recognition and remuneration and the PGCA is lobbying the congress and senate to address these concerns.
>
> (See Table 6.2)

Various entry-level job descriptions of guidance counsellor, teacher, psychologist, nurse, medical doctor, and lawyer entail the minimum educational qualification, licensure examination, professionalization laws, entry-level position, salary grade and the highest possible position. For guidance counsellors and psychologists, the minimum educational qualifications are a specific master's degree in the respective programme, while for teachers and nurses, a bachelor's degree is required from the respective programme. Licensure is backed up by respective professionalization laws with approved salary grades and the highest possible positions (See Table 6.3).

Table 6.3 Comparative Table of Entry-Level Positions as Provided in the DBM-IOS

	Guidance Counsellor	Teacher	Psychologist	Nurse	Medical Doctor	Lawyer
Minimum educational qualification to take the licensure examination	Master's degree in guidance and counselling	Bachelor's degree in education or any bachelor's degree + 18 Education Units	Master's degree in psychology	Bachelor's degree in nursing	Doctor of medicine	Juris doctor (Bachelor of laws)
Professionalization law/s	RA 9258 (Guidance and Counselling Act of 2004)	RA 7836 (Teachers Professionalization Act of 1994) as amended	RA 10029 (Psychology Act of 2009)	RA 9173 (Philippine Nursing Act of 2002)	RA 2382 (Medical Act of 1959)	Rule 138, revised rules of court
Entry-level position and salary grade	Guidance counsellor I (SG-11)[a]	Teacher I (SG-11)[a]	Psychology I (SG-11)[a]	Nurse I (SG-15)[a]	Medical officer I (SG-16)[a]	Attorney I (SG-16)[a]
Highest possible position and salary grade	Guidance counsellor III (SG-13)[b] Guidance coordinator III (SG-16)[c]	Teacher III (SG-13) Head teacher VI (SG-17)[b] Master teacher IV (SG-21) Principal IV (SG-22)[^] Education programme supervisor/public schools district supervisor (SG-22)[^^]	Psychologist III (SG-18)	Nurse VII (SG-24)	Medical officer V (SG-25)	Attorney VI (SG-26)

(Continued)

School Counselling in the Philippines 103

Table 6.3 (Continued)

Guidance Counsellor	Teacher	Psychologist	Nurse	Medical Doctor	Lawyer
*Education, library, and archival service – school, college, university Teaching **if the school has less than seven Guidance counsellors ***if the school has at least seven Guidance counsellors	*Education, library, and archival service – school, college, university teaching **Teacher III can reach as high as Head Teacher VI if they opt to for administrative specialized track ***Teacher III can reach as high as Master Teacher IV if they opt to stay in the classroom specialized track ^ a Head teacher or Master teacher can shift and advance into Principal position ^^ a Principal or a master teacher can advance as an education programme supervisor or public schools district supervisor	*Social Sciences and Welfare Service – Sociology	*Medicine and health service – nursing	*Medicine and health service – medical	*Judicial and legal service – attorneys

a Department of Budget and Management Index of Occupational Services, Occupational Groups, Classes, and Salary Grades, Calendar Year 2022 Edition
b Based on Republic Act 11466, otherwise known as the Salary Standardization Act of 2019, commonly called as Salary Standardization Law V or SSL V. The fourth and last tranche is implemented on January 1, 2023,
c Exchange rate of PhP 56.07 = 1 USD as of January 2024.

Table 6.4 Alternative Guidance-Related Positions that can be Adopted

Items	Guidance services (GS)[a]		
	Salary Grade	Philippine Peso (PHP)[b]	US Dollar (USD)[c]
Guidance services associate I	SG-12	29,165	509.69
Guidance services associate II	SG-14	33,843	591.45
Guidance services specialist I	SG-16	39,672	693.32
Guidance services specialist II	SG-18	46,725	816.33
Guidance services specialist III	SG-20	57,347	1,001.90
Guidance services specialist IV	SG-22	71,511	1,249.12
Guidance services specialist V	SG-24	90,078	1,573.75

Note.

[a] Department of Budget and Management Index of Occupational Services, Occupational Groups, Classes, and Salary Grades, Calendar Year 2022 Edition

[b] Based on Republic Act 11466, otherwise known as the Salary Standardization Act of 2019, commonly called as Salary Standardization Law V or SSL V. The fourth and last tranche is implemented on January 1, 2023,

[c] Exchange rate of PhP 56.07 = 1 USD as of January 2024.

Potential guidance counsellors are not attracted to applying for the vacant posts because of the low assigned salary grade (SG 10). Although now raised to SG 11 by the Department of Budget and Management Circular No. 521 series of 2009, the salary grade is insufficient and not proportional to the minimum educational requirement of a Master of Arts in Guidance and Counselling for Registered/Licensed Guidance Counsellors. Furthermore, there is a lack of career progression schemes for guidance counsellors who are already working in the government.

The career progression for counsellors offers opportunities for career movement, professional growth, and financial stability for Filipino counsellors. The PRC, in collaboration with the PGCA, is currently working on professional quality standards in terms of the selection, hiring, and promotion of counsellors in assessing their performance, planning, and providing professional development interventions and in rewarding counsellors. Its major aim is to create more opportunities for promotion while upholding its commitment to the quality of counsellors.

The CSC Resolution No. 1100651 and subsequent amendments for qualification standards for guidance counsellor positions are important steps taken by the Civil Service Commission to update the eligibility requirements for guidance counsellors. This collaboration with the Professional Regulation Commission, Philippine Guidance and Counselling Association, and other sectors aims to improve the quality of guidance counselling services provided in the country and enhance the professional development that will provide role clarity and competencies for the recognition of Filipino counsellors.

Future Directions for School Counselling in the Philippines

Proposal and Creation of Government-Approved Positions for Guidance Counsellors in Schools

Guidance and counselling are valuable in the holistic development of a learner. Counselling addresses the students' personal, social, academic, and career needs vis a vis the schools' educational programme. School guidance and counselling seek to realize students' potential, assist learners with various day-to-day concerns, and contribute to the development of the school's curriculum, student experience, engagement, mental health programmes, and academic services. Guidance counsellors aim to increase students' school participation by determining and addressing factors for absences, failures, drop-outs, and mental health tendencies, as well as conducting evidence-based interventions for special target groups.

Other challenges faced by the Philippine public education system include improving the quality of education, concerns about online learning during the pandemic, and students' transition to face-to-face learning post-pandemic. Moreover, there is a need to cater to underachievers and children with learning and other disabilities. These challenges highlight the urgent need for a sufficient number of registered guidance counsellors with the competencies, training, and education necessary to support students' holistic development.

Republic Act 9258, or the Guidance and Counselling Act of 2004 (Official Gazette, 2004), provides for a policy of promoting the "improvement, advancement, and protection of the guidance and counselling services profession by undertaking and instituting measures that will result in professional, ethical, relevant, efficient, and effective guidance and counselling services for the development and enrichment of individuals and group lives." However, several barriers exist to meeting the growing demands in schools.

First, the government offers limited guidance counsellor resources for elementary schools. Despite the lack of experience, training for the position, and eligibility for guidance and counselling, public school teachers are typically given the responsibility of organizing and providing direction, and this is done even if it adds to their workload. Currently, only guidance coordinator I–III and guidance counsellor I–III staffing items, which are the government-approved listings of positions, are available countrywide through the DepEd.

Second, despite having the required qualifications, knowledge, skills, values, attitudes, and competencies, few counsellors are applying for guidance-related positions due to the low pay offered (minimum Salary Grade 11). Despite their specialization and high credentials, guidance counsellors' compensation grade was reduced to Teacher III in 1989 when the Salary Standardization Law was enacted. As a result, most qualified guidance counsellors work at selected private schools since they can be paid well.

Third, counsellors are bound to uphold the potential and worth of the individuals in the various settings they serve. The Philippine Guidance and Counselling Association Code of Ethics 2021 expresses the ethical principles and standards of ethical conduct for which counsellors are responsible and accountable. The Code of Ethics reflects values such as dignity and the common good, integrity, competence, responsibility, and an understanding of and respect for the cultural diversity of society. Counsellors are responsible for ensuring that they are knowledgeable about this Code of Ethics, understand its application and implications for their professional and personal conduct, and strive to adhere to the principles and values. They should also be familiar with other sources of information that will assist them in making informed professional decisions. These include the laws, rules, regulations, and professionally relevant policies in their working environment.

The Legislative Agenda

In the 18th Congress (2019–2022), House Bills 10327, otherwise known as the "Basic Education Mental Health and Well-being Promotion Act," and 10284, otherwise known as the "State Universities and Colleges (SUCs) Mental Health Service Act," were passed by the House of Representatives. These measures seek to create a Mental Health and Well-Being Office in every school division throughout the country to address the mental, emotional, and developmental needs of learners. The office is headed by a qualified mental health professional with the position of Guidance Services Specialist V (SG 24). It also provides guidance counsellors and psychologists more attractive entry-level positions and the creation of Psychometrician items in the government service.

To address the scarcity of guidance counsellors and other mental health professionals and to ensure the delivery of mental health and well-being services to schools, the aforementioned measure would allow the hiring of graduates with relevant backgrounds in psychology or similar fields to provide school-based mental health services. They are mandated to meet the relevant qualifications and are licensed as mental health professionals within three years from their date of hiring.

To ensure the effective and efficient delivery of mental health and other support services, a Joint Congressional Oversight Committee (JCOC) will be created to monitor and oversee the implementation of the law. The DepEd is also mandated to provide a substantial annual appropriation for mental health programmes and services along with the other rights and privileges of mental health professionals following existing laws that would include hazard pay, leave benefits, and professional development opportunities. The PRC, PGCA, and DepEd will also have meetings to address the lack of guidance counsellors and improve the salary grades of guidance counsellors in the country.

Conclusion

There are increasing mental health and well-being concerns brought about by the pandemic, the changing landscape of education, and disruptions at home and in the community. After 17 years of the passage of Republic Act 9258 (Official Gazette, 2004), the Guidance and Counselling Act (2004), four years of the Republic Act 11036 (LawPhil Project, n.d.), the Philippine Mental Health Act that gave way to the continuous development of counselling in the country through information, education, advocacies, and legislative agenda, there is still a scarcity of registered guidance counsellors, role ambiguity, compensation concerns, and lack of career progression.

In the 18th Congress (2019–2022), two house bills were passed by the House of Representatives that seek to create a Mental Health and Well-Being Office requiring mental health professionals such as guidance counsellors. However, this should be passed by both chambers of the Philippine Congress. The 19th Congress (2022–2025) gave a better position to tese measures as it was tackled early by the House, and a parallel measure was filed in the Senate. When these bills are enacted, it ensures an accountable and evidence-based delivery of mental health and well-being programmes, as a Joint Congressional Oversight Committee (JCOC) will be created to monitor and oversee the implementation of the law. It further mandates the DepEd to provide a substantial annual appropriation for mental health services and programmes. To address role ambiguity, the Philippine Guidance and Counselling Association Code of Ethics, 2021, expresses the ethical principles and standards of ethical conduct for which counsellors are responsible and accountable. In terms of career progression, the Philippine Regulation Commission Board of Guidance and Counselling, in collaboration with the Philippine Guidance and Counselling Association and national counselling organizations, are in the process of crafting the Career Progression and Specialization Programme to address the development of knowledge, competencies and career development of counsellors. By requiring the creation of enough staffing positions, salary increases, career progression, and adherence to the ethics of counselling through more legislative endeavours, this will increase the number of guidance counsellors and guidance-related employees in the Philippine school system that will provide responsive, developmental, and comprehensive well-being programmes in schools for a more mentally healthy Philippines.

References

Alves, S., & Gazzola, N. (2011). Professional identity: A qualitative inquiry of experienced counsellors. *Canadian Journal of Counselling and Psychotherapy, 45*(3), 189–207. https://cjc-rcc.ucalgary.ca/article/view/59317

American School Counselor Association. (2012). *ASCA national model: A framework for school counseling programs.* American School Counselor Association.

Baker, S. B. (2000). *School counseling for the twenty-first century* (3rd ed.). New Jersey: Prentice-Hall.

Bustos, Irene G. (2016). Development of the guidance counselors' occupational and life Satisfaction scale. *Journal of Universality of Global Education Issues, 3*, 1–30. https://ugei-ojs-shsu.tdl.org/ugei/article/view/6

Camelford, K. G., & Ebrahim, C. H. (2017). Factors that affect implementation of a comprehensive school counseling program in secondary schools. *Vistas Online*. https://www.counseling.org/docs/default-source/vistas/comprehensive-school-counseling.pdf?sfvrsn=9a9f4a2c

Cardinoza, G. (2017, October 25). PH lack professional counsellors to deal with troubled youths. *Philippine Daily Inquirer*. https://newsinfo.inquirer.net/940335/ph-lacks-professional-counselors-to-deal-with-troubled-youths

Cervoni, A., & DeLucia-Waack, J. (2011). Role conflict and ambiguity as predictors of job satisfaction in high school counselors. *Journal of School Counseling, 9*(1), 1–30. https://eric.ed.gov/?id=EJ914271

Cinotti, D. (2014). Competing professional identity models in school counseling: A historical perspective and commentary. *Professional Counselor, 4*(5), 417–425. https://doi.org/10.15241/dc.4.5.417

Cooper, M., Stafford, M. R., Saxon, D., Beecham, J., Bonin, E. M., Barkham, M., ... Ryan, G. (2021). Humanistic counselling plus pastoral care as usual versus pastoral care as usual for the treatment of psychological distress in adolescents in UK state schools (ETHOS): A randomised controlled trial. *The Lancet Child & Adolescent Health, 5*(3), 178–189. https://doi.org/10.1016/s2352-4642(20)30363-1

DeKruyf, L., Auger, R. W., & Trice-Black, S. (2013). The role of school counselors in meeting students' mental health needs: Examining issues of professional identity. *Professional School Counseling, 16*(5), 271–282. https://doi.org/10.1177/2156759X0001600502

de Miranda, D. M., da Silva Athanasio, B., Oliveira, A. C. S., & Simoes-e-Silva, A. C. (2020). How is COVID-19 pandemic impacting mental health of children and adolescents? *International Journal of Disaster Risk Reduction, 51*, 101845. https://doi.org/10.1016/j.ijdrr.2020.101845

Department of Budget and Management. (2022, April 5). *Index of occupational services, occupational groups, classes and salary grades, CY 2022 edition*. https://www.dbm.gov.ph/index.php/332-latest-issuances/budget-circular/budget-circular-2022/2119-budget-circular-no-2022-2.

Department of Education. (2017, October 18). *DM 165, s. 2017 – Implementation of grade 11 career guidance program for school year 2017–2018*. https://www.deped.gov.ph/2017/10/18/october-18-2017-dm-165-s-2017-implementation-of-grade-11-career-guidance-program-for-school-year-2017-2018/

Department of Education. (2018, October 31). *DM 169, s. 2018. Implementation of the grade 12 career guidance modules*. https://www.deped.gov.ph/wp-content/uploads/2018/11/DM_s2018_169.pdf

Department of Education. (2021, March 3). *Guidelines on the counselling and referral system of learners for SY 2020–2021*. https://depedcar.ph/sites/default/files/announcementFiles/ouci_memo_-_revised_implementation_of_homeroom_guidance_hg_during_crisis_situation_for_s.y._2021-2022.pdf

Department of Education. (2021, August 25). *DM-OUCI-2021-346. Revised implementation of homeroom guidance (HG) during crisis situation for S.Y. 2021-2022*. https://depedcar.ph/sites/default/files/announcementFiles/ouci_memo_-_revised_implementation_of_homeroom_guidance_hg_during_crisis_situation_for_s.y._2021-2022.pdf

Department of Education. (2022, October 17). *On the issuance of an amendatory DepEd order to DO 34, s. 2022.* https://www.deped.gov.ph/2022/10/17/on-the-issuance-of-an-amendatory-deped-order-to-do-34-s-2022/

Fedewa, A. L., Ahn, S., Reese, R. J., Suarez, M. M., Macquoid, A., Davis, M. C., & Prout, H. T. (2016). Does psychotherapy work with school-aged youth? A meta-analytic examination of moderator variables that influence therapeutic outcomes. *Journal of School Psychology, 56,* 59–87. https://doi.org/10.1016/j.jsp.2016.03.001

Felipe, C. S. (2023, January 31). *Student suicides on the rise – DepEd.* Philstar.com. https://www.philstar.com/headlines/2023/02/01/2241662/student-suicides-rise-deped?fbclid=IwAR3WX-qGSxXklun5mP9W6DPKl5MfEm5eJi2dONZhUTU7avEOoLR3Ln3qHAA.

Finning, K., White, J., Toth, K., Golden, S., Melendez-Torres, G. J., & Ford, T. (2021). Longer-term effects of school-based counselling in UK primary schools. *European Child & Adolescent Psychiatry, 31,* 1591–1599. https://doi.org/10.1007/s00787-021-01802-w

Gomez, M.G. (2007). *Defining guidance across professions* [Unpublished Doctoral Dissertation]. University of the Philippines-Diliman.

Guo, Y. J., Wang, S. C., Combs, D. C., Lin, Y. C., & Johnson, V. (2013). Professional counseling in Taiwan: Past to future. *Journal of Counseling & Development, 91*(3), 331–335. https://doi.org/10.1002/j.1556-6676.2013.00101.x

Hilts, D., Kratsa, K., Joseph, M., Kolbert, J. B., Crothers, L. M., & Nice, M. L. (2019). School counselors' perceptions of barriers to implementing a RAMP-designated school counseling program. *Professional School Counseling, 23*(1), 1–11. https://doi.org/10.1177/2156759X19882646

Hue, M. T. (2010). Influence of Taoism on teachers' definitions of guidance and discipline in Hong Kong secondary schools. *British Educational Research Journal, 36*(4), 597–610. http://www.jstor.org/stable/27823634

Javier, S. (2021). *And then there was light: The career transition experiences of guidance designates.* [Unpublished Doctoral Dissertation]. West Visayas State University.

Kanellakis, P., & D'Aubyn, J. (2010). Public perception of the professional titles used within psychological services. *Counselling and Psychotherapy Research, 10*(4), 258–267. https://doi.org/10.1080/14733145.2010.485697

Lambie, G. W., & Williamson, L. L. (2004). The challenge to change from guidance counseling to professional school counseling: A historical proposition. *Professional School Counseling, 8*(2), 124–131. http://www.jstor.org/stable/42732614

LawPhil Project. (n.d.). *Republic Act No. 11036. An act establishing a national mental health policy for the purpose of enhancing the delivery of integrated mental health services, promoting and protecting the rights of persons utilizing psychosocial health services, appropriating funds therefor and other purposes.* https://lawphil.net/statutes/repacts/ra2018/ra_11036_2018.html

Lawson, G., & Myers, J. E. (2011). Wellness, professional quality of life, and career-sustaining behaviors: What keeps us well? *Journal of Counseling and Development, 89*(2), 163–171. https://doi.org/10.1002/j.1556-6678.2011.tb00074.x

Leuwerke, W. C., Walker, J., & Shi, Q. (2009). Informing principals: The impact of different types of information on principals' perceptions of professional school counselors. *Professional School Counseling, 12*(4), 263–271. https://doi.org/10.1177/2156759X0901200404.

Llego, M. A. (2021). *DepEd basic education statistics for school year 2020–2021.* https://www.teach?erph.com/deped-basic-education-statistics-school?year-2020-2021/.

Lung, C. L. (2013). Roles and functions of the class teacher: Guidance for pupils' personal growth on a school basis. In P. Y. Y. Luk-Fong, & Y. C. Lee-Man (Eds.), *School Guidance and Counselling: Trends and Practices* (pp. 175–196). Hong Kong University Press.

Magsambol, B., & Chi, C. (2020). With a shortage of guidance counselors, how will PH students cope with pandemic? *Rappler.* https://www.rappler.com/nation/shortage-guidance-counselors-how-students-cope-pandemic/

Malate, G.V. (2017, October 30). Revisiting the guidance advocate in every teacher. *Slideshare.* https://www.slideshare.net/dlaregetalam/revisiting-the-guidance-advocate-in-every-teacher

Manthei, R., Tuck, B. F., Crocket, A., Gardiner, B., & Agee, M. N. (2020). Exploring counselling outcomes in New Zealand schools. *Counselling and Psychotherapy Research, 20*(4), 615–625. https://doi.org/10.1002/capr.12353

McLaughlin, C., Holliday, C., Clarke, B., & Ilie, S. (2013). Research on counselling and psychotherapy with children and young people: A systematic scoping review of the evidence for its effectiveness from 2003–2011. *British Association for Counseling and Psychotherapy, 89.* https://www.bacp.co.uk/media/1978/bacp-research-on-counselling-psychotherapy-with-children-young-people-systematic-review-2013.pdf

Mendijar, M. P., & Manamtam, S. S. (2020). Awareness and Practice of Guidance Functions by the Teachers in Urdaneta City. *Asian Journal of Multidisciplinary Studies, 3*(1). Retrieved from https://www.asianjournals.org/online/index.php/ajms/article/view/298

Militello, M., Carey, J., Dimmitt, C., Lee, V., & Schweid, J. (2009). Identifying exemplary school counseling practices in nationally recognized high schools. *Journal of School Counseling, 7*(13). Retrieved from http://www.jsc.montana.edu/articles/v7n13.pdf

Official Gazette. (2004). *Republic Act No. 9258 (Guidance and Counseling Act. 2004).* https://www.officialgazette.gov.ph/2004/03/02/republic-act-no-9258/

Official Gazette. (2013a). *Republic Act No. 10533. An act enhancing the Philippine basic education system by strengthening its curriculum and increasing the number of years for basic education, appropriating funds therefor and for other purposes.* https://www.officialgazette.gov.ph/2013/05/15/republic-act-no-10533/

Official Gazette. (2013b). *Implementing rules and regulations of the Enhanced Basic Education Act of 2013.* https://www.officialgazette.gov.ph/2013/09/04/irr-republic-act-no-10533/

Official Gazette. (2018). *Republic Act No. 10968: An act institutionalising the Philippine qualifications framework (PQF), establishing the PQF-national coordinating council (NCC) and appropriating funds thereafter.* https://www.officialgazette.gov.ph/2018/01/16/republic-act-no-10968/

Philippine Guidance and Counseling Association. (2020). *Position paper on Senate Bill 1565 (education in new normal).* https://web.facebook.com/PGCAOfficial/posts/position-paper-the-philippine-guidance-and-counseling-association-pgca-lauds-the/1116287962100077/?_rdc=1&_rdr.

Philippine Guidance and Counseling Association [PGCA]. (2021). *Code of ethics (revised).* https://www.facebook.com/PGCAOfficial/photos/pcb.1300965386965666/1300964633632408.

Professional Regulation Commission. (2007). *Rules and regulations of republic act numbered ninety-two and fifty-eight (R.A. No. 9258), known as the guidance and counseling act of 2004.* https://www.prc.gov.ph/sites/default/files/PRBguidance2007-02.pdf

Professional Regulation Commission. (2016). *Implementing rules and regulations of Republic Act No. 10912, known as the continuing professional development (CPD) Act of 2016.* https://www.prc.gov.ph/uploaded/documents/CPD_IRR_p.pdf

Salazar-Clemeña, R. M. (2002). Family ties and peso signs: Challenges for career counseling in the Philippines. *The Career Development Quarterly, 50*(3), 246–256. https://eric.ed.gov/?id=EJ644591

Secretariat, A. S. E. A. N. (2020). *ASEAN qualifications reference framework (final version). Referencing guideline.* The ASEAN Secretariat. https://asean.org/wp-content/uploads/2017/03/AQRF-Referencing-Guidelines-2020-Final.pdf

See, C. M., & Ng, K. M. (2010). Counseling in Malaysia: History, current status, and future trends. *Journal of Counseling & Development, 88*(1), 18–22. https://doi.org/10.1002/j.1556-6678.2010.tb00144.xC

Suh, S., Darch, E., Huffman, S., & Hansing, K. (2014). School counseling practice in the United States and its implications for Asia-Pacific countries. *Journal of Asia Pacific Counseling, 4*(2), 131–145. https://doi.org/10.18401/2014.4.2.5

Tuason, M. T. G., Galang Fernandez, K. T., Catipon, M. A. D., Trivino-Dey, L., & Arellano-Carandang, M. L. (2012). Counseling in the Philippines: Past, present, and future. *Journal of Counseling & Development, 90*(3), 373–377. https://doi.org/10.1002/j.1556-6676.2012.00047.x

Wingfield, R. J., Reese, R. F., & West-Olatunji, C. A. (2010). Counselors as leaders in schools. *Florida Journal of Educational Administration & Policy, 4*(1), 114–130. https://eric.ed.gov/?id=EJ911435

Yuen, M., Chan, R. T., & Lee, B. S. (2014). Guidance and counseling in Hong Kong secondary schools. *Journal of Asia Pacific Counseling, 4*(2), 103–112. https://doi.org/10.18401/2014.4.2.3

7 Developments in School Counselling Practice in Vietnam

Michael Hass and Hoang-Minh Dang

Mental Health and Academic Needs of Vietnamese Youth

Professional School Counselling in Vietnam is essential for several reasons. First, with more than 100 million people, Vietnam is the 16th most populous nation in the world and the second largest in Southeast Asia. Like many lower- and middle-income countries, Vietnam is a young nation, with 23.7% of its population aged 14 or younger (CIA World Factbook, 2022). Vietnam has undergone dramatic social change since 1986, when the government began modernizing the economy and moving towards more free-market policies. This rapid social change has coincided with an increase in psychosocial problems among Vietnamese youth, including family stress, behaviour problems, and suicidal ideation (Nguyen et al., 2022; La et al., 2022; Thai et al., 2020).

Recent studies suggest that the prevalence of general mental health problems in Vietnam ranges from 8% to 29% for children and adolescents. These rates vary across provinces and by gender (UNICEF & ODI, 2018). One nationally representative epidemiological study of the mental health status of 1,314 children 6–16 years of age from 60 sites across Vietnam (Weiss et al., 2014) estimated that 12% of the over 3 million child and adolescent population have a mental health problem that required support and services.

Emotional and Behavioural Problems

The most common mental health problems among Vietnamese children are emotional or internalizing problems (e.g., anxiety, depression, etc.) and externalizing or behaviour problems (e.g., impulsivity, oppositional behaviour, etc.). Females have higher rates of emotional problems than males, while males have higher rates of behavioural issues (Weiss et al., 2014). A recent study by UNICEF (2022) gathered data from four provinces in Vietnam that represented various geographical regions and urban and rural areas. These regions included Dong Thap in the South, Gia Lai in the Central Highlands, Dien Bien in the Northwest region, and the capital city of Hanoi. Of the 668 adolescent students included in the study, 26% were at moderate or high risk for mental health problems. Problems with peers, including experiences

DOI: 10.4324/9781003352457-7

of bullying and emotional issues (symptoms of depression and anxiety), were the most common at 32% and 31%, respectively. About 14% of these students reported symptoms of hyperactivity, including impulsivity and poor concentration, and 11% reported behaviour problems such as disobedience and lying.

Suicidality

Given the high rates of depression and anxiety, there is great concern about adolescent suicide and non-suicidal self-harm. Data gathered in 2005 and 2010 using the Survey Assessment of Vietnamese Youth (SAVY I and II) reported that the percentage of adolescents with suicidal ideation had increased from 3.4% in 2005 to 4.1% in 2010 (Vietnam UNFPA, 2015). In 2012–2013, a survey of 1,745 students aged 16–18 in Ha Noi found 21.4% of females and 7.9% of males reported suicidal ideation during the prior 12 months. Suicidal plans were reported by 7.8% of females and 4.0% of males (M. T. Le, Holton, Nguyen, Wolfe, & Fisher, 2016). Another study conducted in three high schools in the Cau Giay District of Hanoi (Nguyen Thi Khanh et al., 2020) found that among 661 high students, 14.2% reported suicidal thoughts, 5.5% had made plans, and 3.0% had attempted suicide.

Data from a nationally representative sample of 3,465 Vietnamese students in grades 8 to 12 were gathered as part of a study conducted jointly by the Association of Southeast Asian Nations (ASEAN), UNAIDS, UNESCO, UNICEF, and the United States Centers for Disease Control. The results showed that among Southeast Asian countries, Vietnam was a close second to the Philippines (16.9% vs 17%) in the prevalence of suicidal ideation (Peltzer & Pengpid, 2017). The second wave of this study was conducted in 2019 and included 7,796 similarly aged students who attended 81 schools in 20 provinces. These results found a slight decrease in students who seriously considered attempting suicide from the study's first wave in 2013 (15.6% versus 16.9%). This small downward trend was also seen when the data were disaggregated by gender and level of education. Although not considered statistically significant, this decrease was viewed as promising, especially if the trend continued in future studies (WHO, VN MOH, & VN MOET, 2021).

Non-Suicidal Self-Injury

Non-Suicidal Self-Injury (NSSI) is also believed to be prevalent among adolescents in Vietnam. NSSI is defined as acts of intentional self-harm such as cutting, burning, or scratching, but without the will to die (International Society for the Study of Self-Injury [ISSS], 2018). In a study of 755 students in 6th grade in Hue City, 7.1% responded yes to a question asking if they had deliberately hurt themselves.

In another study in Ho Chi Minh city, using the self-report Functional Assessment of Self-Mutilation (Thai et al., 2021), almost half (43.9%) of 1,316 high school students (15–18 years old) reported engaging in at least one type of NSSI within the preceding 12-month period. More than one quarter (26.1%) of participants were engaged in multiple types of NSSI, including hitting themselves on purpose (23.1%), picking at a wound (17.0%), or biting themselves (16.7%). Severe forms of NSSI, including scraping, burning, and erasing skin, were reported by 17.2% of the sample.

The most common functions for NSSI were to stop bad feelings (56.0%), to punish self (48.7%), to get control of a situation (44.0%), and to feel relaxed (42.2%). Symptoms of depression, anxiety, and stress were significant factors associated with NSSI, particularly for participants who engaged in moderate/severe NSSI and multiple types of NSSI.

Adverse Childhood Experiences

One determinant or driver of mental health problems is adverse childhood experiences (ACEs). The original ACE study (Felitti et al., 1998) found that ACEs such as abuse, violence in the household, or living with household members who were incapacitated or unavailable were remarkably prevalent, even among relatively well-educated and economically secure adults residing in Southern California. The researchers found that the more exposure to ACEs, the higher the risk was for various negative health outcomes in adulthood. These included adverse psychosocial effects such as suicidality, substance abuse, pregnancy, and medical problems such as heart disease, cancer, emphysema, hepatitis, and even bone fractures.

Studies of ACEs among Vietnamese adolescents also showed that ACEs are common and strongly associated with depression, psychological distress, and suicidal ideation. For example, in a cross-sectional study conducted among 4,720 secondary schools in four provinces in the south of Vietnam (Ho Chi Minh City, Long An, Tay Ninh, Buon Ma Thuot), about 86% of participants experienced at least one ACE, and 56% reported multiple ACEs (Thai, Cao, Kim, et al., 2020).

Students with four or more ACEs had far higher odds of depression, psychological distress, and suicidal thoughts (Thai et al., 2020). In the north of Vietnam, researchers using the WHO Adverse Childhood Experiences-International Questionnaire (Le, Dang, & Weiss, 2022) found that among 644 Vietnamese high-school students in Hanoi and Hung Yen, about 74% of participants reported experiencing at least one ACE, with 27% reporting experiencing three or more ACE. The most common adversities reported were witnessing domestic violence (36%), emotional neglect (34%), and community violence (23%). The prevalence of sexual abuse was above 10% for both males and females.

Focusing only on child maltreatment, including all types of abuse and neglect, Tran et al. (2021) found that child maltreatment was common in Vietnam, with rates ranging from 2.6% for sexual abuse to 31.8% for emotional abuse. The likelihood of emotional abuse, witnessing parental conflict, and experiencing multiple types of child maltreatment during a lifetime increased with age. Males had a higher risk than females for lifetime sexual and physical abuse. Living in a single-parent family was the risk factor most strongly related to most types of child maltreatment, including lifetime sexual abuse, neglect, and multiple types of child maltreatment. Interestingly, this study found that low socioeconomic status (SES) and parental unemployment were associated with a decreased risk of experiencing emotional abuse in the past year and during a lifetime, respectively. One possible explanation was that parents with lower SES might have lower expectations regarding academic performance and, thus, put less pressure on their children than parents with higher SES. Less tension in the household about academic performance may lead to lower rates of emotional abuse.

Another ACE that Vietnamese children suffer is bullying, both traditional and cyberbullying. The prevalence of being a victim of conventional bullying in Vietnam ranges from 17% to 23% (Le et al., 2017). Cyberbullying ranged from 18% to 45% (Chi et al., 2020; Le et al., 2017; Tran et al., 2022). Cross-sectional and longitudinal studies focused on bullying have shown that persistent and frequent bullying was strongly linked with poor mental health, including depression, distress, and suicidal ideation for both males and females (Le et al., 2017; Thai et al., 2022) and poor academic achievement (Tran et al., 2022).

Data from multiple studies addressing various psychosocial problems suggest that Vietnamese students require mental health and psychosocial support. However, resources in Vietnam for preventing and treating mental health and academic problems are limited, especially in schools. Although school-based services such as those provided by school counsellors are essential in meeting the needs of Vietnamese youth, Vietnam has few training programmes, and there is no consensus on the role of school counsellors. In addition, although the government has recognized the need, it has not provided adequate funding to hire professional school counsellors. In the next section, we discuss these limitations in the context of the history of counselling and psychological support development in schools in Vietnam.

The History of the Development of School Counselling and School Psychology in Vietnam

Schools provide an ideal setting for addressing adolescent mental health problems and promoting well-being. The Organization for Economic Cooperation and Development (OECD), an intergovernmental organization seeking to stimulate economic progress and world trade, has emphasized that schools are where children and youths develop many social and emotional skills needed to become resilient and thrive later in life (OECD, 2015). With more than 60% of Vietnamese children enrolled in upper secondary schools, increasing school-based services and support has the potential to expand access to services significantly for a large number of Vietnamese youth (Tổng cục Thống kê Việt Nam và UNICEF, 2021).

Government Responses to Perceived Mental Health Needs

Three ministries manage the provision of mental health and psychosocial support for children in Vietnam: The Ministry of Education and Training (MOET), the Ministry of Health (MOH), and the Ministry of Labor, Invalids and Social Affairs (MOLISA). Each ministry has different areas of responsibility, roles, and functions. Each also has distinct programmes, proposals, and models for addressing mental health and psychosocial issues. MOH is responsible for the prevention and treatment of mental disorders. MOLISA has responsibility for the rehabilitation and social services for vulnerable populations, including people with mental illness. MOET is responsible for physical and mental health education, school prevention programmes, and psychological counselling (Nguyen et al., 2019). MOET oversees and coordinates mental health and psychosocial services for school students across the three agencies.

The government of Vietnam has recognized the need for mental health services for many years. In 2005, the MOET of Vietnam issued a series of official correspondences to all K-12 schools, the first on April 4, 2005 (Official Letter 2564/BGDĐT-HSSV) and the second on May 28, 2005 (OF 9971/BGDĐT-HSSV). The latter, titled *Implementing School Counselling for General Students and Higher Education Students* provided guidance for the development of school counselling and prompted the initial development of training in school counselling. The goal was to provide realistic advice to help students release mental stress and feel more stable, confident, and able to resolve their problems in a positive way (MOET, 2005). However, the development of school counselling programmes was left to individual schools, and the number of schools that implemented counselling programmes was limited. Also, there were no standards for school counselling programmes and no research evaluating the efficacy of counselling in Vietnamese schools to guide effective programmes

In 2012, the MOET released Circular 42/2012/TT-BGDĐT on the National Criteria for Accreditation and Quality Assurance of Secondary and High Schools. One of the mandates in this correspondence was that students should be taught about *life skills* through mainstream curricular and extracurricular activities. The goal of implementing life skills was to enhance students' self-awareness and skills in communication, decision-making, critical thinking, problem-solving, coping with stress, goal setting, self-control, and teamwork. In addition, MOET stated that all students should have access to psychoeducation and comprehensive counselling about physical and mental health, sex, love, marriage, and other family matters (MOET, 2012).

These official correspondences were followed in 2017 by the first official legislation on school counselling services. Circular 31 (31/2017/BGDĐT) on *Implementing School Psychology Counselling in 1–12 Schools* clearly defined school psychology and counselling in all public schools in Vietnam. It also proposed a framework and guidance for school counselling services in secondary and high schools in Vietnam. The legislation recommended that all

Vietnamese secondary and high school students receive vocational and psychological counselling services (MOET, 2017). The policy also states that experienced teachers with school counselling skills can assume the role of a school counsellor and provide mental health counselling to their students in addition to their primary teaching duties. Teachers taking on the role of a school counsellor must be provided with relevant professional training by MOET, Schools of Education, and community experts in psychology and counselling. MOET's policy did not specify the specific academic preparation or training needed to provide these services to students.

A study conducted by UNICEF (2022) highlighted that many public schools in Vietnam adopted the standards in Circular 31 in developing programmes that focus on promoting life skills, positive peer and romantic relationships, and student awareness of mental health. However, the study also found that these services were primarily provided by teaching staff with limited training in counselling and psychology. Only a very few schools had dedicated full-time counselling personnel. In addition, three barriers to effective counselling services in schools were identified: (1) school counselling programmes are usually staffed by teachers with little training and time to provide counselling support for students; (2) schools lack dedicated private spaces for student counselling; and (3) the secondary and high school curriculum is focused on rigorous and competitive academic subjects, which contribute to more stress and mental health problems.

More recently, MOET has published several directives related to school counselling. For example, in 2018, Decision 338 and Decision 1438 were published. Both directives sought to address education for students with disabilities; Directive No. 31/CT-TTg, published in 2019, strengthened ethics and lifestyle education for all students. In 2021, Directive No. 800/CT-BGDDT directed the Education sector to carefully attend to student mental health and well-being as a consideration of the impact of the pandemic. Finally, Dispatch No. 136/CD-BGDDT in 2022 focuses on support for students when they return to school after a long period of online learning.

In 2022, the Prime Minister approved the School Health Programme for the 2021–2025 period in Decision No. 85/QD-TTg dated January 17, 2022. A critical component of this programme is a plan to link school health programmes with community healthcare services to improve the quality and effectiveness of student healthcare activities. This programme will also promote mental health awareness among students and strategies for improving mental health.

Although MOET recognizes the need for education reform that includes psychosocial support for students, a comprehensive national model and school counselling standards in Vietnam have been slow to develop (Pham & Akos, 2022). There are several possible reasons for this situation. First, historically, mental health problems have been highly stigmatized in Vietnam. Many Vietnamese consider individuals suffering from mental illness to be "wild, unpredictable, and dangerous people" who are "điên" and "khùng," which translates to "crazy" or "nuts" (Dang et al., 2020). These biases have made mental health a low priority for society and for mental health care not to be integrated into other sectors such as education. Second, Vietnam's lack of clear mental health policy and laws results in the limited provision of mental health care to the whole population, including children (Niemi et al., 2010). Third, the vertical, inflexible, and independent structure of Vietnam's health and educational sectors makes it challenging to change the system to be more open to providing mental health care in schools (UNICEF & ODI, 2018). Finally, the position of school counsellor has not been clearly defined. As such, the provision of mental health and psychosocial service in schools vary greatly depending on individual schools, provinces, cities, and private and public sectors.

MOLISA, through its system of community and social protection centres, addresses social support policies for social protection beneficiaries and provides services for cases in need of urgent protection (Vietnamese Government, 2017). Since 2011, MOLISA has established policies for developing community-based social assistance and rehabilitation for children and adults with mental illness and other developmental and physical disabilities, including autism. Unfortunately, despite the overlap in mission, MOLISA and MOET rarely collaborate in addressing the needs of individual students in schools (UNICEF, 2022). The development of school social work is under the responsibility of MOET, but the profession is not yet fully developed in Vietnam, and few social workers work in schools (Villarreal Sosa & Ha, 2020).

The MOH is responsible for general physical and mental health prevention and treatment for people through its system of hospitals and clinics. The MOH currently has no specific policies regarding student mental health, and neither the MOH nor provincial health departments have school-based programmes to address student mental health (UNICEF, 2022). Since 2006, all schools have been required to have a school health officer (Prime Minister, 2006). The school health officer's role is to organize periodic health examinations, provide first aid and primary health care, inform students about general health issues, and ensure adequate sanitation and food hygiene. They are also responsible for preventing infectious diseases, monitoring school safety, and preventing injuries (MOET, 2007). However, there is no unique training programme for school health officers; and they are not required to have a university degree in public health, medicine, or nursing (MOET & MOH, 2016).

Nguyen and colleagues (2020) found that school health officers generally had little training in psychology and mental health, leaving them ill-equipped to deal with mental health issues that arose among students. In most cases, the school health officers connect students or families to hospitals or other community health resources. Still, these services are not coordinated because of the absence of a collaborative framework between the health and education sectors (UNICEF, 2022).

In summary, the school counselling profession and related fields in Vietnam are in the preliminary stages of development. In addition to legislation and the limited guidance government agencies provide several international collaborations in psychology and mental health have contributed to advancing school-based counselling services, training, policy, and research in Vietnam. These included partnerships with international non-governmental organizations (e.g., UNICEF, UN Women, and Plan International) and collaborations among Vietnamese and international academic institutions. Of these, the Consortium to Advance School Psychology International (CASP-I) has been an especially influential collaboration that strongly influenced training in school counselling and school psychology in Vietnam.

History of School Counselling and the Consortium to Advance School Psychology International

Since its beginnings in the 1950s, the study of psychology in Vietnam has been strongly influenced by a national concern for children's education, including pedagogy and student learning. Many of the early programmes of study were focused on educational or pedagogic psychology and targeted teachers rather than school counsellors or other mental health professionals. As discussed above, although MOET began to recognize the need for school-based counsellors in the 2000s, it did not issue standards for university training programmes or provide funding for schools to recruit qualified candidates for counselling positions. As a result, international collaborations between Vietnamese and mostly American universities often filled this gap.

In 2010, the Consortium to Advance School Psychology in Vietnam (CASP-V) was founded by member institutions in Vietnam and the United States. The goal of CASP-V, which later became the Consortium to Advance School Psychology International (CASP-I), was to promote school-based counselling and psychological services in Vietnamese schools. Between 2010 and 2018, CASP-I organized seven conferences and dozens of workshops in different regions of Vietnam that brought together practitioners, policymakers, university faculty members, leaders of non-profit organizations, and parents to advocate for effective school-based services for Vietnamese youth. In addition, CASP-I members worked collaboratively to establish formal university training programmes in School Counselling and related fields in Vietnam. This collaboration eventually led to the creation of three graduate programmes in school counselling and related fields.

Current Status of Training in Vietnam

Currently, in Vietnam, there are three master's programmes in school psychology. Two programmes are in the capital city of Hanoi, and one is in

Danang. Another programme specifically focused on school counselling is also in Hanoi. For this chapter's purposes, we used a survey to gather data about the current status of these programmes (Dang & Hass, 2023a). Three out of four programme directors, two directors of school psychology programmes, and the school counselling programme director agreed to be interviewed regarding their programmes. Information gathered included (a) title of the degree, (b) when the programme began to accept students, (c) the number of credits, (d) the number of faculty teaching in the programme, (e) the programme description, (f) courses offered in the curriculum, (g) outcome standards of the programme, (h) resources drawn upon to develop the programme, (i) the number of students graduated. and (j) percentage of students employed (see Table 7.1). One programme was launched in 2015, and two in 2018.

Although there is considerable overlap in the curricula, only one programme carries the title School Counselling. This programme also explicitly draws upon the professional standards of the American School Counselling Association and the Council for the Accreditation of Counselling and Related Educational Programmes (CACREP). The programmes vary from 47 to 66 semester credits and have graduated from 10 to more than 100 students. Interestingly, nearly all students work as school counsellors or in related positions while attending their programmes.

Status of School Counsellors in Vietnam

To better understand the status of practice in Vietnam, we conducted an online survey among school-based counselling professionals in Vietnam (Dang & Hass, 2023b). The survey was approved and conducted by the Center for Research, Information, and Services in Psychology, VNU University of Education. The questionnaire asked about (a) the percentage of time school counsellors spend doing different counselling tasks, (b) how comfortable they are in providing each of those services, (c) perceived barriers in their work and (d) proposed solutions to those barriers. Sixteen school practitioners were recruited through snowball sampling. Of 16 participants, three were from Ho Chi Minh City, and 13 were from Hanoi. One participant worked in a private school, seven participants worked in international schools, and eight worked in public schools.

Participants reported an average of approximately six years of experience, ranging between 2 and 16 years. Thirteen identified as school counsellors or psychologists; two said they were counselling teachers, and one responded "other." Their academic backgrounds also varied. Seven had a bachelor's degree, eight had a master's degree, and one reported a Ph.D. These degrees also differed in focus, although all were in fields related to school counselling. One participant had a degree in general psychology and one in social work;

Table 7.1 Description of Training Programmes in Vietnam

Institution	Da Nang University of Education	Hanoi National University of Education	VNU University of Education
Title of Degree	Master of Arts in Psychology, specializing in school psychology	Master of Arts in Psychology, specializing in school psychology	Master of Arts in School Counselling
When the programme began accepting students	2015	2018	2018
Number of graduates	45	100 +	10
Number of academic credits	60	47	66
Number of staff teaching in the programmes	23 faculty members, ten instructors from other institutions	Between 15 and 22 faculty members	15 faculty members Five instructors from other institutions
Goals of the Programme	To train master's level students in psychology with in-depth knowledge of school psychology. Two tracks: Master of Research and Professional master	In-depth training in school psychology theories, assessment, school counselling, internship, and related sections of school psychology.	To train school counsellors with a master's degree. It is an interdisciplinary programme based on CACREP standards and integrated with knowledge and skills in School Psychology, vocational education, and school social work. The graduates will have sufficient professional competence and professional qualifications to meet the psychological, health, and academic needs of students, and vocational guidance, contributing to the formation and development of school counselling professionals in Vietnam who can meet the needs of the current education practices and the country's socioeconomic backgrounds in the context of internationalization. The programme was built on five key competencies according to America School Counselling Association (ASCA): 1) Counselling and coordination 2) Educational leadership 3) Advocacy 4) Team building and collaboration 5) Use of assessment data

Developments in School Counselling Practice in Vietnam 123

Courses			
1) Philosophy 2) Research methods in psychology 3) Theories of learning and psychological development 4) School counselling. 5) Development of preventive programmes for the comprehensive development of students' personality. 6) Applied psychotherapy 7) Child and adolescent psychopathology; School psychology. 8) Intelligence and personality assessment 9) Professional ethics 10) Group psychology. 11) Differential psychology 12) Clinical psychology 13) Management of psychological support activities in the educational system	1) Philosophy 2) Advanced Specialized English 3) Modern teaching theories 4) Psychological research methods 5) Modern theories of personality 6) Theories of human development 7) Introduction to school psychology 8) Modern theories of cognition, learning, and motivation. 9) Advanced counselling theories and skills 10) Crisis prevention and intervention 11) School violence 12) Neurological bases of psychological and behavioural disorders	1) Modern theories in school counselling 2) Human development & diversity 3) Identification & assessment of students' difficulties 4) Professional ethics in school counselling 5) Individual counselling techniques & case development, 6) Theory and Practice in Group Counselling, 7) Research methods in school counselling. 8) Career counselling and career development 9) Intervention with externalizing & internalizing problems 10) Inclusive and special education in schools 11) Social work in schools 12) Homeschool-community collaboration 13) Development and evaluation of school counselling programmes, 14) Practicum	

(Continued)

Table 7.1 (Continued)

Institution	Da Nang University of Education	Hanoi National University of Education	VNU University of Education
	14) Socio-emotional competence education for students
15) Social work in school
16) Methods of educating children
17) Classroom behaviour management
18) Practicum
19) Graduation project.
20) Master of Research includes a course in Data analysis and publication of research results and a thesis rather than a project	13) Development and implementation of school-wide programmes on emotional, learning, and cognitive development.
14) Assessment and Socio-emotional behavioural intervention.
15) Assessment and intervention for cognitive and learning, and developmental disorders
16) Career counselling at the university and high school level
17) Consultation and coordination with existing services in the school and community
18) Diagnosis and treatment of psychological disorders
19) Psychopharmacology in children and adolescents.
20) Practicum
21) Master thesis	

Outcome standards	1) Applying advanced and modern knowledge in school psychology to adopt a scientific perspective on psychological research and practice	The output standards were based on the standards of the international and Vietnamese school psychology	Training full-time school counsellors with' master's degrees, qualified and capable of participating in:
	2) Conducting applied psychological research.	1) Understanding of theoretical foundations for practice and research in school psychology	1 Personal counselling, career counselling, and school social work activities
	3) Implementing prevention programmes for psychological difficulties and comprehensive development of learners' personality	2) Knowledge and skills in diagnostic assessment and intervention, counselling, and prevention	2 Educational consultation in educational settings at all levels,
	4) Implementing interventions	3) Practicum	3 Identifying students with difficulties.
	5) Applying information technology and foreign languages	4) Have a sense of respect and follow the professional ethics and qualities of school psychologists	4 Scientific research
	6) Developing soft skills to support research and application of school psychology		5 Work as university instructors or researchers in the fields of School Counselling, Career Counselling, School Social Work, and Educational Counselling in higher education institutions, colleges, and scientific research departments; or staff members who are in charge of school counselling activities in educational agencies, socio-political organizations, socio-professional organizations, and non-governmental organizations.
	7) Demonstrating the qualities and ethics of school psychologists.		

(*Continued*)

Table 7.1 (Continued)

Institution	Da Nang University of Education	Hanoi National University of Education	VNU University of Education
Resources for programme development	1. Existing bachelor's programmes in the department, existing programmes in the country, and programmes in other countries 2. A survey of learners' actual needs 3. Actual demand in the central region of Vietnam. 4. Needs assessment of former students and school psychologists. 5. School psychology programme of RMIT-Australia, Chapman University – USA	Documents from 1. ISPA (International School Psychology Association) 2. American Psychological Association and other countries, 3. Programme at Saint Joint University, USA	1. American Counselling Association 2. Consultation with experts from CASP-I (Dr.Le Nguyen Phuong, Dr.Michael) 3. Documents regulating school counselling and social work of the Ministry of Education and Training 4. Needs assessment of psychologists working in the field of education in Vietnam
Percentage of students employed after graduation	100% of students have jobs because all of them are working while entering the programme, – 90% are working at schools – 10% are working at hospitals	98% of students are professionals when entering the programme; 2% go to work immediately after graduation (50% work at schools, 50% work outside of school). Some work in schools as teachers, administrators, and communication staff.	100% of students have jobs because they are professionals when entering the programme.

Table 7.2 Background Information on School Counsellors in Vietnam

Workplace	
Hanoi	13 (81.25%)
HCM	3 (18.75%)
Type of schools	
Public	8 (50%)
Private	1 (6.25%)
International	7 (43.75%)
Positions	
School counsellors/psychologists	13 (81.25%)
Teachers of counselling	2 (12.5%)
Other	1 (6.25%)
Degree	
Bachelor	7 (43.75%)
Master	8 (50%)
Ph.D.	1 (6.25%)
Academic background	
General psychology	1 (6.25%)
Clinical psychology	7 (43.75%)
School psychology	4 (25%)
School counselling	3 (18.75%)
Social work	1 (6.25%)

seven had degrees in clinical psychology; four had degrees in school psychology, and three had degrees in school counselling.

In addition to the above questions about background and experience, participants were also asked to estimate the percentage of time they spent engaging in different counselling tasks. They were also asked to rate their comfort level in providing these services on a scale ranging from 1 = not comfortable at all, 2 = somewhat comfortable, 3 = moderately comfortable, 4 = very comfortable, and 5 = completely comfortable (see Table 7.2). The participants in this sample reported spending 40% of their time providing personal counselling to individual students, about 30% developing, planning, and implementing the whole school programmes to promote well-being, and 23% giving social-emotional learning lessons in classrooms. The results suggest that participants spent little time providing academic assistance, college advising, or career counselling.

Among the listed activities, participants reported being most comfortable providing individual counselling, consulting with teachers, and consulting with parents (Table 7.3). They reported feeling less comfortable with career counselling and college advising, where they spent less time. Interestingly, two areas participants reported feeling relatively confident with, consultation with teachers and consultation with parents, were not activities they devoted significant time to in their positions.

128 Michael Hass and Hoang-Minh Dang

Table 7.3 Counselling Activities, Percentage of Time, and Comfort in Providing Services

Activities	Means and SD of the Percentage of Time Spent on Different Counselling Tasks	Means and SD of Perceived Level of Comfort Providing Services
Providing personal counselling to individual students	38.8 (27.46)	4.44 (.89)
Providing personal counselling to groups of students	9.28 (10.49)	4.14 (.66)
Providing social-emotional lessons in classrooms	23.29 (19.76)	4.13 (0.74)
Responding to crises, including the threat of self-harm	10.09 (8.5)	3.88 (1.02)
Providing academic assistance to individual students	15.19 (22.59)	3.62 (1.12)
Providing academic assistance to groups of students	4.1 (10.82)	3.58 (1.16)
Helping students choose and apply to college or university	2.35 (4.1)	2.44 (1.33)
Providing career guidance other than college or university	4.67 (7.9)	3.00 (1.26)
Consulting with teachers regarding students	18.39 (13.92)	4.3 (.83)
Consulting with parents about their children	19.75 (16.1)	4.25 (1.06)
Developing, planning, and implementing the whole school programmes to promote well-being	29.44 (27.06)	4.2 (0.86)

The participants were also asked to identify the challenges they perceive in their current work as school counsellors. We identified four participant themes using QDA miner to analyse emergent themes (Table 7.4). These included mental health resources, mental health knowledge on the part of school staff and parents, system support for school counselling, and constraints on the role of school counsellors.

Participants were also asked about potential solutions to these challenges. The solutions suggested by the participants included: raising mental health literacy among stakeholders; enhancing the communications and information about the role of school counsellors; training teachers to provide essential psychological support to students, classroom management, and social-emotional lessons; accessibility for community resources for severe cases; self-study to improve knowledge of mental health and school psychology; seeking professional supervision outside of school; educating leaders and teachers about school psychology and mental health so that they are better able to collaborate; making the responsibilities and job description of school counsellors more apparent to school leaders; and negotiating with school leaders about workload.

Table 7.4 Challenged perceived by school counsellors in their work

Challenges Faced by Practitioners	Count[a]	% Codes
Mental health Resources		
Lack of assessment tools	1	1.4
Lack of community resources	6	8.7
Mental health (MH) knowledge		
Stigma from students	2	2.9
Parents refuse services	2	2.9
MH is not a priority	3	4.3
lack of MH leadership in schools	2	2.9
Support for school counselling		
Lack of support from leadership	1	1.4
Lack of private space for SC	3	4.3
Lack of collaboration among different stakeholders	2	2.9
Constraints on the role of school counsellors		
Lack of framework for practice	9	13.0
Lack of opportunities for continued education	1	1.4
Lack of professional network	2	2.9
Lack of training	7	0.1
Stakeholders lack understanding of the role and responsibilities of school counsellors and psychologists	7	10.1
	5	7.2
	6	8.7
Too many roles to play	2	2.9
Too many responsibilities	8	11.6
Too many school events per year		
Too many students per school		

[a] Count: number of times the theme was mentioned in the survey.

Conclusion

Data from various sources suggest that children and youth in Vietnam could benefit from expanded mental health services. Providing these services and supports in schools makes them much more accessible to students in need. Thus, school-based practitioners such as school counsellors are essential in meeting these needs. The profession of school counselling is in the early stages of development, and Vietnam needs significant investment in school counselling education programmes and training for those already working in schools. Although the Vietnamese government has recognized the need for school-based services, Vietnam still lacks a standard definition of school counselling and accepted standards for training and practice. Despite this, the three programmes surveyed for this chapter have similar coursework and expectations for their graduates. The work done by these institutions could provide a framework for the training of school counsellors nationwide.

Also, the practitioners surveyed for this chapter appear to provide similar services as school counsellors in countries such as the United States or the United Kingdom, where school counselling is well-developed. Yet they also have reported facing multiple challenges, again suggesting the need for a clear framework for practice and more training and supervision. Practitioners also face the task of explaining the importance of mental health services and the relation of those services with improved academic functioning.

For school counselling services to expand, we would like to propose three recommendations. The first would be for practitioners, school leaders, and government officials to collaborate to establish consistent nationwide guidance on school counsellors' roles and scope of practice. Second, there is a need to implement uniform standards for training school counsellors. Third, although studies conducted in the United States, Japan, and Iran show that small-group interventions provided by school counsellors can improve academic and social self-efficacy (Martin et al., 2022), social resilience and emotion regulation (Martinez et al., 2021), general mental health (Fariba Shahraki-Sanavi et al., 2020), and decrease in depression and generalized anxiety (Kiun Kato, 2022), no research has been conducted that confirms the effectiveness of school counselling in Vietnam. Studies on the efficacy of school counselling in Vietnam can help convince school leaders and other stakeholders that school counselling services can help improve students' mental health and academic achievement.

References

Chi, P. T. L., Lan, V. T. H., Ngan, N. H., & Linh, N. T. (2020). Online time, experience of cyberbullying, and practices to cope with it among high school students in Hanoi. *Health Psychology Open, 7*(1): 2055102920935747. https://doi.org/10.1177/2055102920935747

Dang, H.M., & Hass, M. (2023a). *School counselling in Vietnam: Interviews of program directors of graduate programs in school counselling and related fields* [Unpublished manuscript].

Dang, H.M., & Hass, M. (2023b). *School counselling in Vietnam: A survey of practitioners* [Unpublished manuscript].

Dang, H. M., Lam, T. T., Dao, A., & Weiss, B. (2020). Mental health literacy at the public health level in low and middle-income countries: An exploratory mixed methods study in Vietnam. *Plos One, 15*(12), 1–16. https://doi.org/10.1371/journal.pone.0244573

Fariba Shahraki-Sanavi, Alireza Ansari-Moghaddam, Mahdi Mohammadi, Nour-Mohammad Bakhshani, & Hamid Salehiniya. (2020). Effectiveness of school-based mental health programs on mental health among adolescents. *Journal of Education and Health Promotion, 9*(142), 1–6. https://doi.org/10.4103/jehp.jehp_421_19

Felitti, V. J., Anda, R. F., Nordenberg, D., Williamson, D. F., Spitz, A. M., Edwards, V., & Marks, J. S. (1998). Relationship of childhood abuse and household dysfunction to many of the leading causes of death in adults: The Adverse Childhood Experiences (ACE) study. *American Journal of Preventive Medicine, 14*(4), 245–258.

International Society for the Study of Self-Injury. (2018, May). *What is self-injury?* https://itriples.org/about-self-injury/what-is-self-injury

Kato, K., Matsumoto, Y., & Hirano, Y. (2022). Effectiveness of school-based brief cognitive behavioral therapy with mindfulness in improving the mental health of adolescents in a Japanese school setting: A preliminary study. *Frontiers in Psychology, 13*, 1–16. https://doi.org/10.3389/fpsyg.2022.895086

La, N. L., Shochet, I., Tran, T., Fisher, J., Wurfl, A., Nguyen, N., & Nguyen, H. (2022). Adaptation of a school-based mental health program for adolescents in Vietnam. *PLoS One, 17*(8), e0271959. https://doi.org/10.1371/journal.pone.0271959

Le, H. T. H., Nguyen, H. T., Campbell, M. A., Gatton, M. L., Tran, N. T., & Dunne, M. P. (2017). Longitudinal associations between bullying and mental health among adolescents in Vietnam. *International Journal of Public Health, 62*(1), 51–61. https://doi.org/10.1007/s00038-016-0915-8

Le, M. T., Holton, S., Nguyen, H. T., Wolfe, R., & Fisher, J. (2016). Poly-victimisation and health risk behaviours, symptoms of mental health problems and suicidal thoughts and plans among adolescents in Vietnam. *International Journal of Mental Health Systems, 10*(1), 1–12. https://doi.org/10.1186/s13033-016-0099-x

Le, T., Dang, H. M., & Weiss, B. (2022). Prevalence of adverse childhood experiences among Vietnamese high school students. *Child Abuse & Neglect, 128*, 105628. https://doi.org/10.1016/j.chiabu.2022.105628

Martin, I., Choi, J., Zyromski, B., Campos, L., Mansheim, S., Cunningham, P. D., & Callahan, W. (2022). Small-group investigation of the True Goals Curriculum with elementary and middle school students: A randomized control study. *Professional School Counselling, 26*(1), 2156759X2211342. https://doi.org/10.1177/2156759X221134259

Martinez, R. R., Jr., Marraccini, M. E., Knotek, S. E., Neshkes, R. A., & Vanderburg, J. (2021). Effects of Dialectical Behavioral Therapy skills training for emotional problem solving for adolescents (DBT STEPS-A) program of rural ninth-grade students. *School Mental Health, 14*(1), 165–178. https://doi.org/10.1007/s12310-021-09463-5

MOET. (2005). *Official Letter No. 9971/BGD-DT-HSSV regarding the implementation of school counselling programs for all levels of students.* Hanoi: Ministry of Education and Training.

MOET. (2007). *Decision number 73/2007/QĐ-BGDĐT dated 04 December 2007 on school health activities in primary, secondary and high schools* (Quyết định số 73/2007/QĐ-BGDĐT ban hành ngày 04 tháng 12 năm 2007 về việc ban hành qui định về hoạt động y tế trong các trường tiểu học, trường trung học cơ sở, trường trung học phổ thông và trường phổ thông có nhiều cấp học).

MOET. (2012). *Cicular number 42/2012/TT-BGDĐT dated 23 December 2012 on quality assessment and accreditation of schools* (Thông tư số 42/2012/TT-BGDĐT ban hành ngày 23 tháng 12 năm 2012 về tiêu chuẩn đánh giá chất lượng giáo dục và quy trình, chu kỳ kiểm định chất lượng giáo dục cơ sở giáo dục phổ thông, cơ sở giáo dục thường xuyên).

MOET. (2017). *Cicular number 31//2017/TT-BGDĐT dated 18 December 2017 on school counselling in schools* (Thông tư số 31/2017/TT-BGDĐT ban hành ngày 18 tháng 12 năm 2017 về việc hướng dẫn thực hiện công tác tư vấn tâm lý cho học sinh trong trường phổ thông).

MOET & MOH. (2016). *Joint Circular No. 13/2016/TTLT-BYT-BGDDT dated May 12, 2016, regulations on healthcare activities in schools.*

Nguyen, C. T. T., Yang, H. J., Lee, G. T., Nguyen, L. T. K., & Kuo, S. Y. (2022). Relationships of excessive internet use with depression, anxiety, and sleep quality among high school students in northern Vietnam. *Journal of Pediatric Nursing, 62*, e91–e97. https://doi.org/10.1016/j.pedn.2021.07.019

Nguyen, D. T., Wright, E. P., Pham, T. T., & Bunders, J. (2020). Role of school health officers in mental health care for secondary school students in Can Tho City, Vietnam. *School Mental Health, 12*(4), 801–811. https://doi.org/10.1007/s12310-020-09386-7

Nguyen, H. T. L., Nakamura, K., Seino, K., & Vo, V. T. (2020). Relationships among cyberbullying, parental attitudes, self-harm, and suicidal behavior among adolescents: Results from a school-based survey in Vietnam. *BMC Public Health, 20*(1), 1–9. https://doi.org/10.1186/s12889-020-08500-3

Nguyen, T., Tran, T., Tran, H., Tran, T., & Fisher, J. (2019). Challenges in integrating mental health into primary care in Vietnam. In S. Okpaku (Ed.), *Innovations in Global Mental Health* (pp. 1–21). Springer International Publishing.

Nguyen, T. K. H., Nguyen Thanh, L., Pham Quoc, T., Pham Viet, C., Duong Minh, D., & Le Thi Kim, A. (2020). Suicidal behaviors and depression among adolescents in Hanoi, Vietnam: A multilevel analysis of data from the youth risk behavior survey 2019. *Health Psychology Open, 7*(2), 1–11. https://doi.org/10.1177/2055102920954711

Niemi, M., Thanh, H. T., Tuan, T., & Falkenberg, T. (2010). Mental health priorities in Vietnam: A mixed-methods analysis. *BMC Health Services Research, 10*(1), 1–10. https://doi.org/10.1186/1472-6963-10-257

Organization for Economic Cooperation and Development. (2015). *Skills for social progress: The power of social and emotional skills.* OECD Publishing.

Peltzer, K., & Pengpid, S. (2017). Suicidal ideation and associated factors among students aged 13–15 years in Association of Southeast Asian Nations (ASEAN) member states, 2007–2013. *International Journal of Psychiatry in Clinical Practice, 21*, 201–208. https://doi.org/10.1080/13651501.2017.1301486

Pham, A. K., & Akos, P. (2022). Professional school counselling in Vietnam public schools. *Journal of Asia Pacific Counselling, 10*(2), 37–49. https://doi.org/10.18401/2020.10.2.6

Prime Minister. (2006). *Directive number 23/2006/CT-TTg dated 12 July 2006 on school health in schools* (Chỉ thị về việc tăng cường công tác y tế trong các trường học).

Thai, T. T., Cao, P. L. T., Kim, L. X., Tran, D. P., Bui, M. B., & Bui, H. H. T. (2020). The effect of adverse childhood experiences on depression, psychological distress, and suicidal thought in Vietnamese adolescents: Findings from multiple cross-sectional studies. *Asian Journal of Psychiatry, 53*, 102134. https://doi.org/10.1016/j.ajp.2020.102134

Thai, T. T., Duong, M. H. T., Vo, D. K., Dang, N. T. T., Huynh, Q. N. H., & Tran, H. G. N. (2022). Cyber-victimization and its association with depression among Vietnamese adolescents. *PeerJ, 10*, e12907.

Thai, T. T., Jones, M. K., Nguyen, T. P., Van Pham, T., Bui, H. H. T., Kim, L. X., & Van Nguyen, T. (2021). The prevalence, correlates, and functions of non-suicidal self-injury in Vietnamese adolescents. *Psychology Research and Behavior Management, 14*, 1915–1927. https://doi.org/10.2147/PRBM.S339168

Thai, T. T., Vu, N. L. L. T., & Bui, H. H. T. (2020). Mental health literacy and help-seeking preferences in high school students in ho Chi Minh City, Vietnam. *School Mental Health, 12*(2), 378–387. https://doi.org/10.1007/s12310-019-09358-6

Tổng cục Thống kê Việt Nam và UNICEF. (2021). *Điều tra các mục tiêu phát triển bền vững về trẻ em và phụ nữ Việt Nam 2020–2021: Báo cáo kết quả điều tra.* Hà nội: Tổng cục Thống kê.

Tran, C. V., Weiss, B., & Nguyen, N. P. (2022). Academic achievement, and cyberbullying and cyber-victimization among middle-and high-school students in Vietnam. *International Journal of School & Educational Psychology, 10*(1), 118–127.

Tran, N. K., Van Berkel, S. R., van IJzendoorn, M. H., & Alink, L. R. (2021). Child and family factors associated with child maltreatment in Vietnam. *Journal of Interpersonal Violence, 36*(5–6), NP2931-NP2953. https://doi.org/10.1080/21683603.2020.1837700

UNICEF (2022). *Study on school-related factors impacting mental health and well-being of adolescents in Viet Nam: A comprehensive study.* https://www.unicef.org/vietnam/reports/study-school-related-factors-impacting-mental-health-and-well-being-adolescents-viet-nam.

UNICEF & ODI (2018). *Mental health and psychosocial well-being of children and young people in selected provinces and cities in Viet Nam.* https://www.unicef.org/vietnam/reports/mental-health-and-psychosocial-well-being-among-children-and-young-people-viet-nam.

Vietnam UNFPA (2015). *National report about Vietnamese adolescent.* https://bit.ly/3eytpMG

Vietnamese Government. (2017). *Decree number 14/2017/NĐ-CP dated February 17 2017 on stipulating functions, duties, authorities and organization structure of the Ministry of Labour - Invalids and Social Affairs.*

Villarreal Sosa, L., & Ha, N. T. (2020). School social work in Vietnam: Development and capacity building through international collaboration. *International Journal of School Social Work, 5*(2), 1–12. https://doi.org/10.4148/2161-4148.1065

Weiss, B., Dang, M., Trung, L., Nguyen, M. C., Thuy, N. T. H., & Pollack, A. (2014). A nationally representative epidemiological and risk factor assessment of child mental health in Vietnam. *International Perspectives in Psychology: Research, Practice, Consultation, 3*(3), 139–153. https://doi.org/10.1037/ipp0000016

WHO, VN MOH, & VN MOET. (2021). *Report of the 2019 global school-based student health survey in Viet Nam: Report* (WHO Ed.). Hanoi: WHO: Regional Office for the Western Pacific.

8 Professional School Counselling in Vietnam
A Preliminary Model

Anh Kim Pham and Hong Thuan Nguyen

Acknowledgement

The research presented in this chapter was funded by the University of Social Sciences and Humanities, Vietnam National University Ho Chi Minh City under grant number NCM2023-01.

History of School Counselling in Vietnam

Disruptive eco-social changes are transforming many aspects of educational settings, families, and students' learning and career orientation (Becirović & Akbarov, 2015; UNESCO, 2021). In Vietnam, the government's initiatives in education have improved only the mainstream curriculum and the quality of textbooks rather than resolved many critical issues, including bureaucracy, national standardized tests, and psychological stress in schools (Huynh et al., 2019; Le et al., 2016). High school students in the complex developmental stage of adolescence are more influenced by these emerging socio-psychological problems (Bui, 2014; Tran, 2016a, b; Nguyen, 2005).

In Vietnam, the term *school psychology counselling* has been used interchangeably with *school counselling*, an inclusive concept describing helping to improve students' academic, personal/social, and career development. In most public schools, the activities of *school psychology counsellors* have focused on supporting high school students who experience problems in personal/social development, especially peer relationships and school bullying or violence, and future career preparation, (Le et al., 2016; Nguyen, 2005, 2014 ; Pham & Truong, 2016; Pham & Akos, 2020). Since the need for psychological counselling has been significantly increasing every year in Vietnam, education policymakers, educators, psychologists, and counsellors should collaborate and provide appropriate solutions or services to help students overcome poor learning motivation, boredom, disturbance, depression, and deviant behaviours (Le et al., 2016; Nguyen, 2014, 2016). In 2011, the Vietnam Ministry of Education and Training (MoET) enacted the *Charters for Public Secondary Schools* and officially affirmed the usage of *school psychology counselling* terms and the compulsory counselling activities that must be implemented in public secondary schools (middle and high schools).

DOI: 10.4324/9781003352457-8

In 2017, MoET published Circular No. 31/2017/TT-BGDDT which provided guidance for the establishment of a *School Counselling Team* in all public primary and secondary schools across Vietnam. Team members are school board representatives, homeroom teachers, youth union representatives, school nurses, and parent associate representatives. The key role of this team is to help students with psychological matters, including gender awareness, psychological problem resolving skills, and job-seeking skills. An education statistics report for the school year 2019–2020 published by the MoET noted that 20,000 out of 26,500 public and private primary and secondary schools have successfully established *School Counselling Teams* as a result of the MoET's initiatives in enhancing school counselling in Vietnam (MoET & UNICEF, 2021). This report highlighted a significant gap in school counselling quality between urban and rural regions, and private and public education settings. While many schools in large urban cities and provinces such as Ha Noi, Ho Chi Minh, Da Nang, and Hai Phong are increasingly aware of the importance of school counselling services and have invested to improve the quality of school counselling activities, schools in some suburban and rural regions are still struggling with issues such as constrained finance and personnel, and very poor facilities for school counselling activities. The students' need for school counselling services has significantly increased every school year but most students, particularly those from public schools, have received little support (Hagans, Powers, & Hass, 2011; Le et al., 2016; MoET, 2020; Nguyen, 2014; Pham & Akos, 2020).

Findings from some recent studies (Nguyen, Huynh, Nguyen, & Sam, 2018; Nguyen, Huynh, Giang, & Bui, 2020; Nguyen, Huynh, Do et al., 2020; Pham & Akos, 2020) on professional school counselling in Vietnam have indicated a need for the development of a national Vietnam School Counselling Model (VSCM) and a Vietnam Association of School Counselling (VASC). A national VSCM will help to define the professional identity of school counsellors and their responsibilities in the delivery of counselling programmes for students in public schools, and the necessary standards for school counsellors and other stakeholders such as counselling psychologists, homeroom teachers, and Youth Union representatives or specialists (Nguyen, 2014, 2017; Pham & Akos, 2020; Pham, 2021).

In this chapter, we introduce a *Preliminary Model of Professional School Counselling in Vietnam* (VSCM), the aim of which is to help public schools improve the quality and effectiveness of school counselling for students' success in both their learning, career readiness, and lives outside school.

A Preliminary Model of Professional School Counselling in Vietnam (VSCM)

The Fundamental Framework for VSCM

The low quality of school counsellors has negatively affected school counselling in most public schools in Vietnam, and educational issues of school violence,

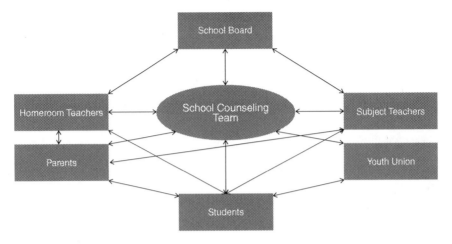

Figure 8.1 A matrix of school counselling activities in secondary schools

student bullying, and stress have become serious in the complex and unique educational context of Vietnam. Many studies related to school counselling have been conducted, but a national model and comprehensive programme of school counselling for public schools has not been developed (Cao & Truong, 2016; Nguyen et al., 2020; Pham & Akos, 2020; Pham, 2021). In Vietnam, the Vietnamese Association of Psychology (VAP) and the Vietnam Psycho-Pedagogical Association (VPPA) are the main associations promoting *school psychological counselling* and collaborating with governmental agencies and some universities to develop professional development programmes for school psychologists across Vietnam (Le, 2016; Le et al., 2016; Nguyen, 2014; Pham & Do, 2004; Tran, 2016c). Education policymakers and educators have recognized the urgent need to develop a national model of school counselling, and to set standards for school counsellors. A model of school counselling for secondary schools was proposed by Nguyen Hong Thuan in 2017 (Figure 8.1), followed by a *fundamental framework* for developing a *Vietnam School Counselling Model* (Nguyen, 2014, 2017; Pham & Akos, 2020; Pham, 2021).

The school counselling model proposed by Nguyen Hong Thuan (Nguyen, 2014, 2017; Pham & Akos, 2020), reflected the unique educational context of Vietnam that emphasized the vital role of the *homeroom teachers* in delivery of school counselling to students. Most public schools in Vietnam assign homeroom teachers to work as *interim school counsellors* due to the lack of professional school counsellors. These interim school counsellors have some counselling skills and collaborate with other school stakeholders such as school principals, subject teachers, and sometimes with youth union representatives, to support students with psychological matters. The *fundamental framework* (Appendix 1) for developing the VSCM provided a concrete foundation for the development of a VSCM through a comprehensive meta-analysis of the educational history, context, and conceptualization of school counselling between the American School Counselling Association's (ASCA) National Model (ASCA, 2016, 2019a; Martin & Carey, 2014) and the preliminary framework or matrix for developing a school counselling model proposed by Nguyen Hong Thuan (Nguyen, 2014, 2017; Pham & Akos, 2020; Pham, 2021). This *fundamental framework* was developed with four components, similar to the ASCA National Model's Themes "Define – Manage – Deliver – Assess" (ASCA, 2019b), and based on two important documents on school psychological counselling – the Official Letter No. 9971/BGDĐT-HSSV and Circular No. 31/2017/TT-BGDĐT published by the MoET (MoET, 2005, 2017).

The VSCM in Figure 8.2 is a preliminary model. Additional studies on the standards for school counselling, and the descriptors and rubrics for assessing effective implementation within Vietnam's educational context and culture, are needed.

VSCM Themes

The VSCM reflects the current educational environment and specific culture of Vietnamese society, family, and relationships. The model consists of *four themes* and *nine components* that help schools successfully foster a school environment with a positive impact on students' achievement and well-being (Figure 8.2).

Management. The first component, management, refers to the efficiency of the school counselling programme at the school level. The VSCM supports all school stakeholders in effectively managing and designing the comprehensive school counselling programmes and implementation plan, professional development programmes for homeroom teachers and interim counsellors, and other issues related to counselling programme administration. The management theme of VSCM is similar to the Manage theme of the ASCA National Model in that it helps to clarify how the school counselling programme could be effectively delivered and efficiently managed (ASCA, 2019b; Pham & Akos, 2020; Pham, 2021).

Management is the most crucial theme of the VSCM model due to the unique characteristics of Vietnam's heavy bureaucracy. This theme satisfies the objectives of school counselling and the administration of counselling programmes stipulated by Vietnam Education Law No. 43/2019/QH14 (National Legislative Documents, 2019), the Charters of Primary and Secondary Schools Circular No. 12/2011/TT-BGDĐT (MoET, 2011), and other related legislative documents issued by the MoET and the city and provincial Departments of Education and Training (DoET) (Pham & Akos, 2020; Pham, 2021). The administration system is formed and managed by the *School Counselling Team* which consists of school administrators (principals or vice principals), homeroom teachers, and interim counsellors (MoET, 2005, 2017). This team is responsible for developing and implementing school

Figure 8.2 The Vietnam School Counselling Model (VSCM)

programmes aligned with the schoolwide philosophy, strategy, and teaching and learning plans published early in a school year. School principals play a crucial role in consulting the school counselling team on the assessment of counselling needs and the implementation or delivery plans, providing professional development for interim counsellors and homeroom teachers, and collaborating with DoET officials and other school stakeholders to ensure the necessary funding and facilities for school counselling activities. Further studies on the management standards or descriptors for school administrators, teachers, and interim counsellors to clarify their roles and performance, especially duties and responsibilities in the implementation of school counselling programmes, should be conducted.

Workforce. The second theme, workforce, refers to all members of the School Counselling Team or the personnel responsible for developing and implementing policies, programmes, and assessments of school counselling in schools. The workforce theme is similar to the *Define* theme of the ASCA National Model which helps to clarify standards for school counselling programmes, implementation plans, and assessment tools (ASCA, 2016, 2019b; Pham & Akos, 2020; Pham, 2021).

Workforce is also a core theme of the VSCM that helps to define student standards and professional and ethical standards for school counsellors. Vietnamese education policymakers, educators, school psychologists, and school counsellors have recognized these important standards or descriptors that need further in-depth studies and evaluation (Nguyen, 2014, 2017; Pham & Akos, 2020; Pham, 2021). The *workforce* theme satisfies the provisions of definitions and the application scope of school counselling as outlined in Circular No. 31/2017/TT-BGDĐT published by the MoET in 2017 (MoET, 2017). This legislative document highlighted the crucial role of the *School Counselling Team* in schools. The team should include a diverse workforce from various groups, such as the school board representatives (principal or vice principal), homeroom teachers, school counsellors, representatives of youth union, school nurses, parents, and outside specialists; and the school principals have the authority to approve and evaluate the performance of this team.

The *workforce* theme can be considered as the unique characteristic of the VSCM model, specifically reflecting Vietnamese collectivism and family-centred culture as it impacts the educational environment and the social lives of students and other stakeholders.

Services. The ASCA National Model offers school counselling services that enhance students' academic development, social/emotional development, and career development (ASCA, 2017, 2019a). The services theme with two components of prevention and counselling is similar to the Deliver theme in the ASCA National Model, highlighting the delivery of appropriate activities and services to students to promote their achievement and success.

Given the specific culture, educational systems, and history of school psychology development in Vietnam, the *services* theme of the VSCM focuses on two basic activities to help students in schools: prevention counselling (psychological diagnosis, psychological development, and adjustment), and psychological counselling (individuals and groups). This theme satisfies the provisions of the implementation or delivery of school counselling programmes and the methods of school counselling as outlined in Circular No. 31/2017/TT-BGDĐT published by the MoET in 2017 (MoET, 2017; Pham & Akos, 2020; Pham, 2021). Like the ASCA National Model, the school counselling services of VSCM also focus on comprehensive activities that are embedded into mainstream instruction and extra-curricular activities, appraisal and advisement, counselling, consultation, collaboration, and referrals to help students develop cognitive ability and behaviours for their success.

Assessment. The *Assess* theme of the ASCA National Model provides assessment tools with comprehensive standards and appraisal criteria to evaluate the school counselling programme, counselling results, school counsellor professional standards and competencies, and school counsellor performance appraisal (ASCA, 2017, 2019a). *Assessment* is also a crucial theme of the

VSCM, focusing on measuring the effectiveness or efficiency of school counselling and the standards or competencies to evaluate the performance of school counsellors. The essential conceptualization of this theme is to assess students' improvement and success and school counsellors' mindsets and behaviours for ongoing professional development (MoET, 2017; Pham & Akos, 2020; Pham, 2021).

In Vietnam, the profession and standards for school counsellors have not yet been defined and stipulated in any legislative documents. Therefore, schools can develop an assessment system aligned with their vision and mission, and the principal has the authority to oversee the effectiveness of the *School Counselling Team* (Nguyen, 2009), evaluate team members and interim counsellors, and assess students' improvement. The principal can also assess the progress or outcomes of the school counselling programmes and motivate the school counselling team to achieve the school's goals and students' success.

Further in-depth studies on the profession, competencies for school counsellors, assessment standards for a comprehensive school counselling programme, and students' improvement will help to affirm this *assessment* theme of the VSCM. This theme will also give school counsellors a broader view of an effective school counselling programme, focusing on how they can effectively establish good relationships with students, parents, and other school stakeholders, and how they can successfully help students in their academic, social/emotional, and career development.

VSCM Components

THE SCHOOL COUNSELLING PROGRAMME

In Vietnam, undergraduate educational psychology and psychology programmes have been offered to students since the early 1980s (Le, 2016; Huynh et al., 2016; Nguyen, 2014; Pham & Do, 2004). The first undergraduate programme of school psychology was launched in 2006 under the consultation of UNESCO and with support from the University of Saint John and the University of Hofstra. Students in this programme learn essential contemporary knowledge and research methodologies in general psychology and school psychology. Circular No. 31/2017/TT-BGDĐT 2017 provides detailed guidelines for developing and implementing the school psychological counselling or school counselling programme for secondary school students in Vietnam (Do, 2006; MoET, 2017). The objectives of the school counselling programme focus on supporting students' development of cognitive abilities, good relationships within the family, with teachers, friends, and other social communities, effective learning methods, and career orientation (Nguyen, 2014, 2017; Pham & Akos, 2020; Pham, 2021). School counselling programmes help students understand the diversity of age, gender, and correlations between adolescent health, marriage, and family relationships; particularly, school counsellors must effectively help students to improve their learning ability, communication, value orientation, and resolve psychological matters.

The *school counselling programme* is one of three important components of the VSCM management shaping the vision, strategy, and objectives of the school counselling policy and complements other components of the implementation plan and professional development programmes for school counsellors (ASCA, 2016, 2019a; Pham & Akos, 2020; Pham, 2021). This component should be viewed as a framework for other components, and it should focus on preventing school violence, bullying, and sexual abuse by fostering a healthy and caring educational environment. School counsellors should successfully support students through intervention and appropriate resolution, especially collaborating with external psychologists for cases of students with psychological disorders that cannot be resolved by the school counsellors.

Public schools in Vietnam are operated and supervised by two main governmental agencies, the Ministry of Education and Training (MoET) and the provincial or city Department of Education and Training (DoET). The heavy bureaucracy of the administrative system creates significant obstacles and less autonomy for public schools in the employment of professional school counsellors (Le et al., 2007; Nguyen, 2014; UNICEF, 2021a). Most public schools choose alternative solutions for the lack of professional school counsellors by appointing homeroom teachers to perform the role of school counsellors, and only a few schools with strong financial resources hire a qualified school psychologist (Nguyen, 2014, 2017; Nguyen et al., 2020; Pham & Akos, 2020; Pham, 2021). School administrators, to successfully develop a comprehensive school counselling programme, should collaborate with the school counselling team and all other school stakeholders to utilize available resources to provide the most benefit for their students.

IMPLEMENTATION PLAN

The component of the *implementation plan* of the VSCM *management* theme reflects the complexity of the legislative system and the unique culture of collectivism in conceptualizing the benefits of school counselling services. The implementation plan of school counselling programmes is significantly affected by the legislative system or education laws and other related guidance of school counselling enacted by MoET and the conceptualization of school counselling in Vietnam.

Legislative Perspectives on School Counselling. The effectiveness of school counselling has been recognized as one of the key educational factors that significantly affects students' academic achievements and social behaviours in communities (Le, 2016; Le et al., 2016; Nguyen, 2014; Nguyen et al., 2020). In Vietnam, MoET has continuously attempted to improve the quality of school counselling programmes. In 2005, MoET published guidance *Implementing counselling services for primary and secondary students and undergraduate students* providing the essential principles for developing and delivering school counselling programmes. This document emphasized the importance of an implementation plan that covers all aspects of students' achievement and success, including career orientation and development, college, and university information, gender and romantic relationships, interpersonal relationships within the family, school, and social environments, learning methods, community activities, and morality (MoET, 2005). More importantly, homeroom teachers, youth union representatives, and outside counsellors should be able to help students deal with mental stress and increase confidence and identify and proactively resolve matters related to their learning and social lives. In 2011, the MoET enacted the *Charter of Secondary Schools* or the Circular No. 12/2011/TT-BGDĐT officially stipulating the standards for school counsellors in middle schools (MoET, 2011) and clarified that "*All educational settings must empower the role of homeroom teachers, youth union representatives, academic counsellors, and local communities to help students enhance their social development skills through moral education, psychological counselling and career guidance...*" as outlined in the Official Letter No. 1537/CT-BGDDT published later in 2014 (MoET, 2014, p.2).

In 2017, MoET issued Circular No. 31/2017-BGDDT provided comprehensive guidelines on the implementation of school (psychological) counselling activities in primary and secondary schools across Vietnam (MoET, 2017). The school counselling programmes should focus on specific topics on cognitive awareness of gender, marriage, family, and adolescent reproductive healthcare, appropriate behaviours towards violence and sexual abuse in an educational environment, positive relationships and problems solving skills in relationships within the family, schools, and social communities, and effective learning methods and career orientation. The delivery of school counselling should be flexible to meet the diverse needs of students, it could be designed as specific lessons or integrated into mainstream subjects, experiential learning activities, and extra-curricular such as seminars, clubs, and forums based on students' needs of counselling. Effective implementation of school counselling should include all related stakeholders, including parents, local communities, and external experts, and the utilization of technology. Findings from a study conducted by Nguyen et al. (2020) and another survey conducted by the MoET (2021) showed that many public schools in Vietnam, with the consultations from MoET and school boards, had successfully carried out a variety of psychological counselling services for their students. (MoET, 2021; Nguyen et al., 2020). Specially, the study conducted by Nguyen and her associate researchers (2020) highlighted the need for psychological counselling has been significantly increasing, and many public rural schools are still struggling with huge challenges in providing comprehensive counselling programmes that satisfy the high demands from families and students with dramatically constrained resources of professional counsellors and funding. The DoETs across the country must review and evaluate the effectiveness of the implementation of psychological counselling programmes for ongoing improvement.

Conceptualization of School Counselling. Within a highly diverse society, school counselling has become more crucial and significantly impacted not only students' learning outcomes but also the family and society. Therefore, the governmental agencies in Vietnam, including the Ministry of Education and Training (MoET), the Ministry of Labour Invalids and Social Affairs (MoLISA), the Ministry of Home Affairs (MoHA), and the Ministry of Health (MoH) have to effectively collaborate in developing and implementing school counselling programmes. In many cities and provinces, the DoETs have been diligently working with school administrators to improve the quality of school counselling activities. However, different conceptualizations of school counselling programmes remain, with inconsistency or inefficient coordination between governmental agencies like the MoET and DoET, the ambiguity of authority and responsibility, and inappropriate evaluation criteria for the quality of the school counselling programmes in different regions in Vietnam (Nguyen, 2014, 2017; Nguyen et al., 2020; Pham & Akos, 2020; Pham, 2021).

The *implementation plan* component of VSCM highlights the importance of effective collaboration between the governmental agencies and schools that enables school counsellors to successfully identify the psychological development and issues of students and the need for counselling, and to then proactively work with parents for efficiency improvement (Pham & Akos, 2020; Pham, 2021). This component also emphasizes the concrete collaboration between school counsellors and other school stakeholders in developing and implementing school counselling programmes. The information monitored through the homeroom teachers and subject teachers helps school counsellors quickly detect and prevent early signs of psychological problems in students. In addition, the school counselling teams should coordinate with outside organizations and experts such as professional psychological counselling centres, therapy, and clinical centres, psychologists, and experts to jointly carry out psychological counselling activities to provide the most benefit for students.

PROFESSIONAL DEVELOPMENT FOR SCHOOL COUNSELLORS

The Need for Professional Development. Most public schools in Vietnam do not have professional school counsellors, and homeroom or subject teachers are often assigned to perform the role of a school counsellor – the *"interim school counsellor"* (Le, 2016; Le et al., 2016; Nguyen, 2014, 2017; Pham & Akos, 2020; Pham, 2021). The homeroom teachers are forced to take on a counselling job to satisfy the mandatory number of working hours stipulated by the MoET, DoET, and school rather than by their competencies or professional skills of counselling. These *interim school counsellors* can be replaced by any other homeroom or subject teachers with little knowledge and few skills in school counselling. In addition, the high workload, the collectivist culture in workplace, and the social complexity create more challenges for the interim counsellors (Le et al., 2016; Pham & Akos, 2020; Pham, 2021).

144 *Anh Kim Pham and Hong Thuan Nguyen*

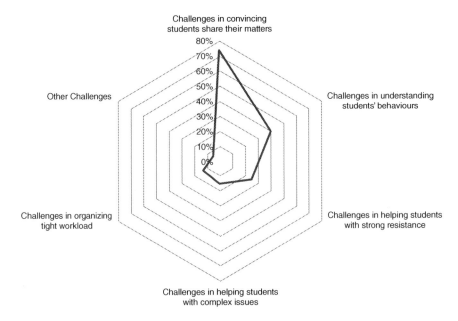

Figure 8.3 The challenges of interim school counsellors in providing the school counselling services for students

Figure 8.3 presents data from a nationwide survey on the implementation of school counselling by 393 interim school counsellors (or homeroom teachers) conducted by MoET and UNICEF from October 2021 to March 2022, and shows some major challenges that interim school counsellors coped with in conducting school counselling (MoET & UNICEF, 2021).

Findings from this survey showed that 73.5% of students were "less willing to share" their problems with adults, 39.5% had difficulty in building rapport, and 24.7% of students had a resistant attitude. These challenges could be explained from two perspectives: the counsellors' competency and students' characteristics. Most interim counsellors lack professional counselling knowledge and skills, so they are not able to effectively build rapport with students, and even negatively influence students, leading to resistance. On the other hand, today's students have a higher awareness of their psychological development than in the past. Especially, the rapidly changing world and disruptive technology have led to a profound conceptualization gap between generations – students may have become more introverted and may shy away from sharing with the older generations – teachers, counsellors, and parents.

Most public schools have been aware of these issues and have offered various professional development programmes to improve the quality of interim counsellors and counselling programmes (Nguyen, 2014, 2017; Pham & Akos, 2020; Pham, 2021). However, this professional development consists of short training courses in interpersonal communication skills rather than professional development for improving counselling competencies. In addition, with the national unique culture and lack of school counselling standards affirmed by the MoET and DoET, most interim counsellors can provide counselling services based on their individual experiences rather than by professional counselling abilities. The need for professional development programmes for school counsellors to improve their counselling competencies is high.

Professional Development for School Counsellors. The transition from the role of teacher to school counsellor is a long, challenging journey, and the quality of school counselling programmes depends on the counselling competencies and the effective collaboration between school administrators, teachers, students, and parents. Many studies on the effectiveness of school counselling have indicated a quality gap in counselling between urban or large cities with high quality versus suburban and rural regions with low quality (Nguyen et al., 2020; Nguyen, 2014, 2017; Pham & Akos, 2020; Pham, 2021). Circular No. 31/2017/TT-BGDĐT and Decision No. 1876/2018/QĐ-BGDĐT officially provided a national framework for developing a professional development programme of school counselling for homeroom teachers or interim counsellors in public schools across Vietnam (MoET, 2017, 2018). These legislative documents highlighted a specific professional development programme, which is developed and approved by MoET, to enhance the counselling competency of teachers or interim counsellors in public schools.

First, primary and secondary homeroom teachers, professional counsellors, or interim counsellors who have not received mainstream education in school counselling are required to take the professional development programme. Second, the purpose of the programme is to help teachers and interim counsellors master the vital role of the school counsellor, including the duties and responsibilities of a school counsellor, the nature of counselling work, and the content, methods, principles, and process of school counselling. Also, the practicum covers professional knowledge and skills such as psychology, education, career guidance, and social work in school counselling activities. Third, the topics of the programme focus on strengthening counselling competency with 8 modules (i.e., 16 credits or equivalent to 240 periods) as outlined in below Table 8.1.

The MoET's professional development initiative has led to positive movements in school counselling activities in public schools in Vietnam. Many cities, provinces' DoETs and schools, in the delivery of these formal professional development programmes, have proactively created more learning activities to help the participants gain more contemporary knowledge and the latest trends in school counselling from developed countries (Nguyen et al., 2020; Nguyen, 2014, 2017). A universally adopted ASCA National Model from the United States has been also introduced to the school counselling community in Vietnam (Pham & Akos, 2020; Pham, 2021). Some certain schools invite outside experts in school psychology to talk with school psychologists, parents, and students about the best practices of interpersonal communication and behaviours in diverse cultural contexts; others send their interim counsellors

Table 8.1 Professional Development Programme for School Counsellors

Modules	Credit(s)	Theory	Practicum
Current issues of school counselling	2	10	20
Understanding and assessing students' psychological matters	2	10	20
Basic skills of school counselling	2	10	20
Counselling students with deviant behaviours	2	8	22
Counselling students with psychological problems	3	10	35
Academic and career counselling	2	10	20
Counselling on sexual and reproductive health	1	5	10
Practicum and final exam	2	5	25
Total	**16**	**68**	**172**

to training centres or institutions with more relaxing and comfortable learning environments and learning motivation. However, the number of interim counsellors or homeroom teachers who participate in MoET's professional development programmes is not high due to their workload; more importantly, trained interim counsellors may take back their key role of teaching whenever they feel overwhelmed by their extra duties of school counselling (Nguyen et al., 2020; Nguyen, 2014, 2017; MoET & UNICEF, 2022).

The *professional development* component helps to improve the counselling competencies of school administrators, teachers, parents, and local communities who are involved in providing school counselling services to students (Nguyen, 2014, 2017; Pham & Akos, 2020; Pham, 2021). Standardized professional development with a comprehensive curriculum will help school counsellors increase their confidence in conducting assessment, prevention, and intervention programmes for their students. Moreover, school counsellors have opportunities to do research and practicums at high-quality institutions of psychology and school counselling across the country (Le et al., 2016). The professional development of school counsellors should be viewed as an imperial agenda for MoET and school administrators to leverage available sources for improving the quality of school counsellors and the effectiveness of school counselling services.

SCHOOL COUNSELLING TEAM

Most public schools in Vietnam use *interim school counsellors* whose primary roles are school administrators, homeroom teachers, and Young Union Specialists (also called *Young Communists*) with some specific skills of counselling to play the role of a school counsellor (Le et al., 2016; Nguyen et al., 2020; Nguyen, 2014, 2017). The interim school counsellors work directly with all other school stakeholders, parents, and local communities to identify and help students to prevent any psychological problems, and to ensure they gain the necessary knowledge and skills, competencies for personal development and growth. The *school counselling team* has a vital role in developing and implementing school counselling services for students in schools (Nguyen et al., 2020; MoET, 2017). This component helps clarify the key role of internal school counsellors in designing and implementing school counselling programmes to help students with their psychological issues, and in their academic and career development.

The school board (normally inclusive of the principal, vice principal, and headteachers) has the authority to select team members and collaborate with them to develop, implement, and assess the effectiveness of school counselling programmes. The school board can also seek consultation from outside experts to review or evaluate the counselling programme's effectiveness.

OUTSIDE SPECIALISTS

The outside school counselling specialists are defined as professional school counsellors or school psychologists who have and in-depth knowledge of school counselling with a master's degree (or higher) and have at least five years of practical experience in the field of professional school counselling (MoET, 2017).

The school board can hire outside counselling specialists to help the internal school counselling team in developing the programmes and practicum or internship opportunities, professional development programmes, assessments, and other specific counselling services such as intervention and therapy for all school stakeholders. Within the educational and cultural contexts of Vietnam, the outside specialists may include students' family members who can effectively build trust and collaborate with the school to offer the best counselling services for students.

PREVENTION

Vietnam is highly multicultural with 54 ethnic minority groups, and some studies have shown a failure or inefficiency in implementing the school counselling in some unprivileged regions with specific customs, beliefs, and school capabilities (Le et al., 2016; Nguyen et al., 2020; Nguyen, 2014, 2017; MoET & UNICEF, 2022). Other geographic and eco-social factors such as poorly educated parents and unprivileged family circumstances also seriously affect the effectiveness of school counselling programmes. Findings from a recent *Report of school counselling implementation* conducted by the MoET and UNICEF in early 2022 have shown a vivid picture of school counselling activities implemented in different regions across Vietnam. The cities and provinces' DoET have considered the eco-social conditions and the schools' capability as two key factors that affect the effectiveness of school counselling and social work programmes in public schools. For example, Hanoi is the capital of Vietnam with thousands of years of historical heritage and unique culture compared to other regions of Vietnam; thus, school counselling activities for more than 2 million students should be designed to reflect the diverse and unique characteristics of people and family relationships in this city (MoET & UNICEF, 2022).

This *prevention* component is very important in school counselling activities, and the MoET has continuously attempted to provide appropriate guidelines and regulations to help schools and counsellors in prevention programmes in both urban and rural regions. This *prevention* component emphasizes the importance of diversity awareness from the school counsellors in building rapport with students and parents with different family circumstances, particularly ethnic minority students in rural regions with their unique languages and cultures. The prevention programme should be designed to meet the needs of students' academic, personal/emotional, and social development.

COUNSELLING SERVICES

The *counselling services* component consists of individual counselling and group counselling. Students are the main target clients of s *individual Counselling* activities, but most students in Vietnam perceive school counselling negatively (Nguyen, 2014, 2017; Pham & Akos, 2020; Pham, 2021). Some students feel extremely shy and are afraid to share their interests, concerns, or personal and social conflicts with their homeroom teachers or counsellors; some do not want their teachers to know about the issues they are experiencing, and others are forced to seek counselling services only when their teachers observe a problem. In some specific cases, a female student might not feel comfortable sharing certain issues with a male counsellor due to the universal conceptualization of Confucianism, or so called the traditional "Eastern cultures" about the gender discrimination in daily social activities (Kim & Ko, 2007; Koç & Kafa, 2019). The need for *individual counselling* has significantly increased since the blooming of technological devices and social networks: students and parents are more aware of emerging social issues and trends, and they trust only in homeroom teachers and counsellors who have relevant knowledge and experiences of these issues (Pham & Akos, 2020; Pham, 2021).

School counsellors in public schools in Vietnam often have challenges in gaining trust from their students and parents (Nguyen, 2014, 2017; Pham & Akos, 2020; Pham, 2021). In particular, social distancing due to the COVID-19 pandemic has caused obstacles to many school counsellors in their counselling activities (Huynh et al., 2019; UNICEF, 2021b). A significant number of students have more serious problems in their academic development, personal development, and social/emotional development due to a lack of interpersonal relationships; and parents tend to hide their children's mental health conditions (Nguyen, 2014, 2017). Successful individual counselling requires school counsellors who are certified with high standards of professional counselling knowledge and core competencies of collaboration, motivation, and inspiration that help build trust and effective relationships with students and parents within the unique Vietnamese culture and social contexts.

Group counselling is more difficult to implement than individual counselling because of the Eastern culture of unique conceptualization of the "self-expression" which is not commonly encouraged in most East Asian cultures, including Vietnam (Kim & Ko, 2007; Koç & Kafa, 2019; Pham & Akos, 2020). This component emphasizes the importance of collaboration between the school counsellors and students and parents, and the school counsellors and other stakeholders such as school administrators, teachers, and local communities to ensure the effectiveness of the counselling programme.

Group counselling helps to enhance the collaboration between all school stakeholders and between the counsellors to ensure provide the best solutions for students. However, studies have shown the diverse conceptualization of parents and students in group counselling and the limitations of collaboration in school counselling activities in different eco-social contexts and regions across Vietnam (MoET, 2021; Nguyen, 2017; Pham & Akos, 2020; Pham, 2021). With a heavily bureaucratic system and closed-family culture, Vietnamese students usually admire and trust in only their parents that causes dramatical obstacles for school counsellors in collaborating and delivering counselling services to their students (Le et al., 2016; Huynh et al., 2019). School counsellors in public schools often have huge challenges in the delivery of prevention and intervention counselling due to a lack of corporation from parents, and accurate information or data on their students' academic progress and status of well-being.

SCHOOL COUNSELLING EFFECTIVENESS

The *effectiveness of school counselling* is one of two important components of the assessment theme that helps to evaluate the success of school counselling programmes. This component consists of counselling methods, counselling delivery, and counselling facilities.

Counselling methods refer to typical counselling methods commonly used such as psychological diagnostic methods (quizzes, questionnaires, tests), psychological counselling (listening, understanding, interpreting, empathizing, eliciting, assuming), psychological adjustment (psychotherapy, experiment, psychological practicing), and psychotherapy treatment (psychoanalysis and behaviour, behavioural therapy, group therapy, family therapy) (Le et al., 2016; MoET, 2005, 2017). Public schools in Vietnam adopt the legislative guidelines from the MoET to develop the school counselling system and they have autonomy or flexibility in using the appropriate counselling methods ensure to alignment with the MoET's requirements and the practical conditions of schools such as the available workforce or interim school counsellors, fundings and facilities. Some typical counselling methods such as lecturing, psychological diagnosis, psychological development and adjustment, and individual and group psychological counselling have been universally used in Vietnam (Le et al., 2016; Nguyen, 2016, 2020; MoET & UNICEF, 2022). The MoET should collaborate with education policymakers, educators, school counsellors, and other related counselling experts to develop appropriate standards or criteria for assessing the effectiveness of school counselling programmes through the methods used in school counselling.

Counselling delivery is the process of conducting counselling activities. In essence, counselling delivery should be defined as the key role of school counsellors – they can deliver counselling in either individual or group forms, directly with the student indirectly with the student's parents, or even through the homeroom teacher who has a close relationship with the students (Le et al., 2016; MoET, 2005, 2017). There are many forms of group counselling such as extracurricular activities, field trips, academic and psychological clubs, parent-teacher clubs, and career orientation events that can help students learn how to effectively build relationships, share, and practise positive thinking to eliminate stress and psychological matters. Homeroom teachers with their specific role in public schools in Vietnam should collaborate closely with school counsellors in the counselling delivery process (Ngo & Nguyen, 2009; Nguyen, 2017; Nguyen et al., 2020; Pham & Akos, 2020; Pham, 2021). Homeroom teachers can help school counsellors identify students with psychological problems, build rapport, and communicate with parents and other related school stakeholders to find suitable solutions for students. In case the homeroom teachers themselves cannot help students to resolve the problems, they can escalate the case to the school counselling team. The *school counselling team* collaborates with all related stakeholders and find the best solutions to help students resolve their psychological problems and improve academic outcomes, and support homeroom teachers or interim school counsellors improve their counselling competencies through continuing professional development programmes and practicum (MoET, 2017; Nguyen, 2017). The team can also help organize seminars or workshops on school counselling topics that enhance the awareness of the importance of psychological issues and counselling services in schools for all school stakeholders.

Counselling facilities refer to the tools and resources, technology, and counselling time used in counselling activities also one of the correlative factors that significantly affects the effectiveness of school counselling in public schools in Vietnam (MoET, 2005, 2017). The school counselling sessions should be carried out in dedicated rooms to ensure privacy for students and a comfortable atmosphere for building rapport and trust, an important step in a professional counselling process, particularly within the specific perceptions and characteristics of Vietnamese students and parents on the school counselling services (Nguyen, 2017; Nguyen et al., 2020; Pham & Akos, 2020; Pham, 2021). The ideal time for counselling can be flexible during class recess time or after class time, corresponding to the counselling need of students and the tight learning and teaching in most public schools in Vietnam.

SCHOOL COUNSELLOR COMPETENCIES

The component of school counsellor competencies refers to the mandatory standards or abilities that a professional school counsellor must have for offering school counselling services to students. The competencies could be classified into two levels: *interim school counsellor* (or homeroom teacher who is assigned to play the role of a school counsellor due to the lack of a professional workforce as stipulated by the MoET), and *professional school counsellor*.

Interim School Counsellors. Many public schools in Vietnam appoint homeroom teachers to play the role of *interim school counsellors* due to the serious shortage of professional school counsellors. These interim school counsellors can provide counselling services for students to focus on gender and sexual orientation, psychology, interpersonal relationships, and social skills development (MoET, 2005, 2017; MoET & UNICEF, 2022; Nguyen, 2017; Nguyen et al., 2020). The interim school counsellors have intensive knowledge, skills, and experience that help them effectively support their students. However, they are often overwhelmed with a high workload of homeroom administration, afterschool activities, professional development programmes, and mentoring for junior teachers.

A nationwide survey on the implementation of school counselling with 393 interim school counsellors (or homeroom teachers) conducted by the MoET and UNICEF from October 2021 to March 2022 (see Figure 8.4) showed that most homeroom teachers considered themselves to be "very overwhelmed" to "absolutely overwhelmed" when taking the additional role of interim counsellors (95.7%) and a few of them considered themselves "not overwhelmed" (4.3%) (MoET & UNICEF, 2021). With a highly stressful workload, most interim counsellors often focus on their main teaching jobs and provide counselling only when they have available time which leads to inconsistency and inefficiency of school counselling offered to students. A positive sign is that at a high rate, 44.3% of primary and secondary homeroom teachers have strong career passion despite the high workload; whilst a significant percentage 18.8% of homeroom teachers are overwhelmed with their teaching job.

Findings from this survey highlight the significant stress of homeroom teachers when they perform the role of interim counsellors and the negative impact of stress on the quality of school counselling services offered to students in public schools.

Homeroom teachers or/and interim counsellors should have opportunities for professional development to improve their skills in developing plans, and effectively managing and performing multiple tasks (Nguyen, 2017; Pham & Akos, 2020; Pham, 2021). Some relevant standards or criteria for assessing persistence and resilience, passion, or willingness in providing school counselling services for their students should be also included in the competency framework for interim counsellors.

Professional School Counsellors. In Vietnam, the profession of school counselling has not yet been legally affirmed by the government (MoET); therefore,

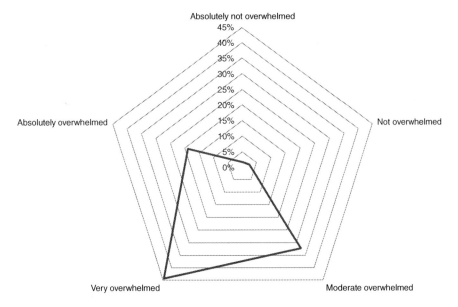

Figure 8.4 The stress of interim school counsellors (or homeroom teachers) in primary and secondary schools

school counselling in public schools across the country focuses on the mere implementation of some guidelines or regulations published by the MoET on school counselling services for students (Nguyen, 2017; Pham & Akos, 2020; Pham, 2021). Once the profession of school counselling is affirmed, then the standards for school counsellors, including duties, responsibilities, and competencies can be identified accordingly.

The COVID-19 pandemic has dramatically impacted all aspects of society, families, educational settings, teachers, students, and the perception of school counselling for students, and there has been a significantly increased demand for mental health counselling from parents and students (Huynh et al., 2019; Nguyen et al., 2020; Pham, 2021; UNICEF, 2021a). Therefore, the role of school counsellors has become more crucial and complex. School counsellors should possess a higher level of competencies, with the knowledge, abilities, skills, and attitudes to successfully perform all 4 themes and 9 components of VSCM. Beyond the essential competencies of planning, organizing, implementing, and evaluating, professional school counsellors must have strategic vision and leadership, efficient collaboration and inspiration, and sustainable passion for assisting students.

Conclusion

As in other countries with a Confucian heritage and a collectivist culture in the Asian region, Vietnam views education as one of the imperative drives for being a wealthy nation (McAleavy et al., 2018), and school counselling has been recognized as one of the success factors in school operations (Pham, 2021). In Vietnam, the need for comprehensive school counselling in public schools has significantly increased, especially after the COVID-19 pandemic, but the existing counselling programmes and initiatives from the MoET have shown many constraints and obstacles in terms of management, workforce, delivery, and assessment (MoET & UNICEF, 2022; Nguyen et al., 2020; Pham, 2021). Therefore, developing a national model of school counselling has become an urgent agenda for the MoET and educators across Vietnam.

In 2017, the Vietnam National Institute of Educational Sciences (VNIES) introduced a *school counselling model* for secondary students in the Northern region of Vietnam – the model merely described the existing practices of school counselling activities in public secondary schools based on some legislative documents published by the MoET (Nguyen, 2017; Pham, 2021). This model illustrated the complex collaboration and involvement of various school stakeholders in implementing school counselling without any fundamental framework or identification of themes and components (Pham & Akos, 2020; Pham, 2021). In 2019 and 2021, an in-depth meta-analysis of the ASCA model of the United States and the legislative documents and guidance on the school counselling programmes published by the MoET provided a *fundamental framework for developing the Vietnam School Counselling Model (VSCM)* as an initial concept for developing a preliminary model of professional school counselling for public schools across the country (Pham & Akos, 2020; Pham, 2021).

The preliminary VSCM helps the MoET, educators, and school counsellors in Vietnam understand what the best practices and models of school counselling in developed countries are, such as the ASCA National Model from the United States, and how all school stakeholders effectively collaborate, develop, and implement comprehensive school counselling programmes to meet the increased needs of parents and students in today's disruptive changing world. The VSCM model's 4 themes 9 components should be viewed as interactive domains or integral modules that help to develop comprehensive school counselling programmes for the best interests of students. This preliminary model is introduced as a part of the roadmap towards a formal professional school counselling model within the Vietnam context and is accepted by global school counselling communities. The education policymakers, MoET, and the city or provincial DoETs have a vital role in supporting and promoting this VSCM to all public schools, and collaborating with school administrators, homeroom teachers, and school counsellors to develop necessary standards or descriptors for each theme and component, especially the standards for school counsellors and the assessment system to affirm its validity and reliability.

As a result of ongoing educational reforms, Vietnam is a developing country with a unique culture and a young population in the Asian region. Increased demand from students and parents for more qualified school counselling services is a force urging education policymakers and educators to consider developing a formal model of professional school counselling for Vietnamese public schools.

References

American School Counsellor Association. (2012). *School counsellor competencies.* https://www.schoolcounsellor.org/asca/media/asca/home/SCCompetencies.pdf.

American School Counsellor Association. (2016). *Ethical standards for school counsellors.* https://www.schoolcounsellor.org/asca/media/asca/Ethics/EthicalStandards2016.pdf

American School Counsellor Association. (2019a). *The ASCA national model: A framework for school counselling programs* (4th ed.). ASCA.

American School Counsellor Association. (2019b). *The ASCA national model: Implementation guide: Foundation, management, and accountability* (2nd ed.). ASCA.

Becirović, S., & Akbarov, A. (2015). Impact of social changes on teacher's role and responsibilities in the educational system. *Journal of Linguistic and Intercultural Education – JoLIE, 8,* 21–34. https://doi.org/10.29302/jolie.2015.8.2

Bui, M. H. (2014). *History of Vietnam education* (3rd ed.). Hanoi University of Education – Educational Leadership and Learning. University of Education Publishing House.

Cao, T. T. X., & Truong, T. T. T. (2016). Application of model theory in the establishment of a school counselling organization in high schools. In *Innovative Education and Development of Trans-Cultural Workforce – Science Seminars Yearbook* (pp. 315–322). Ho Chi Minh National Universities Publications.

Do, V. B. (2006). The reality of counselling services in Ho Chi Minh City. In *Proceedings of the Conference on Building and Developing a School Counselling Network* (pp. 70–73). Ministry of Education and Training.

Hagans, K., Powers, K., & Hass, M. (2011). Developing school psychology in Vietnam. *Bethesda: National Association of School Psychologists, 39*(6), 8–10. https://www.proquest.com/docview/863405333?accountid=34574&sourcetype=Other%20Sources

Huynh, V. S., Giang, T. V., Do, T. T., Tran, L., & Dinh, D. H. (2019). The stress problems and the need for stress counselling of high school students in Vietnam. *European Journal of Educational Research, 8*(4), 1053–1061. http://doi.org/10.12973/eu-jer.8.4.1053

Kim, H. S., & Ko, D. (2007). Culture and self-expression. In C. Sedikides & S. J. Spencer (Eds.), *The Self* (pp. 325–342). Psychology Press. https://psycnet.apa.org/record/2007-02340-015.

Koç, V., & Kafa, G. (2019). Cross-cultural research on psychotherapy: The Need for a change. *Journal of Cross-Cultural Psychology 50*(1), 100–115. https://doi.org/10.1177/0022022118806577.

Le, M. C. (2016). Operational model of school psychology in 1–12 schools. In *Innovative Education and Development of Transcultural Workforce – Science Seminars Yearbook* (pp. 221–231). Ho Chi Minh National Universities Publications.

Le, S., Le, H. M., & Nguyen, T. T. (2016). *School counselling: Fundamental issues.* Thanh Nien Publishing House.

Le, T. K. D., La, T. B., & Dinh, D. H. (2007). Study of some factors that affect middle school students' mental health. In *Proceedings of the Conference on Mental Health Prevention and Interventions for Weinomese Children* (pp. 35–42). Hanoi, Vietnam: Vietnam National University.

Martin, I., & Carey, J. (2014). Development of a logic model to guide evaluations of the ASCA national model for school counselling programs. *The Professional Counsellor, 4*(5), 455–466. http://dx.doi.org/10.15241/im.4.5.455.

McAleavy, T., Tran, T. H., & Fitzpatrick, R. (2018). *Promising practice: Government schools in Vietnam*. Education Development Trust. https://files.eric.ed.gov/fulltext/ED588856.pdf

Ministry of Education and Training (2005). *Official Letter No. 9971/BGD-DT-HSSV regarding the implementation of school counselling programs for all levels of students*. http://www.MoET.gov.vn/tintuc/Pages/tin-tong-hop.aspx?ItemID=4300

Ministry of Education and Training (2011). *Circular No. 12/2011/TT-BGDĐT charter of secondary schools*. https://moet.gov.vn/van-ban/vanban/Pages/chi-tiet-van-ban.aspx?ItemID=1077

Ministry of Education and Training (2014). *Enhancing the effectiveness of education quality for all levels of students in national educational settings and vocational schools*. http://www.moet.gov.vn/tintuc/pages/tin-tong-hop.aspxiItemid=4300

Ministry of Education and Training (2015). *The result of the nationwide conference regarding the development of psychological counselling in 1–12 educational settings and collaboration between schools, families, and society*. http://pbc.MoET.gov.vn/?page=12.4&view=1091&opt=brpage

Ministry of Education and Training (2017). *Circular No.31/2017/TT-BGDĐT guidance of school psychology counselling programs for students in 1–12 schools*. http://MoET.gov.vn/van-ban/vanban/Pages/chi-tiet-van-ban.aspx?ItemID=1269

Ministry of Education and Training (2020). *Educational statistics of middle school and high school in the school year 2019–2020*. https://moet.gov.vn/thong-ke/Pages/Thong-ke-giao-duc-trung-hoc.aspx?ItemID=7387

Ministry of Education and Training, & UNICEF (2022). *Survey results of school counselling implementation in Vietnam*. Vietnam Education Publisher.

National Legislative Documents (2019). *Education Law No. 43/2019/QH14* https://vbpl.vn/TW/Pages/vbpq-toanvan.aspx?ItemID=136042

Ngo, T. D., & Nguyen, H. N. (2009). Development of school counselling model: Supporting student in learning and career planning. *The Journal of Psychological Sciences*, (11/2009). https://vjol.info.vn/index.php/TLH/article/view/5941/5635

Nguyen, H. T. (2014). *Suggestions for developing a model of school counselling in middle schools*. The Vietnam Institute of Educational Sciences (VNIES). http://vnies.edu.vn/tin-tuc/tin-hoat-dong-khoa-hoc/16220/nghiem-thu-nhiem-vu-%E2%80%9Cxay-dung-mo-hinh-tu-van-hoc-duong-trong-nha-truong-trung-hoc-co-so%E2%80%9D

Nguyen, H. T. (2017). *A model of school counselling in middle schools*. Hanoi National University Publisher.

Nguyen, T. B. P. (2020). *Research overview on school counselling model*. https://sti.vista.gov.vn/tw/Lists/TaiLieuKHCN/Attachments/324442/CVv436S1722021108.pdf

Nguyen, T. H. (2005). Solutions for managing school counselling in middle schools in Binh Thanh District, Ho Chi Minh City. *The Vietnam Institute of Educational Sciences (VNIES)*.

Nguyen, T. H. H. (2016). School counselling at high schools in Ho Chi Minh City. In *Innovative Education and Development of Trans-Cultural Workforce - Science Seminars Yearbook* (pp. 232–243). Ho Chi Minh National Universities Publications.

Nguyen, T. M. (2009). *Building model of school counselling department in high schools*. The Ministry of Education and Training: Hanoi National University of Education (HNUE).

Nguyen, T. M. H., Huynh, V. S., Do, T. T., Nguyen, Mai, M. H., Tran, L., Nguyen, T. D. M., Tran, C. V. L., Nguyen, T. M. L., & Sam, V. L. (2020). *A study on* the solutions for developing school counselling programs that meet the requirements of the new secondary curriculum. http://chuongtrinhkhgd.moet.gov.vn/content/dauthaudautucong/Lists/DuAn/Attachments/86/025.%20B%C3%A1o%20c%C3%A1o%20tom%20tat.pdf

Nguyen, T. M. H., Huynh, V. S., Giang, T. V., & Bui, H. Q. (2020). Many social problems in Vietnam stem from the communication problems among high school students while no school counselling support is provided – the urgent need of forming a school counselling model for Vietnamese high school students. *European Journal of Contemporary Education, 9*(1), 102–113. https://files.eric.ed.gov/fulltext/EJ1249457.pdf

Nguyen, T. M. H., Huynh, V. S., Nguyen, T. D. M., & Sam, V. L. (2018). Solutions to developing the school counselling staff in Vietnam. *Journal of Science: Education Science, 15*(10), 5–16. https://vjol.info.vn/index.php/sphcm/article/view/39109/31519

Pham, K. A. (2021). *Introduction to professional school counselling in Vietnam.* Exceller Books.

Pham, K. A., & Akos, P. (2020). Professional school counselling in Vietnam. *Journal of Asia Pacific Counselling 10*(2), 37–49. http://doi.org/10.18401/2020.10.2.6

Pham, M. H., & Do, L. (2004). Psychology in Vietnam. *The Psychologist, 17*(2), 70–71. https://cms.bps.org.uk/sites/default/files/2022-11/viet04.pdf

Pham, T. T., & Truong, N. X. Q. (2016). Building a model of school counselling for high schools in Ho Chi Minh City – an approach of social work. In *Innovative Education and Development of Trans-Cultural Workforce – Science Seminars Yearbook* (pp. 275–287). Ho Chi Minh National Universities Publications.

Taylor, W. K. (2013). *A history of the Vietnamese.* Cambridge University Press.

Tran, A. T. (2016a). The training model of master's degree for school counsellors in Vietnam: Real situation and solutions. *Research Journal of Hanoi National University: Educational Research, 2,* 83–95.

Tran, A. T. (2016b). Career guidance counsellors: Reality and need. In *Innovative Education and Development of Trans-Cultural Workforce - Science Seminars Yearbook* (pp. 288–295). Ho Chi Minh National Universities Publications.

Tran, M. D. (2016c). *The curriculum of psychological counselling* (2nd ed). Hanoi University of Education – Educational Leadership and Learning. University of Education Publishing House.

United Nations Children's Fund (UNICEF) (n.d.). *Comprehensive study on school-related factors impacting mental health and well-being of adolescent boys and girls in Vietnam.* https://www.unicef.org/vietnam/media/9831/file

United Nations Children's Fund (UNICEF) (2021a). *Mental health and psychosocial well-being among children and young people in selected provinces and cities in Vietnam.* https://www.unicef.org/vietnam/media/976/file

United Nations Children's Fund (UNICEF) (2021b). *Situation analysis on the effects of and responses to COVID-19 on the education sector in Asia: Vietnam study case.* https://www.unicef.org/eap/media/9346/file

Appendix
Framework for Vietnam School Counselling Model (VSCM)

	ASCA National Model	*Fundamental Framework for Vietnam School Counselling Model (VSCM)*
	The framework of the ASCA National Model Fourth Edition consists of four components: define, manage, deliver and assess.	The Official Letter No. 9971/BGDĐT-HSSV 2005 (major contents): The implementation of school counselling for students in secondary schools, vocational schools, colleges and universities. The Circular No. 31/2017/TT-BGDĐT 2017 (the entire wordings): The guidelines for implementing the school psychological counselling for secondary school students.
Define	Three sets of school counselling standards define the school counselling profession. These standards help new and experienced school counsellors develop, implement and assess their school counselling programme to improve student outcomes. **Student Standards**	School counselling (for secondary and higher education students) is an educational-oriented approach that helps students with psychological and emotional matters, problems of adolescence, difficulties in learning, social relationships, career readiness and job hunting. Those who have knowledge and skills of counselling can help students to choose the appropriate behaviours, effectively handle their mental and emotional behaviours as their aspirations. **Article 1. Scope of application** 1. This circular defines the objectives, implementation principles, content, methods and conditions for develop and implement school psychology counselling for upper secondary students (grade 10–12). 2. This circular is applied to students, school administrators, teachers, psychological counsellors, and other school staff members working at primary schools, lower secondary schools (grade 6–9), upper secondary schools (grade 10–12), continuing education settings, vocational schools, and other educational organisations.

(*Continued*)

(Continued)

ASCA National Model	Fundamental Framework for Vietnam School Counselling Model (VSCM)
ASCA Mindsets & Behaviours for Student Success: K–12 College- and Career-Readiness for Every Student **Professional Standards** ASCA Ethical Standards for School Counsellors ASCA School Counselor Professional Standards & Competencies.	**Article 2. Definitions** 1. School psychological consulting is a psychological assistance that helps students improve their personality, family context, social relationships for enhancing positive emotions, and decision-making skills to resolve challenges or difficulties during their learning at school. 2. School psychological counselling is the interaction, psychological assistance, intervention (when necessary) provided by the school staff and counselling teachers that helps students enhancing positive emotions, and self-esteem and decision-making skills to resolve challenges or difficulties in their learning, as well as problems in their social relationships and family circumstances. **Article 3. The objectives of school psychological counselling** 1. To prevent, assist and intervent (when necessary) psychological matters and learning difficulties for students through providing appropriate solutions to minimize negative impacts, fostering a safe, healthy, and caring learning environment to prevent school violence. 2. To help students improve their life-skills and enhance their will, beliefs, bravery, behaviour, social relationships, as well as physical and mental health in order to gain the best of personality and morale. **Article 8. School Counselling Workforce** 1. The school should have a Student Support & Counselling Team and arranges school staff and teachers (as additional duty) to help students with psychological matters. The Student Support & Counselling Team is led by a Team Leader – a representative of the school leadership team, and operated by team members who are school administrators, teachers with additional duty of psychological counselling, school clinic staff, communist youth specialists, representatives of students' parents committee, and some students who are class leaders or and communist youth's outstanding students.
Manage To be delivered effectively, the school counselling programme must be efficiently and effectively managed. The ASCA National Model provides school counsellors with the following programme focus and planning tools to guide the design and implementation of a school counselling programme that gets results. **Programme Focus** Beliefs Vision Statement Mission Statement	The Provincial Department of Education and Training should issue the guidance on school counselling to the lower and upper secondary schools, and vocational secondary schools within the region; the universities, colleges, vocational secondary schools under the administration of the ministries and agencies have not implemented school counselling can launch a pilot implementation phase and then formulate the counselling programme in the next phase. The schools have already implemented school consulting can assess the effectiveness for improvement based on this guidance.

2. School staff and teachers concurrently working as school counsellors should have experience or and to be trained in psychological counselling (professional psychology counselling certificates issued by the MoET). Teachers with additional duty of psychological counselling are entitled to a reduction in teaching period prescribed by the MoET.

Article 9. Facilities and Funding

1. The school arranges a separate psychological counselling room (for elementary schools, the counselling room can be arranged according to the size and conditions of the school) to ensure privacy, discreet, easily accessible and suitable for organizing consulting activities; equip necessary facilities, equipment, and learning materials to ensure the effectiveness of school counselling.
2. The funding for psychological counselling is utilized from the following sources:
   a) The school's regular expenditure sources;
   b) Financial aids from domestic and foreign organizations and individuals as prescribed by law;
   c) Other lawful revenue sources.
3. Funding for psychological counselling is managed and used for the right purposes and according to the regimes prescribed by law.

Article 10. The Accountability of the School and the Principal

1. Set up the Student Support and Counselling Team and formulate the functions, tasks, coordination mechanism as well as develop the implement plan and programme of school counselling.
2. Conduct surveys and build initial psychological data for first-grade students of each education level; classify, monitor, regularly update students' psychological characteristics and developments and psychological matters.
3. Prepare reports to the immediate superior management authorities periodically in each school year.

(Continued)

Programme Planning
School Data Summary
Annual Student Outcome Goals
Action Plans: Classroom and Group, Closing the Gap
Lesson Plans
Annual Administrative Conference
Use of Time
Calendars: Annual, Weekly
Advisory Council

ASCA National Model	Fundamental Framework for Vietnam School Counselling Model (VSCM)
(Continued)	**Article 11. The Accountability of the Provincial Department of Education and Training, and the District Office of Education and Training** 1. Lead and organize the implementation of this Circular at schools within the respective management authority. 2. Guide, inspect and supervise the psychological counselling at the schools within the respective management authority. 3. Do research and consult the People's Committees on relevant policies and regimes to support and motivate school staff and teachers with additional duty of counselling in accordance with local economic and society conditions. 4. Regularly organize professional training and development of school psychological counselling for school staff and teachers, contracted psychological counsellors, communist youth specialist, homeroom teachers and other school staff members additional duty of counselling in providing psychological counselling services for students. 5. Conduct preliminary reviews and prepare reports to the immediate superior management authorities periodically for each school year, and irregular reports on the implementation of this Circular in schools within the respective management authority.

Article 12. The Accountability of the MoET's Agencies

1. The Department of Political Education and Student Affairs shall assume the prime responsibility for, and coordinate with the respective schools and educational organisations in leading and advising the implementation, inspection and supervision of the implementation of this Circular to ensure the school counselling activities relevant to the national education and training for all students at all levels; conduct the preliminary and final reviews of psychological counselling effectiveness for upper secondary students (or high school, grade 10–12). Assume the prime responsibility for, and coordinate with the Department of Teachers and Education Administration Officers in leading and inspecting the professional development and the issuance of school psychological counselling certificates.
2. The Departments of Primary Education, Secondary Education, Continuing Education collaborate with the related authorities in advising the development of integrated curricular with school counselling contents in teaching mainstream subjects and extra-curricular activities as outlined in Circular and within the respective management authority.
3. The Department of Teachers and Education Administration Officers shall assume the prime responsibility and coordinate with the related authorities and agencies in elaborating professional training programmes for teachers who provide psychological counselling to students in schools.

Article 13. The Accountability of the Universities in Providing the Educational Psychology Course

1. Conduct surveys, develop educational plan and design curriculum of professional school psychological counselling to ensure effectively support local authorities and educational institutions in school psychological counselling needs.
2. Develop teaching and learning materials, organize professional training courses of school psychological counselling, and grant certificates of professional school counsellors for school staff and teachers who are qualified.

(*Continued*)

(Continued)

ASCA National Model	Fundamental Framework for Vietnam School Counselling Model (VSCM)
Deliver School counsellors deliver developmentally appropriate activities and services directly to students or indirectly for students as a result of the school counsellor's interaction with others. These activities and services help students develop the ASCA Mindsets & Behaviours for Student Success and improve their achievement, attendance and discipline. **Direct Student Services** Instruction Appraisal and Advisement Counselling **Indirect Student Services** Consultation Collaboration Referrals	**Section I. For Students at Secondary Schools (Grade 6–12)** The career guidance and social psychological counselling (or so called "consulting") are defined as "school counselling" provided for lower secondary students (grade 6–9) and upper secondary students (grade 10–12). The content of counselling (or consulting) should focus on the following matters: 1. Career guidance, career selection and admissions (enrolment) information, 2. Love, gender and relationship with the different gender friends, 3. Relations, communication, relationship with family members, teachers and friends, 4. Learning methods, 5. Social community activities, 6. Beauty, etc..... **Article 4. Implementation** 1. To ensure the highly collaborative coordination between the school staff and the involvement of the guardian/parents and external psychological counselling experts. 2. To ensure the right of students in school counselling: their participation, voluntariness, autonomy and self-determination, as well as the privacy right (confidential information) in psychological counselling activities as prescribed by law. **Article 5. School Counselling Programme** 1. Psychological counselling for age, gender, marriage, family, adolescent reproductive health suitable for ages. 2. Counselling, skills consultation, appropriate behaviours, preventing and combating violence and sexual abuse help building a safe, healthy and caring educational environment. 3. Counselling to improve the ability to cope with and solve problems that arise in family relationships, teachers, friends and other social relationships. 4. Consulting skills, effective learning methods and career orientation (depending on the level of education). 5. Psychological counselling for students in need of support through intervention and appropriate resolution. Introduce and support students to the external psychosocial counselling organisations and experts for cases of students with psychological disorders that cannot be resolved by the school counsellors.

Article 6. School Counselling Methods

1. Develop specific topics on psychological counselling for students and design as specific lessons or integrate into class activities and activities under flags solute event. Design integrated teaching of psychological counselling for students in formal subjects and experiential learning activities, and extra-curricular.
2. Organize seminars, extracurricular activities, clubs, forums on topics related to the counselling content based on students' needs of counselling.
3. Support parents with helpful materials, establish communication channel and regularly collaborate with parents about their children's psychological matters and necessary assistance.
4. Provide individual and group consultation and counselling services directly at school's facilities or and indirectly via intranet, school website, email, social networks, phones and other media virtually.
5. Collaborate with other external professional experts and organizations in organizing psychological counselling programmes for students.

Section II. For Students at Vocational Schools, Colleges, Universities

Consult the Principal about the implementation of the following counselling services:

1. Career guidance (by leaflets, advertisements or through job fairs) to help students understand their learning goals and be prepared their future careers.
2. Employment guidance during their enrolment at the school through facilitating regulations or instructions students' rights and obligations about part-time while studying.
3. Utilize the final week of last semester for job search counselling for students through providing the information of potential employers and job vacancies, and organizing job fairs, etc.
4. Counselling on social and psychosocial issues as outlined in the Section I.2, 3, 4, 5, 6 through organizing group counselling, regular group counselling talks with external experts to answer students' questions.
5. Schools should have a "Standing Counselling Team" provides regularly (or periodically) consulting to students who need help.

(Continued)

(Continued)

ASCA National Model	Fundamental Framework for Vietnam School Counselling Model (VSCM)
Access To achieve the best results for students, school counsellors regularly assess their programme to: determine its effectiveness inform improvements to their school counselling programme design and delivery show how students are different as a result of the school counselling programme. School counsellors also self-assess their own mindsets and behaviours to inform their professional development and annually participate in a school counsellor performance appraisal with a qualified administrator. The ASCA National Model provides the following tools to guide assessment and appraisal. **Programme Assessment** School Counselling Programme Assessment Annual Results Reports **School Counselor Assessment and Appraisal** ASCA School Counselor Professional Standards & Competencies Assessment School Counselor Performance Appraisal Template.	**Article 7. Collaboration in School Counselling** 1. Collaboration within schools School staff and teachers in charge of school psychological counselling closely coordinate with homeroom teachers, communist youth specialists, subject teachers and other personnel in schools in providing psychological counselling activities for students. 2. Collaboration with external school counselling experts and organizations a) Collaboration with parents: Regularly exchange information about their children; enhance the parents' knowledge of the characteristics of psychological development of age and the impact of such changes on their children; regularly pay attention, detect and provide timely assistance to the abnormal manifestations of their children. b) Collaboration with experts, professional psychological counselling and clinic centres, and judicial and legal protection agencies for psychotherapy treatment and deep intervention when necessary, c) Collaboration with external agencies and organizations in psychological education research, as well as the qualified schools of education and professional school counselling experts and scientists in providing professional development for teachers and psychosocial counsellors about knowledge and skills, appropriate attitude needed in professional consultation and psychological counselling in schools; d) Collaboration with communist youth specialists and other socio-political organizations in providing psychological counselling activities; e) Collaboration with other professionals and local authorities in organizing psychological counselling activities relevant to the school's educational objectives and the counselling needs of students.

9 Pioneering an Experiential Training Programme for Career Counsellors and Facilitators in Hong Kong

Design, Programme Development and Challenges

Queenie Lee, James Yu and Mark G. Harrison

The Career Education Landscape in Hong Kong – Past and Present

School-based counselling and guidance programmes have a relatively short history in Hong Kong. It was not until the beginning of the 1960s that specific guidance programmes commenced in Hong Kong schools and related supports such as school social work service were not available until the 1970s (Yuen et al., 2014, Yuen et al., 2018). Career education and life planning, which is one important component of school guidance and counselling, also had a late start. It was in 1958 that the first batch of career guidance masters and mistresses was appointed in Hong Kong, and the Hong Kong Association of Career Masters and Guidance Masters (HKACMGM) – a professional body composed of teachers who were taking up the role of career and/guidance personnel in schools – was established.

In the 1990s, the Education Bureau of the government of Hong Kong promulgated a Career and Life Planning Grant (CLP Grant) to support the enhancement of career counselling services and life education in schools. This policy is welcomed as many schools, especially public sector ones, did not have stable funding to hire teachers or guidance personnel to conduct career-related programmes for students before. In recent years, many schools are using this grant to hire regular teachers to provide career education and services to students and develop appropriate school-based resources to respond to the learning needs of students in the realm of career education and life planning.

Situated in these historical contexts, some career counsellors and facilitators working in secondary schools are teachers who possess different credentials related to career counselling in addition to their teacher qualifications. These positive changes and funding support has provided schools with more financial and human resources for designing and implementing suitable career guidance programmes and activities for students. However, the challenges faced by many schools and teachers in Hong Kong are that many frontline

DOI: 10.4324/9781003352457-9

teachers who are delivering career-related guidance programmes and services are still without adequate professional training. In this chapter, we attempt to describe some challenges in school counselling, particularly in the realm of career education and counselling, in Hong Kong. In addition, we aim to provide some ideas about professional training for teachers that can respond, at least in part, to the need for such training in career counselling for students.

Professional Training for Career Education and Life Planning in Hong Kong

As noted above, school counselling and career guidance in Hong Kong have been in place since the late 1950s when the government recognized the need to appoint career masters/mistresses in school to assist students in their career development and exploration. In the past five decades, several key providers have offered professional training for career guidance personnel in schools, notably the Education Bureau, tertiary institutions with teacher-training programmes, and charitable organizations such as the Hong Kong Jockey Club.

Playing a leading role in education policies and school operations in Hong Kong, the Education Bureau – formerly known as the *Education Department* in the 1980s and the *Education and Manpower Bureau* in the 1990s – has regularly offered training to teachers in career and life planning. Courses are offered at different levels such as basic level courses and certificate courses to meet the different training needs of the teachers. These courses are often contracted to local universities and faculty members with relevant expertise are assigned to conduct the training for the teachers.

Presently, four out of nine government-funded universities in Hong Kong have a faculty or department of education which offers teacher training programmes and, relatedly, school guidance and counselling certificate courses or postgraduate courses for teachers. However, teachers' exposure to the knowledge and skills specifically related to career counselling in these programmes are often limited with only one or two courses offered in this specialized area. Teachers who aspire to deepen their knowledge in career counselling must turn to other organizations for more information and resources (Ho, 2008, 2014; Yuen, 2006).

One example is the Hong Kong Association of Career Masters and Guidance Masters (HKACMGM) which has brought together educators with expertise in designing career exploration materials for school students and providing up-to-date information to different stakeholders, such as parents, teachers, and students, on matters related to further studies, job-search skills, and career development across the life-span. The HKACMGM also produces career-related materials such as occupation cards and self-understanding workbooks with relatively low cost which allows easy access for teachers to use these tools for supporting students. These well-designed resources are made available online by the Education Bureau on its official website for public access, showing the recognition of the endeavours by the local government (EDB, 2023).

Since 2015, the Hong Kong Jockey Club, as the largest charitable organization, has implemented a project called Career and Life Adventure Planning (CLAP) to assist adolescents in their exploration of personal interests, potentials, and career aspirations. As a joint venture with different universities in Hong Kong, the CLAP project has adopted a research-based design that informs its implementation and trajectory in programme development. During the first five years since the programme has been launched, the project has successfully engaged 30,000 young people and trained over 4,000 teachers and 1,800 social workers and school guidance personnel. In the long run, the project aims to benefit 160,000 youths with the vision that the younger generation would be able to achieve meaningful lives and make positive contributions to society (CLAP, 2023). The project is unprecedented in terms of the scope of service and breadth of influence. We await further research to investigate the specific positive outcomes and how, if possible, the model of implementation can be used in other countries and regions to help youngsters better explore and develop their career.

Professional Training Programme Provided by a Local Tertiary Institution

One of the universities in Hong Kong has devised and introduced a training programme to meet the market demands. Since 2014, the institution has started to offer professional training to school teachers, career or school counsellors, social workers, human resources personnel and people who aspire to become career facilitators. Starting from 2019, the Facilitating Career Development (FCD) programme has been launched to provide more extensive training in career counselling and facilitation. Graduates of the programme are expected to master the 12 core competencies set forth by the National Career Development Association (NCDA) in the States: (1) career development models and theories; (2) ethical and legal issues in career facilitation; (3) multicultural awareness and the ability to serve diverse populations; (4) appropriate use of assessment in career facilitation; (5) access to and dissemination of labour market information and resources; (6) helping skills; (7) consultation and supervision; (8) use of technology; (9) promotion and public relations; (10) programme management and implementation; (11) training clients and peers; and (12) employability skills (NCDA, 2009). These competencies are not only important for in-service career services provider but essential for teachers and social workers who are responsible to designing and implementing career programmes and services to students of different grade levels and developmental needs.

Sample Training Materials of the "Group Facilitation for Career Development" Module

The first author of this chapter has been involved in the training of career facilitators at the institution. Among the many modules offered in the career facilitation training, she has been primarily involved in using a group approach for career exploration and development. This is important as most counsellor education courses cover micro-skills in individual counselling and many counselling professionals have not been trained to use a group approach to conduct career counselling in private and school settings. Gladdings (2020) emphasizes that group counselling is a counselling speciality and that professional training ought to be offered to counsellors-in-training and also practising ones to benefit more clientele. To respond to this training need, the following section describes a module "Group Facilitation for Career Development" which was written and implemented by the first author to train novice career facilitators.

This eight-hour module (see Table 9.1) is designed on the premise that course participants would first learn as group members the relevant knowledge and skills which are then put into practice as they role-play the leader in a career exploration group. This is an experiential-learning approach in which participants learn about the processes, ethical considerations and dynamics of group work through direct experience in both the leader and member roles. The module is also designed with the principles of co-constructivism whereby participants play an active role in the learning process and benefit from the dialogue and collaboration with their peer learners in the construction of new knowledge (McMahon, 2017). Essentially, the learning process is grounded in direct experience and reflective dialogues.

The importance of ice-breaking activities. In the morning session, the course participants began with an ice-breaking activity starting with a brief self-introduction. Premised on Super et al.'s (1996) concept of "life roles", they were instructed to talk about their different life roles such as student, worker, and parent, with another participant who had similar experiences. This part of the session provided an opportunity for the participants to mingle with one another who were initially strangers. They reported feeling more relaxed while sitting in a round circle after the ice-breaking activity and much less isolated and insecure compared with the first minutes of the class.

Setting up ground rules. After the warm-up activities, the instructor divided the members into small groups of three and four and each group was asked to propose a few ground rules to be followed by all members in the training module. Then the participants were invited to think from the perspective of a group leader the following questions: (1) What is the importance of ground rules (2) What is the best timing to set up ground rules with the group? (3) Should the rules be set solely by the group leader or should the members be involved? (4) Should the age of the participants be considered when setting up the ground rules? (5) What should be done in response to violations of the rules? These questions are important for career counsellors and facilitators as ground rules protect the welfare of the group participants and the group leader (Gladdings, 2020; Yalom & Leszcz, 2005). The contemplation about the importance of ground rules and how they should be set offers career facilitators direct experience and reflection about this needed but often neglected procedure in group work.

Training Programme for Career Counsellors and Facilitators   169

Table 9.1 Outline of the Module "Group Facilitation for Career Development"

Duration	Activity	Rationale behind the Activity
Session One		
30 min	Ice-breaking activity (see Appendix A)	To warm up the participants and familiarize them to one another for the group processes that follow
30 min	Round-group self-introduction from the participants	To let each participants share a piece of themselves so the whole group can get to know one another
30 min	Setting ground rules with the participants and discussion about the importance of setting ground rules	Let participants experience what it is like to set ground rules as group members; then they think about the importance of such as a group leader in the future
30 min	"Self-thoughts Journal" (see Appendix B) and sharing in small groups	Participants answer questions in the "Self-thoughts Journal" to understand themselves more. Then sharing in a small group about their responses to the questions in the journal
60 min	Big group sharing of ideas from "Self-thoughts Journal"	Trainer demonstrates micro skills in group work to let participants experience the power and dynamics of a career facilitation group
30 min	Round-group sharing of learning and observations	Consolidation of learning in the first session
Session Two		
30 min	Introduction of stages of group development	Career facilitators get to know the four stages of group work
60 min	Career facilitators work in small groups to plan a career facilitation group for a specific target group by following the four stages of group development	Career facilitators apply the knowledge about group development to design a career exploration or career facilitation group
75 min	Presentations by individual groups	Each group shares the ideas in their design of the career facilitation group; each member role-plays being the group leader to demonstrate the skills in conducting a career facilitation group
30 min	Closure and summary of learning	Trainer summarises the key ideas in the module; participants share their takeaways from the eight-hour training module

Micro-skills in group work. As members became more familiarized with one another, the group proceeded to the "working stage" for which the module is intended (Corey et al., 2018). To prepare members for deeper personal reflection and sharing, a "Self-Thoughts Journal" adopted from Niles et al. (2011), was given to the participants. The participants were asked to record their own brief answers to a list of questions before sharing with a small group of three to four people. Then, the instructor invited all members to sit in a big circle and share their responses. It is during this time that the instructor demonstrated different micro-skills that are commonly used in a career exploration group such as active listening, reflection of feelings, paraphrasing, questioning, reframing, self-disclosure, and affirmation.

Putting theory into practice. The afternoon session began with an overview of "stages of group development" (Corey et al., 2018) and the course participants learned about the different stages of group development and common occurrences in each of the stages. This exercise was designed to familiarize them with the relevant stages of group work and the common obstacles and issues encountered by a group leader (e.g., the resistance of members in the transition stage and the sadness and/or anxiety of members in the termination stage).

Designing a career exploration/development group. The highlight of the training is when course participants worked in small groups to design a career exploration or development group. Focusing on the characteristics and needs of a target group of interest, they worked together to develop an appropriate career-related programme accordingly. Coming from diverse backgrounds like school teachers, social workers or human resources personnel, the participants came up with creative ideas for very specific target groups– for example, an exploration group for teenage mothers who need information and skills to enter the workforce, and a career development group for retiring professionals to find new interests and meaningful engagements in post-retirement life. Each group has to present ideas of the career exploration group at the end of their discussion.

Implications for Professional Training of Career Counsellors

The training detailed in the section above is an example of how participants from diverse backgrounds can be trained with a group approach to conduct career exploration and development. It represents a valuable training opportunity as most counsellors are more extensively trained to work with clients on an individual basis (Berg et al., 2018). Given that many in-service teachers and frontline social workers in Hong Kong have to conduct career exploration groups or personal growth workshops regularly with students, the demand for quality training is understandably high. The training offered represents a major endeavour to meet this demand.

The experiential-learning approach in the training module is based on the premise that in-depth learning of career counselling skills, ethical decision-making and group dynamics can be achieved by a combination of reflective activities and role-play exercises. On the other hand, the principles of co-constructivism underlying the training module is important for the training of career counsellors and facilitators in contemporary societies which are undergoing massive changes in the labour market as a result of mega-trends and forces such as automation of many types of work, the emergence and prevalence of artificial intelligence and metaverse in education and the world of work, and the challenges posed by unprecedented happenings such as COVID-19. The influence and implication of these mega-trends is that the meaning and purpose of work has changed for modern-day workers from traditional job-seekers who enjoy work stability over a life-span to slashers who may be hired on shorter-term work contracts and projects in the course of constructing a life of meaning and agency that is unique to each individual (Hartung et al., 2015; Savickas, 2012, 2019). Hence, the active involvement and reflection of the course participants in the module echoes the trending needs of the workers which include meaning-making, building a sense of personal agency, finding a career as a result of personal choice and life construction, and other issues which career facilitators have to deal with their clients (e.g., resolving conflicts in the workplace, transition between jobs, etc.).

Challenges in Career Education and Counselling in Hong Kong

This chapter attempts to fill the gap in career counsellors' training by presenting a module indigenous to Hong Kong. While the training programme could provide frontline teachers and counsellors with some professional training by using a group approach for career exploration, we still face a number of challenges in counselling in the school setting.

First, the provision of professional training for career teachers and counsellors is still lacking in Hong Kong. Even though the government offers training and seminars for frontline teachers in career education and life planning, there is clearly room for increasing the frequency of the training and the quota available for teachers. Relatedly, both digital and textual materials as well as financial resources to support students' career exploration are not meeting the market needs. Up to now, materials and resources related to career education of school students are mainly provided by HKACMGM which is not a statutory association funded by the government. It is an organization highly dependent on voluntary services and support from a few in-service principals and senior teachers. Another non-government organization (NGO) known for its dedication to adolescents' career exploration is St. James' Settlement, which has offered a number of career services and programmes to students in Hong Kong. On top of that, the organization has converted part of its headquarter for the development of the simulated working environment of different industries such as medical clinics, Chinese medicine centres, passenger airlines and arenas for e-sports. To extend these efforts in promoting career education and planning for students, it is recommended that the government consider providing long-term funding to these organizations and to establish an academy for career education.

Lastly, the issues concerning career education and life planning of primary school students and those in early childhood settings seem to be left unanswered. In 2021, the government introduced policies to promote the career education of upper primary school students. However, it was not explained how career exploration and education for younger students would be integrated into the whole-school approach (WSA) to school guidance and counselling. The WSA model, which has been increasingly adopted and implemented in Hong Kong Schools (Yuen et al., 2014), has four main components in its design, namely: (1) a guidance curriculum which covers students' personal, social, academic, and career development; (2) organization and planning of guidance activities; (3) development, management, and accountability of the guidance programmes; and (4) manpower and resources considerations. Although school guidance and counselling operated under the WSA is well-structured and promoted by the Education Bureau, frontline teachers and students had differing opinions as to how well the WSA to school guidance is followed and whether or not it is effective. For example, Hui (1998) found that some teachers did not perceive that the actual guidance programme was consistent to its intended emphasis on prevention which represents a shift from the remedial focus that has been in place for a long time. What is more concerning is that, whereas teachers believed they were helping students devise practical strategies to deal with academic and life issues, students did not share the same perception. On the contrary, students reported that guidance teachers were, to some extent, overlooking their emotional and behavioural problems.

This points to a concerning problem with school counselling in Hong Kong that has lasted for many decades, namely a mismatch of the services provided and the actual needs of the students. According to Hui (1998) and Yuen (2018), guidance teachers have spent a considerable amount of their time on handling more serious student cases that require one-on-one counselling. When it comes to career education, usually whole-school programmes which are intended to enhance students' life skills and personal development (e.g., emotional management, self-understanding, stress management, and financial management) are organized. However, there seems to be a lack of group counselling for students as most teachers are not equipped with the skills to conduct group sessions for students' career exploration and/or personal problems. Leung (2002) summarized some of these issues as follows:

> Due to the packed school curriculum, most secondary schools do not have the option of integrating career guidance materials into a formal guidance curriculum. Individually tailored career interventions such as career guidance groups and individual counselling were uncommon. ... most of the career guidance programmes focused narrowly on information dissemination (e.g., knowledge about educational opportunities and career) and very little on self-exploration. In addition, extensive effort was directed toward helping students to know about different educational opportunities and to assist students to complete their applications.

There was comparatively less effort directed toward helping students to know more about different career opportunities.

One of the reasons why individualized career guidance and counselling were "uncommon" is that school teachers are not appropriately trained to provide tailor-made developmentally sensitive interventions for students. The schools' expectation for teachers to do so is nonetheless very common, especially for homeroom teachers as the first person school children and adolescents may confide in with their problems. Yuen (2007a, 2007b) found that as many as 31% of class teachers and 15% of Life Education coordinators had not received any training in school guidance and counselling. Yuen and colleagues (2018) pointed to *"a pressing need for teachers, especially those who are in charge of student guidance work, to receive proper and adequate training in the theory and practices of school guidance and counselling"* (p. 288).

Conclusion

With the advent of the Information Age and the rapid changes in the global labour market, the Hong Kong government, like many governments around the globe, has recognized the need to provide more comprehensive career education and life planning services to support school children and adolescents facing a variety of work and life challenges in the 21st century. The CLP Grant as previously discussed represents a notable strategy adopted by the government, but there is certainly still a long way to go before the funding support and other interventions can meet the needs. As Ho (2016) asserts,

> the discussion on a policy level on how quality career guidance could be delivered has been lacking. Areas worth exploration and development include professional competence expected from career guidance teachers or practitioners, effective models of career interventions in line with student developmental and transition needs, outcomes of career guidance in students, and systemic issues of actualization of career guidance in school.
> (p. 217)

This chapter has shed some light on what has been done and achieved and what lies ahead. It is hoped that more school teachers and guidance personnel can receive proper training to deliver effective career services to help children and adolescents to manoeuvre and thrive in their life trajectories.

References

Berg, R. C., Landreth, G. L., & Fall, K. A. (2018). *Group counseling: Concepts and procedures* (6th ed). New York: Routledge.

CLAP. (2023, December 8). *About clap @ JC*. https://charities.hkjc.com/charities/english/charities-trust/trust-initiated-projects/clapor-youth-at-jc.aspx

Corey, M. S., Corey, G., & Corey, C. (2018). *Groups: Process and practice* (10th ed.). Boston, MA: Cengage Learning.

Education Bureau. (2023, December 9). *Finding your colors of life.* https://lifeplanning.edb.gov.hk/uploads/page/attachments/2010JISP_engSample.pdf

Gladding, S. T. (2020). *Groups: A counseling specialty* (8th ed.). New Jersey: Pearson.

Hartung, P. J., Savickas, M., & Walsh, W. B. (2015). *APA handbook of career intervention* (1st ed.). Washington, DC: American Psychological Association.

Ho, Y. F. (2008). Reflections on school career education in Hong Kong: Responses to Norman C. Gysbers, Darryl Takizo Yagi, and Sang Min Lee & Eunjoo Yang. *Asian Journal of Counselling, 15,* 81–103. https://citeseerx.ist.psu.edu/document?repid=rep1&type=pdf&doi=1602f1fa6682380f8b1d0b0b2619f63b11cefe1c

Ho, Y. F. (2014). Career education for all? A review of career education development in Hong Kong within the context of the new academic structure. *CAISE Review, 2,* 1–36. https://doi:10.12796/caise-review.2014V2.007

Ho, Y. F., & Leung, S. M. A. (2016). Career guidance in Hong Kong: From policy ideal to school practice. *The Career Development Quarterly, 64*(3), 216–230. https://doi.org/10.1002/cdq.12056

Hui, E. K. P. (1998). Guidance in Hong Kong schools: Students' and teachers' beliefs. *British Journal of Guidance & Counselling, 26*(3), 435–448. https://doi.org/10.1080/03069889808253854

Leung, S. A. (2002). Career counseling in Hong Kong: Meeting the social challenges. *The Career Development Quarterly, 50*(3), 237–245. https://doi.org/10.1002/j.2161-0045.2002.tb00899.x

McMahon, M. (2017). *Career counselling: Constructivist approaches* (2nd ed.). Oxon: Routledge.

National Career Development Association. (2009). *Career counseling competencies.* https://ncda.org/aws/NCDA/pt/sd/news_article/37798/_self/layout_ccmsearch/true

Niles, S. G., Norman E. A., & Roberta A. N. (2011). *Career flow: A hope-centered approach to career development.* Boston, MA: Pearson.

Savickas, M. L. (2012). Life design: A paradigm for career intervention in the 21st century. *Journal of Counseling and Development, 90*(1), 13–19. https://doi.org/10.1111/j.1556-6676.2012.00002.x

Savickas, M. L. (2019). *Career counseling* (2nd ed.). Washington, DC: American Psychological Association.

Super, D. E., Savickas, M. L & Super, C. M. (1996). The life-span, life-space approach to careers. In D. Brown, & L. Brooks (Eds.), *Career Choice and Development: Applying Contemporary Theories to Practice,* 121–178. San Francisco: Jossey-Bass.

Yalom, I. D., & Leszcz, M. (2005). *The theory and practice of group psychotherapy* (5th ed.). New York: Basic Books.

Yuen, M. (2006). School counselling in Hong Kong: History, policy, current implementation status, and future directions. In C. H. So (Ed.), *School Counselling and Career Guidance* (pp. 44–70). University of Macau, Faculty of Education.

Yuen, M. (2007a). Evaluating life skills development curriculum and activities. In P. S. Y. Lau, M. Yuen, R. M. C. Chan, T. K. M. Leung, E. K. P. Hui, P. M. K. Shea, & N. C. Gysbers (Eds.), *Life Skills Development and Comprehensive Guidance Programme: Assessment and Applications* (pp. 8–20). The University of Hong Kong, Faculty of Education Life Skills Development Project.

Yuen, M. (2007b). Assessing students' life skills development. In P. S. Y. Lau, M. Yuen, R. M. C. Chan, T. K. M. Leung, E. K. P. Hui, P. M. K. Shea, & N. C. Gysbers (Eds.), *Life Skills Development and Comprehensive Guidance Programme: Assessment and Applications* (pp. 21–39). The University of Hong Kong, Faculty of Education Life Skills Development Project.

Yuen, M., Gysbers, N. C., Chan, R. M. C., Lau, P. S. Y., & Shea, P. M. K. (2010). Talent development, work habits, and career exploration of Chinese middle-school adolescents: Development of the career and talent development self-efficacy scale. *High Ability Studies, 21*, 47–62. https://10.1080/13598139.2010.488089

Yuen, M., Leung, S. A., & Chan, R. T. (2014). Professional counseling in Hong Kong. *Journal of Counseling and Development, 92*, 99–103. https://doi.org/10.1002/j.1556-6676.2014.00135.x

Yuen, M., Yau, F., Tsui, J., Shao, S., Tsang, J., & Lee, B. (2018). Career education and vocational training in Hong Kong: Implications for school-based career counselling. *International Journal for the Advancement of Counselling, 41*, 449–467. https://doi.org/10.1007/s10447-018-9361-z

Appendix A
Ice-breaking Activity

Instructions:

1 Finish Part 1 First.
2 Then go around the classroom to find five people who has interesting answers to the five statements in the table.

Part 1: Something about myself	Part 2: Find someone who has interesting response(s) to the statements *(Please put down his/her name and brief info about the response)*
When I was a school student, the subject I liked best was _____.	
During my leisure time, I like to _____.	
I work in the _____ industry.	
At home, one household chore I enjoy doing is _____.	
If I can travel outside HK, I would like to go to _____.	

Notes: The ice-breaking activity is written according to the concepts in Donald Super's life space/life role theory of career development which is covered in the preceding modules in the CDF training.

Appendix B
Self-Thoughts Journal

To gain clarity in your inner conversations, start maintaining a daily journal. Try to record at least a few thoughts each day. Begin right now by recording a few words for each of these questions:

1 In what ways do you encourage yourself?

    _____

2 In what ways do you discourage yourself?

    _____

3 What positive statements do you make about yourself?

    _____

4 Conversely, what negative statements do you tell yourself?

    _____

5 In what ways do you feel you do not measure up?

    _____

6 What are your strengths?

    _____

7 What would someone who loves you say are your strengths?

    _____

8 Where do you find enjoyment in your activities?

_____

9 What sort of activities do you prefer to avoid?

_____

10 What do you hope for in your life?

_____

11 What do you fear?

_____

From Niles, S., Amundson, N., & Neault, R. (2011). *Career flow: A hope-centered approach to career development* (pp. 6–7). Boston: Pearson.

10 The Development of Career Education and Counselling in Mainland China

A Brief Overview

Houming Jiang, Queenie Lee and Mantak Yuen

Introduction

The term *career education* has two different translations in Chinese – *zhiye jiaoyu* (职业教育) which is translated as *vocational education* and *shengya jiaoyu* (生涯教育) which is translated as *life education*. The first meaning is associated more with preparing students for an occupation, while the latter is associated more with lifelong learning.

In 2019, the then Premier of China, Li Keqiang, announced that the central government would spend 100 billion RMB to strengthen employees' career skills to improve their adaptability for job transfers (State Council, 2019). This immediately caused unprecedented attention to the provision of career education in schools and vocational colleges in China. Many changes were found in the 2021 Catalogue of Majors for vocational training (Ministry of Education, 2021). While some majors had been merged to form new ones, some brand-new majors had been added as well. For example, in secondary vocational schools, nuclear chemistry and chemical engineering were cancelled while emergent rescue technology was added. On the other hand, electro-mechanical technology and application was merged with electrical operation and control. Most of these adjustments were made because of changes in the global trends and the local job market.

Prior to these changes in course offerings, vocational schools had experienced a decline in popularity among students and their parents because university degrees, rather than vocational training, are now regarded as essential for a prosperous career for young people. In Mainland China there had been a rapid increase of the higher education sector since the late 1990s while enrolment in vocational schools have declined. At the same time, in non-vocational secondary schools there was a lack of effective career education and guidance programmes, so students were often confused about their future career path and the selection of appropriate high school subjects and their later college majors (Luo, 2019).

To seek a better understanding of how career education has developed and the future implications for career education for China, this chapter reviews relevant policy changes for vocational colleges and non-vocational high schools in Mainland China. It is hoped that readers can get a glimpse of the development of policies in the realm of career education in the past 30 years in China.

Different Types of High Schools in Mainland China and Their Role in Career Education

There are significant differences between vocational schools and non-vocational schools in China and between high schools and colleges. The Chinese term *zhongxue* (中学) is equivalent to secondary school in English and it includes junior high (初中) and high school (高中). The Chinese words for high school *gaozhong* (高中) is short for *gaojizhongxue* (高级中学) (senior secondary school) and includes vocational schools with the key role of job preparation and regular high schools for *gaokao*, a country-wide public examination system for admission to universities in China. Included in this senior-secondary-school category are *internationalized schools* for students who plan to pursue baccalaureate programs overseas.

It is interesting to note that internationalized schools in China are not the same as typical international schools that admit foreign students who hold foreign passports. Internationalized schools usually admit ethnically Chinese students who are mainly local passport holders but intend to study in other countries upon their graduation. In this chapter, only internationalized schools that follow China's policies for education will be reviewed and discussed because of the school management experience of the first author. The focus of the paper is on career education and counselling during the high school period in such internationalized schools. The high school years and experience are important because middle adolescence is a prime time when youngsters develop different competencies that prepare them for transitions to college and later work life.

Historical Development of Career Education in Mainland China

Regarding the term *career*, the everyday Chinese translation would be *zhiye* which in most cases refers to vocation (work) while the Chinese words *shengya* carries a broader connotation of career and meaning or purpose in life. According to Cihai which is a classic Chinese dictionary, *zhiye* means "the property, content and pattern of a job through which someone makes a living" (2015, p. 620). Wu (1997) considered *shengya* as a concept of living style, including all activities one does in his or her life. Similarly, Tian (2015) described *shengya* as embodying the life development of an individual as well as the range of jobs he or she may have. In short, Chinese scholars consider the words *shengya* as carrying a broader meaning than *zhiye* which is like how Western scholars conceptualize the terms (e.g., Hall, 1986; Super, 1957).

Closely related to the above, the term *career education* has two different Chinese translations – *zhiye jiaoyu* (*career education* in English) and *shengya jiaoyu* (*life education* in English). In published articles and academic papers in Mainland China, *zhiye jiaoyu* (career education) is more frequently used in the context of vocational schools while *shengya jiaoyu* (life education) is used more frequently in the context of regular high schools including *gaokao* and internationalized schools.

In Mainland China, most government documents have focused on *zhiye jiaoyu* because it had a much earlier start than *shengya jiaoyu* due to the economic needs since the 1980s. The Chinese Ministry of Education has not published policies or papers on *shengya jiaoyu*. However, some documents published by provincial educational authorities have included coverage of career planning that addresses self-exploration, decision-making, self-management skills, and other skill sets required in social and work life after students have left the school. For example, in Henan province, high-school career education should help students understand the importance of planning on one's life, the notion of proactive self-development, and the value of establishing positive beliefs and a responsible attitude towards one's life (Fang et al, 2020).

The Development of Career Education Policies in Mainland China

In order to examine recent advances in career education, this review will mostly cover developments in the field after the Chinese Economic Reform in 1978 although it is important to describe practices that were in place before this time. Prior to the establishment of the People's Republic of China in 1949, apprenticeships played the main role in career development for young people in China (He et al., 2019). Organizations like the China Vocational Education Association (CVEA) made contributions to the field of career education in the early 19th century, focusing on "practical efficiency" as opposed to the outdated "formal education system" that had little relationship with real-world employment (Gewurtz, 1978; Schulte, 2013).

In 1980, the *Report on Reform of Secondary Education Structure* was published by the Ministry of Education and the National Labour Bureau. This reform facilitated the development of new vocational schools and those converted from former regular high schools (He, 2009). At that time, the need for gaining employment after high school or middle school weighed more for most Chinese families than pursuing a university degree because children are expected to enter job market earlier to earn a living. However, it wasn't long before university education gained in popularity and university admission rate rose from below 10% in 1980 to above 70% after 2010 as the country underwent rapid economic and social changes (Zhang, 2017).

The concept of career guidance and its importance in regular high school was first introduced in a national newspaper article (Zhang, 1984). This was seen as the beginning of career education in China because that year heralded the first curriculum framework, teaching pedagogy, and teacher training in the field of career education. The first and second National Conferences on Career Guidance and Counseling were held in Shanghai in 1987 and 1990 respectively (Zhang et al, 2002). Several experts in career education from the United States came to China in 1993 and presented at a conference organized by Beijing Normal University and the State Labour Department (Hu, Krumboltz & Hansen, 1997). The speakers also included high-school career counsellors as well as researchers. This can be seen as the first step in international communication and cooperation in the field of career education which is still going on to this date.

At around the same time, the Ministry of Education formally added career education to the secondary school curriculum (Zhang, 1998). Also, at the beginning of 1990s a series of textbooks on careers and career planning were published by Zhejiang Education Press (Jin, 1991; Shen, 1991; Wen, 1990). These books greatly enriched the resources and ideas in this emerging field. Step by step, the field of career education was developed by the adoption of new textbooks and materials with the good support from provincial government and input from local and international experts.

Another milestone for career education in China was the Career Education Law which was enacted in 1996. The purpose of the Law was to implement the strategy of developing the country through science and education, advancing career education, improving the competence of workforce and facilitating socialist modernization (State Council, 1996). With career education specifically mentioned as a core component of the strategy, the Law served as a tool to establish the right of civilians to receive career education. Clause 16 mentioned that "regular high schools should start career-related courses grounded in the local context or add additional content based on practical needs". With legal endorsement from the Central Government, an ever-increasing number of relevant courses emerged in the country.

Influence from the Progressive Education Movement

In contrast with traditional education, *Progressive Education* in China focuses more on attending to the whole child, community, collaboration, social justice, intrinsic motivation, deep understanding, active learning, and lifelong learning (Kohn, 2015). It is hard to establish a watershed between "traditional education" and "progressive education" in China but John Dewey's visit in China in 1919 could be a marker. The Progressive Education Movement has emphasized liberation in terms of racial and social equality which finds its root in the United States (Garte, 2017). In essence, progressive education is associated with the pedagogy advocated by Locke and Rousseau and later spread in China by Dewey (Guo, 2019). Published in the *School Journal* in 1897, Dewey elaborated on progressive education in five aspects: (1) what education is; (2) what school is; (3) the subject matter of education; (4) the nature of method; and (5) the school and social progress (Dewey, 1897, pp. 77–80). In contrast to lecture-based school system that aims to produce workers for the modern industrial way of life, Dewey's approach was more student-centred, active, and engaging, where student participation should be valued and promoted. Education was to be regarded as the process of living now, not as a passive preparation for future living. Since Dewey visited China in 1919, this can be considered an important paradigm shift in China as to what modern-time education and career education could mean. This is quite a stark contrast with the conception of such that has been in place for hundreds or even thousands of years in the country.

In terms of effective pedagogy in career education in China, Jiang (2017) proposed action-oriented teaching that follows a sequence of the following: providing information, facilitating planning, making decisions, taking action, evaluation, and assessment. This system is based on similar practices in the German education system in which knowledge is not simply input from outside but formed through students' own endeavours. The approach shares similarities with methods that are often regarded as part of the progressive education movement and place students at the centre of learning based on what Dewey has preached (Cremin, 1959).

In terms of curriculum design, according to a teacher's handbook on career education *Career Education Teacher's Teaching Handbook* (Zhao & Bai, 2013), the chapter on the topic introduced the concepts of competency-based education (CBE), competency-based teaching (CBT) and developing a curriculum process (DACUM). In fact, the concept of competency-based education and teaching was introduced in the 1960s in the U.S. (Burke, 1989) and views learning as the mastering a series of skills rather than merely acquiring content knowledge. Using competency as the criterion for career-related curriculum design ensures that teaching focuses on what is most practical and grounded in real employment contexts. DACUM differentiates itself from other methodologies because it respects the needs of employers rather than the assumptions by education "experts" (Norton, 1997). The suggested use of CBE, CBT and DACUM demonstrates international influence in career education in Mainland China.

Another facet of progressive education is the notion of *lifelong learning and education*. This theme emerged after the enactment of the *Education Law of People's Republic of China* (1995). Clause 11 in the Law mentioned the need for the refinement of lifelong education system. However, career education was not fully established until 2010 when the *Action plan of 21st Century Education Revitalization* was proposed (He et al., 2019). Since that time, career education has become an indispensable part of lifelong education and it is one of the objectives of economic and social development in modern China.

Career-Related Resources Offered by Internationalized School in Mainland China

Different from international schools that mostly serve foreign passport holders, internationalized schools mainly cater to the educational needs of Chinese passport holders. Both international schools and internationalized schools charge high tuition, and their target customers are upper middle class and upper-class families. What differentiates internationalized schools from international school nowadays is the focus on Chinese roots in addition to global horizon, represented by more emphasis on Chinese language arts and culture.

As time passes, career education models and textbooks for regular *gaokao* high schools serve as important resources for the relatively new internationalized schools. Founded in 1993, the Shanghai Graduates Vocational Guidance Centre (SGVGC) has regularly disseminated information about employment for college graduates and founded the newspaper *Employment Reports* together with an annual magazine entitled *Career Information: for Gradu*ates and a new website http://www.firstjob.com.cn/ (Zhou et al., 2016). The Center has been serving as a platform to connect resources outside and inside school campuses. Though mostly catering to the needs of college-level students, the work of SGVGC has also provided important ideas and resources for secondary school career education.

The content of the textbook *Teaching and Design of Secondary Students' Career Planning* (Zhang, 2012) included students' personal characteristics, values, interests, exploration of different occupations through fieldwork and internet search, learning about successful people's career path, understanding current employment market, making career plans, cultivating key attributes such as confidence, responsibility, reliability, perseverance, positive mindset, and communication skills, etc. Additional chapters are provided on topics such as time management, critical thinking, and cooperative skills. Different assessment models and resources including lesson plans are provided for the teaching staff. In sum, curriculum and pedagogy of career education in China has become more systematic and institutionalized over the years as a result of the concerted effort from the government, academia, and frontline teachers and career-related personnel who work in schools.

Theory-Based Practices in Career Education in Mainland China

Another textbook in Chinese, *Facing the Future with Ease: High School Career Education Theory and Practice* (Jia, 2019), referred to Holland's Personality-Job Fit Theory where the author developed six modules for career guidance and counselling programmes in Minxing District, Shanghai. The six modules covered the following: (1) My high school; (2) I am who I am; (3) Self-management; (4) Career exploration; (5) College major exploration; and (6) Career portfolios. The publication reflects an increasing awareness of the range of topics that are important in career education beyond simply helping youngsters to find suitable courses and jobs.

Another important publication is *For the Well-being in Life: Secondary Students Career Development Education Research and Practice* (Pan, 2020), which addresses the ground practices of career education in the context of public schools in Minxing District in Shanghai. The general philosophy underpinning the design of these career education books is influenced by a student-cantered approach and an inquiry-based way of learning. The author of the book, Beilei Pan (2020), was also a deputy head of Qibao Secondary School in Shanghai. She pointed out that domestic research on career education in mainland China has focused too heavily on theory while the urgent need is for practice-informed action research that can guide educators to implement effective strategies. She also criticized typical career education in China because it had focused mainly on classroom activities and paid too little attention to the establishment of an overarching curriculum framework that guides career education on a broader level.

To give an example of how career education had developed in China, Qibao School in the city of Shanghai can serve as one example. According to Pan (2020), Qibao School combined a tutorial system with college-major academic advising using Holland's assessment tools co-developed by the school and Shanghai Jiao Tong University. The tutorial system, which involves small-group academic sessions as a method of teaching in addition to lectures, was influenced by a much earlier model used in England by the University of Oxford and the University of Cambridge (West, 1906). The Qibao school tutorial system has been endorsed in the government document *National Mid- and Long-term Education Reform and Development Planning Summary* (2010–2020) which advises schools to create a student-development-and-guidance system that can strengthen students' career aspirations (State Council, 2010). *OH cards* as another tool are playing cards used as prompts for story–telling, guidance counselling, educational aids, and other social interactive activities that can be used in schools, homes, clinics and corporate training centres as a tool for training and coaching self-discovery (Moore, 1999). Xingzhi School in Shanghai has used the OH cards to design a career exploration lesson to explore students' career interest and enhance their engagement in classrooms (Zhao & Bai, 2013).

Cases in the aforementioned schools provide examples of how to design and implement career education in local contexts, especially ways to integrate career guidance into the established national Chinese curriculum framework and how to adapt and utilize international resources in a local community context. This is not typical in China because schools are usually not expected to innovate beyond the established curriculum in the public education system so the above are deemed quite innovative strategies in career education and guidance.

Career assessment tools based on technology platforms have also been utilized in high schools to give more accurate recommendation and guideline to students. For example, in the city of Shanghai, Fudan University Affiliated High School used POLAR (Potential Occupational Assessment Rubric); Hongkou High School used DPA (Dynamics Personality Assessment); and Shanghai No. 2 Industrial University Affiliated Gonglu High School used a Career Development Education Platform (Shen, 2019). COMET (Competence Measurement) developed by University Bremen (similar to PISA used for assessment by OECD) has been used in China and is mentioned in Zhao and Bai's 2013 handbook which details the curriculum, pedagogy, and assessment tools of career education in Chinese context after taking lessons from practices in Germany.

Funding for Career Education in Mainland China

After the end of Cultural Revolution and the start of Economic Reform in 1978, private capital from non-public sectors was used to fund private vocational schools. For example, the first private college in China, Hunan Jiuyi Technical College, was founded by scientist Le Tianyu (Yongzhou Highlight, 2022). The *Report on Reform of Secondary Education Structure* issued in 1980 allowed for the establishment of vocational schools by private entities and persons in addition to public proprietorship. After five years, the government document *Central Committee's Decision on Education System Reform* not only gave permission to start schools using private capital but also allowed schools to raise money by themselves for educational purposes (State Council, 1980b). These two documents were influential and served as catalysts for career education in vocational schools in China. The introduction of private capital in career education was indicated in the *China Education Reform and Development Outline* (State Council, 1993) which states that vocational technical education and adult education mainly rely on industry, enterprises, public institutions and all aspects of the society. It was supplemented by State Council's *China Education Reform and Development Outline: Suggestions on Implementation* (1994) which stated that "vocational education and adult education should cater to social needs and be provided under the supervision of the government. All constituents of society are encouraged to do this".

In the Career Education Law of 1996, it was also mentioned that "The country encourages multiple legal ways to raise funds for career education" (State Council, 1996). The introduction of private capital greatly stimulated the market for career education and created opportunities for relevant courses and programmes to flourish. However, like a double-edged sword, private capital also caused issues in the educational purposes and ownership structures of vocational schools. As a result of these, more stringent regulations were implemented afterwards to govern the aims, missions, and profitability of these schools.

Talent Development in Vocational Schools

Another important component in career education in Mainland China is to assist students to identify their strengths and develop their talents. Talent development in career education in China is seen as developing in three phases: (1) the combination of industry and teaching (产教结合); (2) the combination of industry and learning/the combination of school and enterprise (工学结合/校企结合); and (3) the merging of industry and teaching (产教融合) (He et al, 2019). The shift of focus from the general industry to specific companies marks the main difference between first and second phases. Also, the different wording from using "combination" to "merging" implies a deeper level of cooperation between the school and various industries.

Regarding the development of the three phases, the first phase started from Deng Xiaoping's speech at the National Education Work Conference in 1978 when he pointed out that "in order to cultivate qualified talents needed for socialist development, we have to carefully research how to implement the principle of combining education and production under the new social circumstances" (Deng, 1994). During the period from the 1980s to 1990s, individual entrepreneurs started school and industry at the same time and developed career-related courses in regular schools.

The second phase, which is between 2000 and 2010, leaned towards rural areas and was marked by the government document *The Decision on Further Strengthening Rural Education*, which advocated for the advancement of career education in rural schools (State Council, 2003). "Order-like Talent Development Mode" (订单式人才培养), which refers to schools cultivating talents by following the demand of the enterprises, was mentioned and promoted in *The Opinions on Further Strengthening Career Education by Ministry of Education and Other Six Ministries* (State Council, 2004).

During the third phase, which is after 2010, *Internet Plus* was a keyword and college graduates were encouraged to create startups by themselves. *Internet Plus* is a strategy and concept proposed by the then premier Li Keqiang in his Government Work Report so that China can keep pace with the worldwide Information Age (Post, 2015). It emphasizes the application of internet and other forms of information technology in traditional industries such as automobile manufacturing and agriculture. The term *Internet Plus* then expanded its meaning when other forms of internets (e.g., cloud networking, mobile Internet, Internet of Things, big data, etc.) were added to particular industries to foster new business development and opportunities in China (Daily, 2015). The changes in phases of talent development modes indicate the importance of adjusting career education based on market needs and changing economy.

Career Education and Choosing a College Major in Mainland China

Similar to the talent-development mode in vocational schools, choosing a college major is equally important for students of the *gaokao* track. In 2014, the *gaokao* reform was introduced based on the *Opinions of the State Council on the Implementation of Deepening the Reform of Examination and Enrolment System* (State Council, 2014). The reform was piloted in Shanghai City and Zhejiang Province, and it was stipulated that the two traditional tracks of STEM and humanities should switch to a new mode – "select three out of six" – which means Chinese language and literature, Mathematics and English are the three mandatory *gaokao* subjects for all students while at the same time, students need to choose three from the following six subjects: physics, chemistry, biology, history, geography, and politics. This is quite a big change because in the old *gaokao* system, all STEM-track students took physics, chemistry and biology while all humanities-track students took history, geography and politics. On the one hand, the new policy allows for more flexibility in the choices of subjects compared with original system; on the other hand, the complexity caused by the new system with more than 20 different combinations of choices creates new challenges for school timetabling and staffing matters. In addition, college admission usually requires certain *gaokao* subjects for specific programmes (e.g., biology and chemistry are prerequisites for medical school students) and this requirement varies among different college majors. With the advent of the *gaokao* reform, students need to know what they should study at least two years prior to their college admission. As a result, the decision on the college major makes it more necessary for regular high-school students to explore their career interest much earlier on than the previous generations. To prepare students for choosing the right subjects in *gaokao* and later their college major, different resources and books have been published in Mainland China. In the textbook written by Fang et al. (2020), a chapter is dedicated to the introduction of different combinations of *gaokao* subjects and their impact on choosing college majors across different provinces in China. This is followed by the introduction of different universities in China which includes the various academic departments and their relevance to career opportunities in the future which are deemed important information for students, teachers and school counsellors in Mainland China.

Further to the changes described above, the *National Career Education Reform Plan on Career Education* requires that the "Career Education Catalogue" (职业教育专业目录) be modified every five years. This arrangement matches the five-year economic development plan of the central government. It is noteworthy that in March 2021, the Ministry of Education published a new version of the *Catalogue of Majors in Career Education* for vocational schools that offer bachelor's degrees and associate degrees, as well as secondary vocational schools that offer high school diploma (Ministry of Education, 2021). Compared with elite universities, these vocational schools accept a lower entry score on exams but provide the same level of degrees and diplomas to students. In the latest version, hundreds of majors have been changed as new majors are added, old ones deleted, while some other majors merged or split.

As a result of these changes, the catalogue for secondary vocational schools has 225 majors adjusted, accounting for 61.1% of the total. Moreover, in the catalogue two levels of majors were changed to three levels with more specific categorization. For example, under the first level *energy power and materials*, there is second level *electronic technology*, which includes third level majors like *power plant operations and maintenance, hydropower station installation and operations*, etc. To cite another example, the kindergarten-teaching major was removed but schools are encouraged to add the kindergarten-childcare-worker major because it is more likely that graduates would be able to obtain a childcare worker position rather than a teaching position (usually teaching positions require a bachelor's degree). The purpose of these changes is to cater to the needs of the employment market, changing macro-economic structures, international relations that are getting more intense, and the need for lifelong learning of the citizens so that they can catch up with what the 21st-century labour force requires. With the lifting of restrictions in the post-COVID era, more changes are to be envisaged based on the societal needs of the new normal.

Implications for Career-Education Practice and Research in China

Career education in China has a late start when compared with her Western counterparts; nonetheless, it has developed quite rapidly over the past few decades. It would be fair to say career education in Mainland China has been an arduous journey alongside the economic reforms in the country.

To facilitate further development of career education in China, policy makers and educators need to consider the needs of the local culture when they adapt theoretical frameworks, practices, and resources from Western countries. This is especially important when frameworks and practices in the fields of science and engineering are transferred to the Chinese context as there could be unique economic and societal factors that are quite different from those in the West.

As can be seen in this paper, most extant government documents and literature on career education are about vocational schools and *gaokao*-track high schools. In the future, career education in private internationalized schools should also be the focus of study and research due to the rapid growth of such institutions in China. There is much to learn from studying the interesting differences between internationalized schools and traditional vocational and gaokao-track schools in terms of structure, policies and school practices.

It should be noted that past and existing policies directing career education in China have created room for development and constraints. The constraints can be seen in the current requirement of instructional hours for Grades one to nine students. For example, Grade 1 students are required to receive at least 208-minute Chinese-language-arts instruction and 135-minute Maths instruction per week. However, how schools can allocate extra hours for career education is not detailed in the government policies. Another challenge is how Western theories in career counselling and education can be applied to the Chinese contexts such that good practices from the West can be blended to the existing curriculum that allows indigenous career education to bloom and develop in the local Chinese context. Considering the historical development of career education and counselling detailed in this paper, it will remain a great challenge and a good opportunity to link *shengya jiaoyu* (life education) and *zhiye jiaoyu* (career education) in meaningful ways so that students and adults can be helped and inspired to become life-long workers and learners which is necessary to survive and thrive in the 21st century.

References

Burke, J. W. (Ed.). (1989). *Competency based education and training*. London: Routledge. https://doi.org/10.4324/9780203974261

Cihai Editorial Board. (2015). [Original in Chinese]. https://www.cihaidaquan.com/

Cremin, L. A. (1959). John Dewey and the progressive-education movement, 1915–1952. *The School Review, 67*(2), 160–173. https://doi.org/10.1086/442489

Daily, C. (2015). *Internet plus: China's official strategy for the uberisation of the economy*. http://hdl.handle.net/20.500.11937/50534

Deng, X. (1994). *Selected works of Deng Xiaoping*, vol. 2, p.107. Beijing: People's Press.

Dewey, J. (1897). My pedagogical creed. *School Journal, 54*, 77–80. http://dewey.pragmatism.org/creed.htm.

Fang, X., Zhang, M. & Zhang, W. (2020). *High school students' career planning's theory and practice*. Beijing: Science Press.

Garte, R. (2017). American progressive education and the schooling of poor children: A brief history of a philosophy in practice. *International Journal of Progressive Education, 13*(2), 7–17.

Gewurtz, M. S. (1978). Social reality and educational reform: The case of the Chinese Vocational Education Association 1917–1927. *Modern China, 4*(2), 157–180. https://doi.org/10.1177/009770047800400202

Guo, F. (2019). Dewey's China visit: One hundred years of educational thought [Original in Chinese]. *Educational Research, 4*, 28–33.

Hall, D. (Ed). (1986). *Career development in organizations*. Jossey-Bass. https://doi.org/10.1002/hrm.3930260214

He, Z. (2009). Thirty year overview of China's career education policy [Original in Chinese]. *Education Development Research*, 2009(3), 32–37.

He, Z., Liu, Y., & Wei, M. (2019). *China education reform and opening-up 40 years* [Original in Chinese]. Beijing Normal University Publishing Group.

Hu, X., Krumboltz, J., & Hansen, S. (1997). The status of career counseling in the People's Republic of China. *Career Planning and Adult Development Journal, 13*(2), 13–18.

Jia, Y. (2019). *Facing the future with ease – high school career education theory and practice* [Original in Chinese]. East China Normal University Press.

Jiang, D. (2017). *The gist of career education*. Beijing Normal University Publishing Group.

Jin, Y. (1991). *Career guidance in secondary schools* (textbook for guidance teachers) [Originals in Chinese]. Zhejiang Education Press.

Kohn, A. (2015). Progressive Education: Why it's Hard to Beat, but also Hard to Find. Bank Street College of Education. http://educate.bankstreet.edu/progressive/2

Luo, Y. (2019). Career education exploration and analysis of secondary schools under the new gaokao background [Original in Chinese]. *Secondary and Elementary School Mental Health Education, 17*, 24–26.

Ministry of Education. (2021). *Ministry of education's notice on 2021 version of catalogue of majors in career education* [Original in Chinese]. http://www.moe.gov.cn/srcsite/A07/moe_953/202103/t20210319_521135.html

Moore, J. (1999). OH cards – a game of inner vision. Positive Health Online. http://www.positivehealth.com/article/psychospiritual/oh-cards-the-game-of-inner-vision

Norton, R. E. (1997). *DACUM handbook*. Leadership Training Series No. 67.

Pan, B. (2020). *For the wellbeing in life – secondary students career development education research and practice* [Original in Chinese]. Shanghai Educational Publishing House.

South China Morning Post. (2015, March 5). China unveils targets for 2015: Li Keqiang's speech as it happened. https://www.scmp.com/news/china/article/1729846/live-li-keqiang-unveils-chinas-annual-work-report?campaign=1729846&module=perpetual_scroll_0&pgtype=article

Schulte, B. (2013). Unwelcome stranger to the system: Vocational education in early twentieth-century China. *Comparative Education, 49*(2), 226–241. https://doi.org/10.1080/03050068.2012.713581

Shen, Z. (1991). *Careers guidance in foreign countries* [Original in Chinese]. Zhejiang, China: Zhejiang Education Press.

Shen, Z. (2019). *Ignite the dream in mind – Shanghai high school career education cases* [Original in Chinese]. East China Normal University Press.

State Council (1980a). *Report on reform of secondary education structure* [Original in Chinese]. http://www.gov.cn/gongbao/shuju/1980/gwyb198016.pdf

State Council (1980b). *CPC's central committee's decision on education system reform* [Original in Chinese]. https://baike.baidu.com/item/%E4%B8%AD%E5%85%B1%E4%B8%AD%E5%A4%AE%E5%85%B3%E4%BA%8E%E6%95%99%E8%82%B2%E4%BD%93%E5%88%B6%E6%94%B9%E9%9D%A9%E7%9A%84%E5%86%B3%E5%AE%9A

State Council (1993). *China education reform and development outline* [Original in Chinese]. https://baike.baidu.com/item/%E4%B8%AD%E5%9B%BD%E6%95%99%E8%82%B2%E6%94%B9%E9%9D%A9%E5%92%8C%E5%8F%91%E5%B1%95%E7%BA%B2%E8%A6%81

State Council (1996). *Career education law* [Original in Chinese]. https://baike.baidu.com/item/%E4%B8%AD%E5%8D%8E%E4%BA%BA%E6%B0%91%E5%85%B1%E5%92%8C%E5%9B%BD%E8%81%8C%E4%B8%9A%E6%95%99%E8%82%B2%E6%B3%95

State Council (2003). *The decision on further strengthening rural education* [Original in Chinese]. http://www.gov.cn/gongbao/content/2003/content_62440.htm

State Council (2004). *The opinions on further strengthening career education by ministry of education and other six ministries* [Original in Chinese]. http://www.moe.gov.cn/srcsite/A07/moe_737/s3876_qt/200409/t20040914_181883.html

State Council (2010). *National mid- and long-term education reform and development planning summary* [Original in Chinese]. http://www.gov.cn/jrzg/2010-07/29/content_1667143.htm

State Council (2014). *Opinions on deepening examination and admission system* [Original in Chinese]. http://www.gov.cn/zhengce/content/2014-09/04/content_9065.htm

State Council (2019a). *National career education reform plan on career education* [Original in Chinese]. http://www.gov.cn/zhengce/content/2019-02/13/content_5365341.htm

State Council (2019b). *Li Keqiang: We will spend 100 billion yuan to train workers for career skills and job transfer* [Original in Chinese]. http://www.china.com.cn/lianghui/news/2019-03/05/content_74533602.shtml

Super, D. E. (1957). *The psychology of careers; An introduction to vocational development*. Harper & Bros.

Tian, X. (2015). *Career counseling and guidance: Theory and practice*. Xuefu Culture.

Wen, Y. (1990). *Career guidance in secondary schools* (textbook for pupils) [Original in Chinese]. Zhejiang Education Press.

West, A. F. (1906). The tutorial system in college. *The School Review, 14*(10), 705–716. https://doi.org/10.1086/434928

Wu, Z. (1997). Exploring topics on individual constructed system and career decision via constructivism [Original in Chinese]. *Counseling Quarter, 33*(3): 42–51.

Yongzhou Highlight. (2022). *The first private college in China is in Yongzhou* [Original in Chinese]. http://news.sohu.com/a/574441386_121123913

Zhang, J. (2012). *Teaching and design of secondary students' career planning.* Beijing Normal University Publishing Group.

Zhang, W. (1984, April 24) Suggestions for careers guidance for secondary school pupils [Originals in Chinese]. *Guangming Daily* (Beijing), p.3.

Zhang, W. Y. (1998). *Young people and careers: School careers guidance in Shanghai, Edinburgh and Hong Kong.* Comparative Education Research Centre, The University of Hong Kong.

Zhang, W., Hu, X., & Pope, M. (2002). The evolution of career guidance and counseling in the People's Republic of China. *The Career Development Quarterly, 50*(3), 226–236. https://doi.org/10.1002/j.2161-0045.2002.tb00898.x

Zhang, Y. (2017). Trend and analysis of university unified admission examination system [Original in Chinese]. *Shaanxi Normal University Journal (Philosophy and Social Sciences Section), 4*, 3–4.

Zhao, Z & Bai, B. (2013). *Career education teacher's teaching handbook* [Original in Chinese]. Beijing Normal University Publishing Group.

Zhou, X., Li, X., & Gao, Y. (2016). Career guidance and counseling in Shanghai, China: 1977 to 2015. *The Career Development Quarterly, 64*(3), 203–215. https://doi.org/10.1002/cdq.12055.

11 Conclusion

The Future of School Counselling in East and Southeast Asia

Mark G. Harrison, Queenie Lee and James Yu

Introduction

This book was compiled in response to the rapid developments in school counselling in East and Southeast Asia. As the preceding chapters have shown, change is taking place across many domains of school counselling in different countries across the region. Shifts in societal behaviours and attitudes are being driven by global phenomena such as the astonishing pace of technological innovation, and unforeseen events such as the COVID-19 pandemic. These shifts interact with traditional cultural ways of knowing and behaving in the world to give rise to a myriad of new challenges. Schools are, inevitably, influenced by these profound changes, and respond to them in different ways, sometimes with innovation, sometimes in a more reactionary manner.

Changing Societies and the Changing Needs of Young People

Societies are changing rapidly in many pervasive ways, and these shifts are being reflected in the nature and characteristics of schools and school counselling. The acronym VUCA, meaning *volatile, uncertain, complex, and ambiguous*, was coined as long ago as 1987 by the U.S. Army War College to describe the world emerging from the Cold War, and has since been applied to a wide range of contexts. Young people growing up in East and Southeast Asia in the first quarter of the 21st century doubtless live in environments with these characteristics. As such, their needs are complex. It is impossible here to give a full sense of the scope of these changes, but we highlight four areas very briefly: increasing diversity, the rise of technology, the increasing dominance of discourses related to well-being, and the relationships between schools and parents.

Diversity is increasingly recognised and valued. For example, the presence of LGBTQ students is increasingly being acknowledged in schools, and the distinct needs of this population are becoming more apparent. Schools are also recognising the importance of adopting a social justice perspective in the curriculum, and issues of equity, diversity, and inclusion have become an important strategic focus for many schools. The diverse needs of students with a

DOI: 10.4324/9781003352457-11

wide range of learning difficulties have become clearer. Indeed, the scope of the term learning difficulties has itself become wider.

As we noted in Chapter 1, the rise of technology is a significant driver of contemporary social change. Smartphones have changed the way people communicate and, through the curation of information by social media algorithms, are causing shifts in behaviour. Social media has become deeply embedded into young people's lives, profoundly shaping their experiences and the nature of the societies in which they live. In many cases, schools – and school counsellors – are struggling to keep up.

One area of note is the increasing prominence of the discourse around the notion of well-being itself. Twenty years ago, well-being was seldom mentioned in schools. Indeed, the concept of well-being barely existed in the way it is thought of today. McLeod and Wright (2015) argue that the term well-being has been co-opted to serve a variety of social and economic purposes but, whatever the origins, purposes, and effects of well-being as a concept, it is now often at the heart of schools' mission, vision, and values. As such, school counsellors are at the forefront of making sense of the contested, ambiguous, and loaded set of concepts and practices associated with this nebulous term (Whippman, 2017).

As the role of schools in society has changed, so has the role of parents. Several decades ago, parents might have seen schools as comprising of experts providing a service and might not have been very involved, leaving the business of schooling to teachers. As the neoliberal zeitgeist has pervaded every sphere of life, parents' roles have shifted from the recipients of a service to that of (sometimes paying) customers (Helgøy & Homme, 2017). As such, parents' expectations and needs have changed and, as a result, the roles of counsellors have shifted. A climate of accountability and a move towards evidence-based practice have increasingly pervaded the school counselling sector, providing a challenge to the roles and identity of counsellors.

How best should school counsellors respond to this complex set of challenges? One response to the complex world we inhabit lies in the idea of *21st century skills*, the learning characteristics needed for success in a future characterised by uncertainty, advancing technology, and rapid change, has been increasingly influential in education (Geisinger, 2016). Beyond helping young people to develop skills, however, lies a focus on personal characteristics that can help young people to navigate through an uncertain future. Bill George (2017), a professor at Harvard Business School, has proposed a response to the complex world we now face he has called VUCA 2.0, an acronym for *vision, understanding, courage, and adaptability*. As the authors have explored throughout this book, in the context of the East and Southeast Asian region, the focus would be less on individual growth and development, and more about making sense of who and where we are as a society, recognising the importance of societal, systemic, and organisational contributions to individual well-being, and engaging in advocacy to bring about structural changes (Whippman, 2017). Such an approach would be focused on community and communal action, perhaps drawing on insights from community psychology (Burton et al., 2007). This involves the adoption an ecological perspective, an emphasis on more cooperative ways of living, and an attempt to improve the life conditions of individuals within their communities by enacting interventions to promote well-being (Natale et al., 2016).

Key Challenges Faced by School Counsellors

School counsellors face a significant challenge as they grapple with how to respond to the profound and rapid changes taking place in schools and societies. Counsellors' roles have also become more wide-ranging. The already diverse roles of school counsellors have become even more so in response to the changing need of young people, and their roles are continually evolving as society changes and schools try to adapt. Indeed, schools have themselves become more complex places providing a wider range of services. Whereas schools once concerned themselves almost entirely with academic education and vocational readiness, they are now concerned with a wide range of issues pertinent to child development in contemporary society, including mental health and well-being, child safety, and issues of diversity and social justice. As a result, school counsellors are now expected to play a significant role in areas such as crisis management, suicide prevention, safeguarding, addressing the needs of marginalised groups, and advocating for equitable access to educational opportunities for all young people.

Counsellors in the region are, for the most part, poorly resourced. Many schools in the region suffer from an insufficient number of counsellors. ASCA (2019) recommends a ratio of 1 counsellor to 250 students, but this ratio is seldom achieved. For example, in the Philippines, where school counselling is a legally recognised profession requiring a master's degree and a license to practise, the ratio of counsellors to students in public schools is an astonishing 1:20,000 (See Chapter 6). A lack of resources also hinders the provision of high-quality counselling. Supervision and continuing professional development are seldom available to school counsellors in public schools, who often have to pay from their own pockets to receive training and supervision.

Perhaps the most significant challenge faced by school counsellors in the region is to find a clear purpose, aligned with the cultural and organisational contexts in which they work, and serving the needs of young people in the region as they face a complex and uncertain future. An effective response requires a strong identity and purpose, but counsellors in East and Southeast Asia are a long way from establishing a clear and coherent identity and a role in schools which is understood and valued. School counsellors across the region continue to suffer from role ambiguity, and there is often a weak distinction between school counsellors and other professionals such as social workers and (guidance) teachers (Harrison, 2022). Low pay and poor career progression hinders school counselling in many countries. Whereas teachers mostly have clearer career paths and higher salaries, school counsellors are often employed on temporary, part-time contracts (as is the case in Japan), using discretionary or special funding sources (as in Hong Kong). Even where school counselling is an established and recognised profession (as in the Philippines), pay is often low compared to teachers and other professional occupations. Few countries in the region have licensing arrangements for counselling, which is not recognised legally as a profession in most cases. This is not to say that legal recognition and licensing is a panacea. Such recognition can be something of a double-edged sword. The experience of counsellors in the Philippines, for example, shows that licensing can become a barrier for counsellors, since non-licensed practitioners are unable to practise until they have completed their master's degree in Guidance and Counselling, and passed the licensure examination.

School counsellors lack frameworks and robust codes of ethics to guide their work. Some schools use the ASCA (2019) model, but many have no model at all or a model which is insufficient to support the provision of an effective counselling service (as is the case in Hong Kong, for example, where the Comprehensive School Guidance System (CSGS) fails to specify the roles of school counsellors). Culture-specific frameworks are needed which define counselling and the roles of counsellors in ways consistent with indigenous understandings of well-being and ill-health, and help-seeking behaviours.

Several trends – the rise of evidence-based practice, increasing professionalisation of counselling, and the focus on discourses on well-being – have led to school counsellors being seen as mental health professionals focused on addressing young people's social-emotional needs (DeKruyf et al., 2013). At the same time, school counselling has become increasingly conceptualised as a service focused on short-term interventions, and crisis management, with little focus on longer term, therapeutic work with students (Lambie et al., 2019). In East and Southeast Asia, this way of practising school counselling might also be necessitated by a lack of staffing and resources to enable the provision of a more comprehensive, holistic, and longer-term approach.

There is, therefore, a danger that school counsellors can become narrowly focused on managing issues of mental health in the population of students they serve in a short-term way, jumping from crisis to crisis. But school counselling should be so much more than this. Traditional Asian notions of education are very much concerned with self-cultivation and adopt a long-term orientation. In the Analects, Confucius writes: "At fifteen, I had my mind bent on learning. At thirty, I stood firm. At forty, I had no doubts. At fifty, I knew the decrees of Heaven. At sixty, my ear was an obedient organ for the reception of truth. At seventy, I could follow what my heart desired, without transgressing what was right." This famous quotation illustrates the lifelong pursuit of character in the Confucian mindset and is a call for school counsellors to challenge the dominant Western, short-term orientation with its medicalised notion of ill health and narrow conceptualisation of well-being. Instead, perhaps counsellors might consider their role as one of promoting a good life. Such a practice would involve an exploration of values, an examination of meaning and, ultimately, embracing what the philosopher Chritoph Teschers (2017) describes as living a beautiful life as the broad goal of education.

Key Themes for the Future Development of School Counselling

The challenges faced by school counsellors in East and Southeast Asia described above require a robust and creative response. At the same time, many opportunities exist for the development of the field. In this section, we identify several key themes in the development of school counselling as the field responds to the fast-changing environment in which counsellors work.

This volume has adopted an ecological perspective throughout, and several contributors have written explicitly about the importance of using an ecological framework. The importance of the ecological approach is summarised by Fred Low in Chapter 2: "School counselling is more than just a conversation between a safe and trusted adult and a young person in a small quiet room in the school." In Chapter 4, Boon-Ooi Lee highlighted the importance of an interdependent construal of self in the cultural context of East and Southeast Asia. As such, an approach to counselling which sees all stakeholders as being connected and mutually influential is essential – even more so than is the case in Western contexts. In the work of these authors, we see an increasing recognising the importance of counsellors adopting an ecological perspective in their work.

School counselling is increasingly becoming culture specific. Counselling in the region has tended to develop as a Western import, but an approach is needed which conceptualises, practices, and appraises counselling in more culturally meaningful ways. This involves more than cultural understanding. Counsellors' practice needs to be fundamentally informed by indigenous notions of help seeking, mental health, effective ways of helping, and wellness. To address this aim, the characteristics of cultural humility and epistemological flexibility (see Chapter 4) should be at the heart of counsellors' work with young people. Indigenous school counselling frameworks are in an early stage of development, but there are encouraging signs that this work is being taken seriously and making a difference (see Chapter 8, for example).

The world inhabited by young people is increasing online, and the inevitable rise of technology will continue to do shape our lives in far reaching ways. School counsellors are adapting to the changes brought about by technology and will need to embrace the opportunities these changes provide. It is hard to overestimate the scale of change. Since the year 2000, access to the internet has grown from just 7% globally to over half of the world's population, with mobile telephone subscriptions rising from 740 million to 8 billion in the same period, and the number of users of social media platforms has risen from zero to over 5 billion when combining Facebook, YouTube, and WhatsApp (World Economic Forum, 2020). These developments have profoundly changed that way we communicate and consume information and have significant implications for the life experience and mental health (in both a positive and a negative way) of young people (Haidt & Allen, 2020). The technology of artificial intelligence (AI) is in its infancy: by the middle of the century, it will have transformed our world. This represents an enormous challenge to school counsellors, and an immense opportunity. Counsellors will need to respond to the needs of students as they prepare for a very different future. For example, career guidance will need to adapt to a world in which the work landscape is being profoundly reshaped (Lent, 2018). From the use of big data to inform decision making about good practice to the increasing prevalence of online counselling, and the future development of AI counselling, technology will reshape society and education, and counsellors should be at the forefront of these changes.

Advocacy for school counselling as a profession is increasing. Professional bodies such as the *Philippine Guidance and Counselling Association* (PGCA) and the *Singapore Association for Counselling* are working with governments to improve role clarity and professional status for school counsellors, to develop skills frameworks and codes of practice, to improve pay and conditions, and to promote the public's understanding of counselling. As school counsellors become more connected and organised, advocacy can become more robust and effective. At the school level, counsellors need to see themselves as leaders and establish productive relationships with principals (e.g., see David, 2019). The ASCA (2019) model describes counsellors as agents of systemic change, and counsellors will need to find culturally appropriate ways to influence schools' provision for supporting the communities they serve.

An important part of this change agenda is that counsellors are adopting a more proactive approach as they work with young people, and increasingly playing a more central role as their practice shifts from reactive to proactive and becomes more holistic and developmental. Advocacy for the young people with whom they work is also an important part of this. For example, counsellors will increasingly need to practise from a social justice perspective, as issues of equity, diversity, and inclusion become a more important part of the discourse of schools and societies.

School counsellors in the region are becoming increasingly interconnected, although many barriers need to be overcome. For example, counsellors in international schools (originally set up to serve the children of Western expatriates) and local schools often inhabit two different worlds. For example, counsellors in local and international schools seldom cross paths: their teachers and counsellors and, indeed, their student bodies, are drawn from different populations. While they are physically close to each other, they live in relative cultural isolation. However, as the traditional boundaries between international and local schools change, a challenge for the future will be to bridge this gap, and for counsellors to become part of a more coherent community where diversity is recognised and valued. While collaboration across countries is in its infancy, opportunities for communication and cross-fertilisation are growing, aided by the ease of travel and the rise of technologies which facilitate virtual interactions.

As the role of parents in schools has changed, relationships between parents and counsellors are developing. Social stigma and mistrust of counselling is common in the region, so changing the way parents and counsellors relate to each other and work together is vital (Bryan et al., 2019). Seeing parents as partners is something of a paradigm shift for many counsellors (and school leaders) but such a conceptualisation of the role of parents is essential in overcoming stigma and working in a more systemic way to provide effective counselling. Indeed, working more closely with parents is part of a more culturally responsive indigenous approach to counselling which recognises the importance of community and the social aspects of young people's identities.

Some Recent Developments in School Counselling in the Region

Several recent developments highlight the changes taking place to the school counselling landscape across South and Southeast Asia. Many countries in the region have well-established professional counselling associations, and there is a trend for these associations to become increasingly connected and to share good practice. For example, a memorandum of understanding between several ASEAN counselling associations was signed in November 2023 in Singapore to facilitate cooperation and sharing of good practice. This followed a webinar series titled *Counselling in Southeast Asian Contexts*, organised collaboratively by academics in Cambodia, Indonesia, Malaysia, The Philippines, Thailand, and Singapore, with the aim of exploring how counselling has evolved in the culturally, socioeconomically, and religiously diverse region of Southeast Asia. The 2023 Singapore *Counselling and Psychotherapy Symposium* organised by the Singapore Association for Counselling (SAC) brought together academics and practising counsellors from a wide range of countries in Southeast Asia.

It is hoped that these developments prefigure the establishment of and connections between school counselling organisations. Communication and cooperation between school counsellors across, and even within, countries in the region are not well developed, however. There is a need to develop a network of school counsellors. Few countries have school counselling associations. The PGCA is the most well-established in the region and has been active in advocating for increasing the status, recognition, and remuneration of school counsellors. Elsewhere, such associations tend to be rather small and not very influential. South Korea has the *Korea International School Counselor Association* (KISCA), established in 2012, with members across 34 international schools. The *South East Asia School Counselling Network* (SEASCN) is a network of international school counsellors working in the region and has held an annual conference since 2011. In Hong Kong, the *Asian Professional Counselling and Psychology Association* (APCPA) has a school counselling division, but as of January 2024, only eight counsellors are registered. Informal networks also exist, such as a school counsellor network in Hong Kong, consisting mostly of international school counsellors, which meets two or three times per year. While these associations undoubtedly provide some networking opportunities and are a valuable resource for school counsellors, they are not well resourced, and there is little (if any) coordination or communication between them.

One other positive development is a growing legal recognition of school counselling. In some countries, such as the Philippines, school counselling has been recognised legally for some time. In other countries, school counselling is not regulated legally, but counsellors enjoy a degree of professional recognition. For example, in Singapore, the adoption of a new counselling skills framework in November 2023 brought school counsellors greater government and public recognition as professionals. Elsewhere, however, school counselling is far from being regarded as a professional activity. In Mainland China, for example, school counselling is scarcely recognised as a profession at all, despite government policy mandating counselling in schools to support young people's well-being (Shi, 2018). In Hong Kong SAR, counselling has a poor public recognition and there is limited support from the government for school counsellors, who have been described as having been "invisible in the field of mental health for decades" (Fung, 2019, p. 85).

Research Directions

Research into school counselling in the East and Southeast Asian region is in its infancy. The chapters in this edited book have presented some of the research taking place into school counselling in various parts of the region. Much work is needed to build on this foundation. Here we highlight several key areas for future research.

Very little research into evidence-based practice exists, and high-quality studies addressing the question of which interventions are most effective for different populations need to be undertaken. The little research that does exist, while encouraging, is small in scale and does not reach sufficient statistical power to make meaningful inferences about the efficacy of interventions (e.g., see Harrison & Wang, 2020; Kameoka et al., 2020; Saw et al., 2019; Wong et al., 2018). Counselling interventions are generally imported from Western settings, but it is not clear how such approaches to counselling are transferrable to the very different cultural context of East and Southeast Asia. The little research which has been conducted suggests that modifications are needed (e.g., Naeem et al., 2021). Indeed, the question of what constitutes effective counselling should be given more serious attention.

Apart from investigating the effectiveness of specific interventions, models of school counsellor effectiveness should be developed which define the factors associated with effective practice. For example, there is evidence that professional identity is associated with effectiveness (e.g., Heled et al., 2022), and this might be especially impactful in the region given school counsellors' weak professional identities, but the relationship is unclear. The effect of counsellors' positioning in school ecologies should also be investigated. While studies have found that counsellors' embeddedness in schools promotes their effectiveness (Cholewa et al., 2017; Knight et al., 2018; Spratt et al., 2006), others have found that counsellors' independence from the school can be helpful, given students' concerns about confidentiality and confusion about dual roles (e.g., Griffiths, 2013: Harrison 2020). Other factors such as workloads, role ambiguity, relationships with principals and teachers, autonomy, and the provision of training and supervision, await research.

Research to develop indigenous, ecologically informed frameworks for school counselling is needed across the region. The implementation of a counselling framework is associated with better counsellor job satisfaction (Pyne, 2011) and reduced levels of burnout (Fye et al., 2020). However, many schools in the region are not using any formal framework to plan, implement, and assess their counselling provision. School counselling frameworks should be culture-specific, developed with the input of different stakeholders, and thoroughly trialled.

Little work has been carried out on the impact of relationships with parents. A substantial literature demonstrates the importance of forming partnerships with parents in Western settings (Bryan et al., 2019) but, to our knowledge, no research has been conducted on counsellor-parent partnerships in countries in East and Southeast Asia. Given the high levels of stigma associated with mental health, and the weak help-seeking behaviours found in the region, finding effective ways to work with parents should be a priority.

The experience and impact of counsellor leadership also awaits investigation. Research into counsellor leadership in the U.S. is well established and suggests that counsellors are most effective when they can influence counselling policy and practice through formal and informal leadership roles (Prasath et al., 2021; Wingfield et al., 2010). In the very different cultural context of East and Southeast Asia, counsellor leadership may be quite different in its enactment and impact. Schools in the region are typically very hierarchical organisations with rigid power structures and a strong focus on organisational cohesion and stability, so counsellors need to find ways to exercise soft power by forming strategic relationships.

Finally, more practitioner-based research is needed. In the U.S., the ASCA journal, *Professional School Counselling*, is well established and publishes articles by academics and practising school counsellors. It is uncommon for research in East and Southeast Asia to be conducted by counsellors, however: they typically lack the time, resources, and professional support to carry out research. There is often a divide between university departments and practising school counsellors, so structures are needed to bridge this gap. Universities could partner with schools, for example, to provide support, supervision, and resources for a practitioner-based, action research approach. Some schools (or groups of schools) have established their own, in-house research centres which could be extended to other schools.

Conclusion

We had several aims when compiling this book. We wanted to convey a sense of the rapid development of school counselling in East and Southeast Asia as the field responds to changing societies, changing schools, and the changing needs of young people. We also sought to capture a sense of the rich diversity of school counselling in the region, and the creativity, persistence, and resilience of school counsellors, who often work in difficult and demanding contexts.

The chapters contributed to this edited volume give a sense of the challenges faced by school counsellors, how much work is being done, how rapidly school counselling is changing, and the opportunities which exist for development. As counsellors move into the second quarter of the 21st century, the forces shaping the region will continue to provide a challenging environment for school counselling services. To transform these challenges into opportunities, school counsellors will need to find creative and novel ways to advocate for and empower themselves, carve out clear identities, form partnerships with parents, teachers, and others in the community, and build strong professional communities. We suggest that an approach to school counselling for the future of the region will contain several elements. It will adopt an ecological perspective and will be built on indigenous, culturally meaningful understandings of well-being and human development. This development will be broad, holistic, and will be focused on advocacy for better communities and more sustainable ways of living.

Ultimately, school counselling is about helping young people – and the communities in which they exist – to live well. The challenges are immense, and this is why the opportunities are so great. Counsellors in the region are creative, resilient, persistent, passionate, courageous, and adaptable. These qualities are needed more than ever to provide young people with the resources they need to live well, and in so doing, to give the enterprise of school counselling a bright future.

References

American School Counselor Association (2019). *ASCA national model: A framework for school counseling programs* (4th ed.).

Bryan, J., Griffin, D., Kim, J., Griffin, D. M., & Young, A. (2019). School counselor leadership in school-family-community partnerships: An equity-focused partnership process model for moving the field forward. In S. B. Sheldon & T. A. Turner-Vorbeck (Eds.), *The Wiley Handbook on Family, School, and Community Relationships in Education* (pp. 265–287). Wiley.

Burton M., Boyle, S., Harris, C., Kagan, C. (2007). Community psychology in Britain. In S. M. Reich, M. Riemer, I. Prilleltensky, and M. Montero (Eds.), *International Community Psychology* (pp. 219–237). Springer. https://doi.org/10.1007/978-0-387-49500-2_11

Cholewa, B., Goodman-Scott, E., Thomas, A., & Cook, J. (2017). Teachers' perceptions and experiences consulting with school counselors: A qualitative study. *Professional School Counseling, 20*(1), 1096–2409. https://doi.org/10.5330/1096-2409-20.1.7

David, E. C. (2019). Partnership and collaboration: Understanding the counsellor-principal relationship in the Philippine context. *British Journal of Guidance & Counselling, 47*(6), 698–711. https://doi.org/10.1080/03069885.2017.1413167

DeKruyf, L., Auger, R. W., & Trice-Black, S. (2013). The role of school counselors in meeting students' mental health needs: Examining issues of professional identity. *Professional School Counseling, 16*(5), 271–282. https://doi.org/10.1177/2156759X0001600502

Fung, S. C. (2019). Counsellors in Hong Kong primary schools: On becoming visible counselling professionals. *Global Journal of Health Science, 11*(12), 80–90. https://doi.org/10.5539/gjhs.v11n12p80

Fye, H. J., Bergen, S., & Baltrinic, E. R. (2020). Exploring the relationship between school counselors' perceived ASCA National Model implementation, supervision satisfaction, and burnout. *Journal of Counseling & Development, 98*(1), 53–62. https://doi.org/10.1002/jcad.12299

Geisinger, K. F. (2016). 21st century skills: What are they and how do we assess them? *Applied Measurement in Education, 29*(4), 245–249. https://doi.org/10.1080/08957347.2016.1209207

George, B. (2017, Feb 17). VUCA 2.0: A strategy for steady leadership in an unsteady world. *Forbes Magazine.* https://www.forbes.com/sites/hbsworkingknowledge/2017/02/17/vuca-2-0-a-strategy-for-steady-leadership-in-an-unsteady-world/?sh=7655839213d8

Griffiths, G. (2013). *Scoping report for MindEd: helpful and unhelpful factors in school-based counselling: clients' perspectives.* BACP.

Haidt, J., & Allen, N. (2020, Feb 10). Scrutinizing the effects of digital technology on mental health. *Nature.* https://www.nature.com/articles/d41586-020-00296-x

Harrison, M. G. (2022). The professional identity of school counsellors in East and Southeast Asia. *Counselling and Psychotherapy Research, 22*(3), 543–547. https://doi.org/10.1002/capr.12546

Harrison, M. G., & Wang, Z. (2020). School counselling based on humanistic principles: A pilot randomized controlled trial in Hong Kong. *Asia Pacific Journal of Counselling and Psychotherapy, 11*(2), 122–138. https://doi.org/10.1080/21507686.2020.1781667

Heled, E., Ukrop, S., & Davidovitch, N. (2022). Between academia and the field: The case of school counselling effectiveness of school counselling training and its impact on professional identity. *International Journal of Higher Education, 11*(6), 1–1. https://doi.org/10.5430/ijhe.v11n6p1

Helgøy, I., & Homme, A. (2017). Increasing parental participation at school level: A 'citizen to serve' or a 'customer to steer'? *Nordic Journal of Studies in Educational Policy, 3*(2), 144–154. https://doi.org/10.1080/20020317.2017.1343625

Kameoka, S., Tanaka, E., Yamamoto, S., Saito, A., Narisawa, T., Arai, Y., Nosaka, S., Ichikawa, K., & Asukai, N. (2020). Effectiveness of trauma-focused cognitive behavioral therapy for Japanese children and adolescents in community settings: A multisite randomized controlled trial. *European Journal of Psychotraumatology, 11*(1), 1–10. https://doi.org/10.1080/20008198.2020.1767987

Knight, K., Gibson, K., & Cartwright, C. (2018). "It's like a refuge": Young people's relationships with school counsellors. *Counselling and Psychotherapy Research, 18*(4), 377–386. https://doi.org/10.1002/capr.12186

Lambie, G. W., Stickl Haugen, J., Borland, J. R., & Campbell, L. O. (2019). Who took "counseling" out of the role of professional school counselors in the United States?

Journal of School-Based Counseling Policy and Evaluation, 1(3), 51–61. https://eric.ed.gov/?id=EJ1264175

Lent, R. W. (2018). Future of work in the digital world: Preparing for instability and opportunity. *The Career Development Quarterly, 66*(3), 205–219. https://doi.org/10.1002/cdq.12143

McLeod, J., & Wright, K. (2015). Inventing youth wellbeing. In K. Wight & J. McLeod (Eds.), *Rethinking Youth Wellbeing: Critical Perspectives* (pp. 1–10). Springer.

Naeem, F., Latif, M., Mukhtar, F., Kim, Y. R., Li, W., Butt, M. G., Kumar, N., & Ng, R. (2021). Transcultural adaptation of cognitive behavioral therapy (CBT) in Asia. *Asia-Pacific Psychiatry, 13*(1), 1–8. https://doi.org/10.1111/appy.12442

Natale, A., Di Martino, S., Procentese, F., & Arcidiacono, C. (2016). De-growth and critical community psychology: Contributions towards individual and social well-being. *Futures, 78,* 47–56. https://doi.org/10.1016/j.futures.2016.03.020

Prasath, P. R., Lindinger-Sternart, S., & Duffey, T. L. (2021). Counselors as organizational leaders: Exploring parallels of servant leadership and professional counseling. *Journal of Counselor Leadership and Advocacy, 8*(2), 146–156. https://doi.org/10.1080/2326716X.2021.1904460

Pyne, J. R. (2011). Comprehensive school counseling programs, job satisfaction, and the ASCA National Model. *Professional School Counseling, 15*(2), 88–97. https://doi.org/10.1177/2156759X1101500202

Saw, J. A., Tam, C. L., & Bonn, G. (2019). Development and validation of a school-based cognitive-behavioural therapy (CBT) intervention for Malaysian high school students with depressive symptoms. *Asia Pacific Journal of Counselling and Psychotherapy, 10*(2), 171–187. https://doi.org/10.1080/21507686.2019.1629973

Shi, Q. (2018). School-based counseling in mainland China: Past, present, and future. *Journal of School-Based Counseling Policy and Evaluation, 1*(1), 17–25. https://doi.org/10.25774/p7xm-yg61

Spratt, J., Shucksmith, J., Philip, K., & Watson, C. (2006). 'Part of who we are as a school should include responsibility for well-being': Links between the school environment, mental health and behaviour. *Pastoral Care in Education, 24*(3), 14–21. https://doi.org/10.1111/j.1468-0122.2006.00374.x

Teschers, C. (2017). A beautiful life as an end of education. *Knowledge Cultures, 5*(06), 62–73. https://doi.org/10.22381/KC5620175

Whippman, R. (2017). Where were we while the pyramid was collapsing? At a yoga class: II. Society and politics. *Society, 54*(6), 527–529. https://doi.org/10.1007/s12115-017-0203-0

Wingfield, R. J., Reese, R. F., & West-Olatunji, C. A. (2010). Counselors as leaders in schools. *Florida Journal of Educational Administration & Policy, 4*(1), 114–130. https://eric.ed.gov/?id=EJ911435

Wong, D. F., Kwok, S. Y., Low, Y. T., Man, K. W., & Ip, P. S. (2018). Evaluating effectiveness of cognitive–behavior therapy for Hong Kong adolescents with anxiety problems. *Research on Social Work Practice, 28*(5), 585–594. https://doi.org/10.1177/10497315166583

World Economic Forum. (2020, Nov 18). *How has technology changed – and changed us – in the past twenty years?* https://www.weforum.org/agenda/2020/11/heres-how-technology-has-changed-and-changed-us-over-the-past-20-years/

Index

Note: **Bold** page numbers refer to tables; *italic* page numbers refer to figures and page numbers followed by "n" denote endnotes.

Abu Yazid, A. B. 38
adverse childhood experiences (ACEs) 115–116
Aga Mohd Jaladin, R. A. 37
agnostic-atheist 54
Amat, S. 39
American School Counsellor Association (ASCA) Model 6–7, 9, 98
artificial intelligence (AI) 3, 198
Asian schools counselling, ecological lenses *17*; clinical knowledge 19–23; COVID-19 pandemic 25–26; dual-dimension structure 16; Information Technology & Counselling 18–19; Internal and External domains 17–18, 21–24; Personal domain 18–20, 23, 24; social and demographic changes 23–25; social-political structures 17; Systems domain 22, 24.
asynchronous communication 42

Bhat, C. S. 21
Boman, P. 22
Bowen family systems therapy 58–59
Bullivant, S. 54–55

Career and Life Adventure Planning (CLAP) 167
Career and Life Planning (CLP) Grant 165, 173
career assessment tools 185
Career Construction Interview (CCI) 4
career counselling 2, 91, 98, **123–125**, 127, **146**; China 11; development of 3–4, 11; and facilitation 167; private and school settings 168; programmes 166; services 165; skills 170; Western theories 189
career education 3–4; Group Facilitation for Career Development module 171–173; Mainland China 179–189
career guidance 3–4
Career Progression and Specialization Programme (CPSP) 108
Chan, M. C. R. 89n9
Chen, P. H. 10
Children and Adolescent Risk Screener (CARS) 99
China Vocational Education Association (CVEA) 181
Clavesillas, Elgin 11
codes of ethics 2, 5, 92, 107, 108, 196
collaboration with stakeholders 38–39
collectivism-individualism 56–57
competency-based education (CBE) 183
competency-based teaching (CBT) 183
Comprehensive School Guidance Service (CSGS) 9
comprehensive training 77
Confucian ethics 56
Consortium to Advance School Psychology International (CASP-I) 120
Consortium to Advance School Psychology in Vietnam (CASP-V) 120
counselling framework 9–11, 197, 201
Counsellor Act of 1998 34
COVID-19 1–2, 5, 10, 152, 153, 171, 189, 193; ecological domains 25; global event 18; Japan,

school counselling in 72–88;
Malaysia, school counselling in
32–45; psychological distress 99; SAS
programmes 93; social distancing 148
CPSP *see* Career Progression and
Specialization Programme (CPSP)
CSGS *see* Comprehensive School
Guidance Service (CSGS)
culture/cultural: characteristics 5, 52,
55; diversity 10; humility 52, 59–60;
sensitivity 44
cyberbullying 116

Dang, H.M. 11
David, A. R. 55
Deng Xiaoping 187
developing a curriculum process
(DACUM) 183
Dewey, J. 182–183
distance learning 74, 88
Doi, Y. 73

ecological perspective 6–8, 10, 195, 197,
202
e-counselling service 40–41
Education Consultation Service Referral
Cards 77
embodied culture 55
emotional expressiveness 59
Enhanced Basic Education Act 97
Epstein, J. L. 8
ethical dilemmas 5
ethical practice 5–6
ethics 6, 24, 43, 92, 101, 108, 118
experiential-learning approach 170–171
explanatory models 60, **61–62**,
63–64

face-to-face counselling 18, 33, 41,
43–44
Facilitating Career Development (FCD)
programme 167
Filipino Counsellors 96–97
Filipino school guidance system 94
Frank, J. B. 60
Frank, J. D. 60
Functional Assessment of Self-Mutilation
114–115

Gamage, G. P. 20
George, B. 194
Ghazali, Nor Mazlina 37
Gladding, S. T. 168

Global School-based Health Survey
21–22
gnostic-atheist 54
Gomez, M.G. 101
Griffiths, F. 42
group counselling 149
Group Facilitation for Career
Development module: career
counselling 167–168; career
education 171–173; career
exploration/development group 170;
eight-hour module 168, **169**;
experiential-learning approach 170–171; ground rules 168; ice-breaking
activities 168; micro-skills 170; theory
170
Guidance and Counselling Act 91, 94
Guidance and Counselling Referral
System 98
guidance counsellor certification 79
Gysbers, N. C. 9

Harrison, M. G. 11, 23
Hass, M. 11
Henderson, P. 9
Hirano, Y. 89n9
Ho, Y. F. 173
Hocson, Sheila Marie G. 11
Holmes, J. 36
Hong Kong: career education landscape
165–166; CLAP 167; Group
Facilitation for Career Development
module 167–168, **169,** 170; life
planning 166–167; local tertiary
institution 167; professional training
166–167, 170–171
Hong Kong Association of Career
Masters and Guidance Masters
(HKACMGM) 166, 171
Hsi, T. 22
Hui, E. K. P. 172

ice-breaking activities 168, 176
indigenisation of counselling 6, 101,
197, 199, 201, 202; in East and
Southeast Asia 9–10; healing systems
52, 65, 66, 67n4; Hong Kong 171
indigenous healing systems 52
individual counselling 148
individualism–collectivism 56–57
Indonesia: Global School-based
Health Survey 21–22; YouTube and
WhatsApp 18

Information Technology & Counselling 18–19
informed consent 5
intercultural counselling 35
interim school counsellors 143–145, *144*, 151, *152*
internationalized schools 180, 183–184
Internet Plus 187
interpersonal psychotherapy (IPT) 58–59
Ishikawa, E. 73

Japan, COVID-19 impact 20; comprehensive training 77; cultural and historical factors 73; decision-making 86, 87; distance learning 74, 88; Education Consultation Service Referral Cards 77; ES 80–83; ethical dilemma 84; exploratory investigation 79; GC 83–86; guidance counsellor certification 79; homeroom teachers 73; JACS 78–79; JASC 79; joint licensing system 79; JSCA 78–79; JSSCE 78–79; MEXT policies 75, 77, 86; narrative analysis 80; non-attendance 72; professional communities 72; public certification 78; regulations 74–77; SCs assignment 76; SCs deployment 75; social distancing 86; tele-counselling 88
Japanese Association of Counselling Science (JACS) 78–79
Japanese Association of School Counselling (JASC) 79
Japanese Society for the Study of Career Education (JSSCE) 78–79
Japan School Counseling Association (JSCA) 78–79
Jayawardena, H. K. 20
Jiang, D. 183
Jiang, Houming 11
Joint Congressional Oversight Committee (JCOC) 107, 108
joint licensing system 79

Kato, K. 89n9
Kawai, Hayao 77–78
Kirmayer, L. J. 58
Kitayama, S. 57–58
Knives, Teo 10–11
Komatsu, H. 22
Korea, sexual bullying 21

Kwok, D. K. 24
Kwok, Jin Kuan 10

Lee, B. O. 10, 197
Lee, Queenie 11
Lee, S. M. 21
Lent, R. W. 4
Leung, S. A. 10, 172
Lijadi, A. A. 23
Liu, X. 3
Locke 182
Low, Fred 197
Low, P. K. 10
Low, S. K. 10, 36, 38
Loyalka, P. 24

Macau, TCK 23
Mainland China, career education: college major selection 187–189; funding 186; high schools, types of 180; historical development 180–181; implications 189; internationalized schools 180, 183–184; job market 179; LGBTQ youth 24; policies 181–182; progressive education movement 182–183; social networking sites 24; theory-based practices 184–186; vocational schools, talent development 186–187
Malaysia: academic-related issues 33; asynchronous communication 42; career guidance and developmental issues 33; Counsellor Act of 1998 34; COVID-19 pandemic 39–43; cultural sensitivity 35–36; drug abuse scenario 33–34; e-counselling 40–41; face-to-face counselling 18, 33; formal public-school education 32; guidance services 33–34; legal and ethical considerations 41; misunderstanding and misinterpretation 42–43; multicultural competence 36–37; online counselling, benefits 43–44; parent, school, and community collaborations 38–39; personal mental health wellness 32; psychosocial issues 33; self-efficacy 34; special education needs, service for students 37–38; stigmatisation 35; strengths and shortcomings 44–45; technological barriers and inaccessibility 41–42
Markus, H. R. 57–58
Matsumoto, Y. 89n9

McLeod, J. 194
mental health concerns 20
Ministry of Education and Training (MoET) 117, 118, 134, 135, 141, 142, 145, 153
Ministry of Health (MOH) 117
Ministry of Labor, Invalids and Social Affairs (MOLISA) 117
Missouri Comprehensive Guidance Program 33
Movement Control Order (MCO) 32
multicultural awareness 5, 11
multicultural counselling 34, 37; *see also* Singapore, multicultural school counselling
multicultural school counselling, Singapore 10

National Career Development Association (NCDA) 167
Nguyen, D. T. 119
Nguyen, H. T. 11, 136, 142
Noboru, T. 21, 22
non-suicidal self-injury (NSSI) 114–115
non-verbal behaviour 41

online counselling services 2, 5–6
online learning 3
organisational politics 8
Organization for Economic Cooperation and Development (OECD) 116

Pan, B. 185
Parsons, Frank 3
Pham, A. K. 11
Philippine Association of Guidance Counsellors 91
Philippine Guidance and Counselling Association (PGCA) 91, 92, 99, 105
Philippine Mental Health Act 92
Philippine Qualifications Framework 93
Philippines: Code of Ethics 107; compensation 101; CPSP 108; DepEd 97–99, 102, **102**; educational institutions 94, **95, 96**; educational qualifications 102; entry-level positions 102, **103–104**; Filipino Counsellors 96–97; government-approved positions 106–107; Guidance and Counselling Act 91, 94; guidance counsellor positions 102, **102**; guidance-related positions 102, **105**; JCOC 107; legislative agenda 107; mental health services 92; psychosocial needs 98; role ambiguity 99–101; SAS programmes 93; scarcity, guidance counsellors 98–99; SLE 98; SSL 94
power distance 21
professional ethics **123, 125**
professional identity 7, 11, 22–23, 72, 79, 94, 97, 135, 200–201
professional school counsellors 151–152
professional training 166–167, 170–171
progressive education movement 182–183
psychoeducation 7
Putman, D. A. 35

quality-of-service delivery 34

Rappleye, J. 22
Raupach, Hans 10–11
Richello, M. G. 42
Rousseau 182

Salary Standardization Law (SSL) 94, 106
SAS programmes *see* Student Affairs and Services (SAS) programmes
Schalkwyk, G. J. 23
school counselling: Asian cultures 16–26; East and Southeast Asia 1–12, 193–202; in Hong Kong 166, 172; in Japan 72–88; in Malaysia 32–45; model 153; in Philippines 91–108; programme 140–141; in Singapore 51–66; team 135, 139, 140, 146–147; in Vietnam 113–130, 134–153; *see also* indigenisation of counselling
school counsellors 1–12, 19, 25, 26, 167, 188, 194–202; in Asia 22; Asian school counselling 63; *Aswab* 66; cultural values 55; e-counselling 40–41; employment status 34; in Indonesia 18; Japan 73–88; *Jia Wen*'s case 51–52, 63; in Macau 17, 23; Malaysia 36–39; multicultural competencies 56; online platforms 32; roles and functions 33, 100, 101; salary-related concerns 101; school-based services 116; Singapore 53; Vietnam 120–130, **129**, 135, 136, 139–141, 143–153, **146,** *152*
School Counsellor Utilisation Investigation Research Project 74
self-advocacy 5

self-construal theory 57–59
self-thoughts journal 177–178
Shanghai Graduates Vocational Guidance Centre (SGVGC) 183
Singapore, multicultural school counselling: agnostic-atheist 54; *Aswab's* case 51–52, 64–66, **65**; cultural context 52; cultural humility 52, 59–60; culture, definition 53–54; embodied culture 55; epistemological flexibility 52, 59–60; explanatory models 60, **61–62**, 63–64; gnostic-atheist 54; indigenous healing systems 52; individualism–collectivism 56–57; *Jia Wen's* case 51–52, 63–64, **64**; multicultural competencies 56; non-religionists 54; self construction 57–59; social context 52–53; symbolic healing model 60, **62**; Systems domain 24; third culture kids 54; worldview 56, **57**; youth mental health 20
Singapore Association for Counselling (SAC) 199
social equality 182
social inequality 24, 25
social isolation 3
sociocultural contexts 2
Sokantat, N. 21, 22
SSL *see* Salary Standardization Law (SSL)
standard operating procedures (SOPs) 40
Stoll, J. 43
Structured Learning Experience (SLE) 98
Student Affairs and Services (SAS) programmes 93
Subong, Francis Ray D. 11
Sue, D. W. 36, 56
Suhaila, K. 34
Super, D. E. 168
symbolic healing model 60, *62*

Taiwan, chatbot 19
Tajan, N. 10–11, 20, 78
Tan, E. C. 23
technology 10, 11, 41, 42, 45, 63, 64, 193, 194, 197, 198; career assessment tools 185; challenges and opportunities 2–3; counselling facilities 150; COVID-19 pandemic 5, 32; disruptive 144; electronic 188; emergent rescue 179; psychological services 18; utilization of 142; in workplace 4
tele-behavioural health 2, 3
Teo, Y. 24
Thai culture 21
theory-based practices 184–186
third culture kids (TCK) 23, 54
Tian, X. 180
Tran, N. K. 115
trauma-informed practices 19
Trevisan, M. 21

urbanisation 4

Vietnam **128**; ACEs 115–116; ASCA National Model 145; community resources 128; conceptualization 143; counselling delivery 150; counselling facilities 150; counselling methods 149–150; counselling services component 148–149; COVID-19 pandemic 153; developments in 113–130; disruptive eco-social changes 134; eco-social factors 147; emotional and behavioural problems 113–114; government responses 117–120; group counselling 149; implementation plan 141–143; individual counselling 148; interim school counsellors 143–145, *144*, 151, *152*; large-scale enhancement 20; legislative perspectives 141–142; mental health and academic needs 113–116; MOET 117, 118, 134, 135, 153; MOH 117, 119; MOLISA 117, 119; NSSI 114–115; OECD 116; outside school counselling specialists 147; prevention 147–148; professional in 134–153, **146**; professional school counsellors 151–152; school counselling model 153; school counselling programme 140–141; school counselling team 135, 139, 140, 146–147; school counsellors 121, 127, **127**, 128, **129**; school psychology counselling 134; suicidality 114; training 120–121, **122–126**; VSCM 135–152
Vietnam Association of School Counselling (VASC) 135
Vietnamese Association of Psychology (VAP) 136
Vietnam National Institute of Educational Sciences (VNIES) 153

Vietnam Psycho-Pedagogical Association (VPPA) 136
Vietnam School Counselling Model (VSCM) 135, **157–164**; assessment *138*, 139; components 140–152; fundamental framework 135–137, *136*; management 137–138, *138*; services *138*, 139; themes 137–140, *138*; workforce *138*, 138–139
vocational schools, talent development 186–187

whole-school approach (WSA) model 172
Williams, B. 57
Wright, J. 42
Wright, K. 194

Yeung, W.-J. J. 23
young people, changing needs 193–195
Yu, James 11
Yuen, M. 11, 172, 173

Printed in the United States
by Baker & Taylor Publisher Services